New Paradigms of Peace Research

New Paradigms of Peace Research

The Asia-Pacific Context

Edited by

Akihiko Kimijima

Vidya Jain

RAWAT PUBLICATIONS

Jaipur • New Delhi • Bangalore • Hyderabad • Guwahati

ISBN 978-81-316-0563-9

Published by
Prem Rawat for **Rawat Publications**
Satyam Apts, Sector 3, Jawahar Nagar, Jaipur 302 004 (India)
Phone: 0141 265 1748 / 7006 Fax: 0141 265 1748
E-mail: info@rawatbooks.com
Website: www.rawatbooks.com

New Delhi Office
4858/24, Ansari Road, Daryaganj, New Delhi 110 002
Phone: 011 2326 3290

Also at *Bangalore, Hyderabad* and *Guwahati*

Typeset by Rawat Computers, Jaipur
Printed at Chaman Enterprises, New Delhi

To

Johan Galtung

who has always been a pioneer in peace research,

with deep respect

Contents

Part III
Non-violence: Gandhi and Beyond

Part IV
Conflict Transformation in the Asia-Pacific

Acknowledgements

This book has its origin in the Asia-Pacific Peace Research Association (APPRA) Conference held at Ritsumeikan University, Kyoto, Japan, on October 14–16, 2011. We would like to thank all those who have contributed to the conference. Particularly we would like to express our deep gratitude to three donors – Mr Akio Komatsu, President of the Human, Nature & Science Institute Foundation, Dr Ikuro Anzai and Dr Kazuyo Yamane, both of Ritsumeikan University. APPRA secretarial staff, Ms Yoshiko Tanigawa's contribution has been immeasurable. Support of administrative staff of the Kyoto Museum for World Peace, the Graduate School of International Relations, and the Kinugasa Research Organization of Ritsumeikan University has been extremely important. Students of the Faculty of International Relations, Ritsumeikan University, have helped us enormously. Without their contributions, the APPRA Conference 2011 would not have been possible. It is our pleasant duty to thank them all.

And of course we deeply appreciate all the authors for contributing their cutting-edge research to the book. It is our joy that we could publish these contributions. Last but not least, without the cooperation of Mr Pranit Rawat of the Rawat Publications, this work would not have been possible at all. We thank him from the bottom of our hearts.

Akihiko Kimijima
Vidya Jain

Contributors

Akihiko Kimijima is Professor of Constitutional Law and Peace Studies in the Faculty of International Relations at Ritsumeikan University in Kyoto, Japan. His research focuses on the relations between constitution and peace, the pacifism of the Japanese Constitution and global constitutionalism. He is Secretary-General of the Asia-Pacific Peace Research Association and a board member of the Peace Studies Association of Japan. His recently published essay is "Global Constitutionalism and Japan's Constitutional Pacifism" in Vidya Jain (ed.), *Peace, Non-violence and Gandhian Concerns* (Rawat Publications, 2011).

Francis Daehoon Lee is Research Professor, Peace Studies, SungKongHoe University, Republic of Korea. Currently he is an Executive Member of the Centre for Peace and Disarmament and Coordinator for CENA (Civil Society Education Network in Asia) – a collaborating network of universities committed for peace, human rights and democracy studies in Asia. In 2012, he was nominated as an advisor to the UN Asia-Pacific Regional Advisory Group on Women, Peace and Security. He has also been actively involved in facilitating UNESCO-APCEIU teachers training workshops since 2006.

Ikuro Anzai graduated from the Department of Nuclear Engineering, University of Tokyo, Japan. He is Professor Emeritus in the Faculty of International Relations, Ritsumeikan University, and Director

Emeritus of the Kyoto Museum for World Peace. He was awarded the Medal for Merit by the Government of Vietnam in 2003, the 22nd Kubo Medical Culture Award in 2011, and the 4th No Gun Ri Human Rights Prize in 2011.

Kenji Urata is Professor Emeritus of Constitutional Law at Waseda University, Tokyo, and also Visiting Professor at Lund University, Sweden. He has been Vice President of the International Association of Lawyers Against Nuclear Arms (IALANA). His publications include *Reflections on Global Constitutionalism* (Institute of Comparative Law, Waseda University, 2005), The Moral Responsibility of the United States: Reading Barack Obama's Prague Speech, in *Peace and Conflict Review* (United Nations University for Peace, Fall 2009), and the Spirit of the Japanese Constitution and Its Universalism, in *Peace and Conflict Review* (Fall 2008).

Vidya Jain is Professor of Political Science and Director, Centre for Gandhian Studies, University of Rajasthan, Jaipur, India. She has held many important positions such as the Deputy Secretary General of APPRA (Asia-Pacific Peace Research Association), member of Nonviolence Commission and Global Political Economic Commission of IPRA and the Non-killing Political Science Research Committee, Hawaii (USA). She has several research publications to her credit and has made presentations at many international forums. Her recent book *Peace, Non-violence and Gandhian Concerns* (Rawat Publications, Jaipur, 2011) was released in APPRA Summit, Kyoto, Japan, 2011.

Thomas Weber is an Honorary Associate of the Politics Programme at Melbourne's La Trobe University. He is a regular writer on Gandhian topics. His latest Gandhi-related books include *Going Native; The Shanti Sena; Gandhi, Gandhism and the Gandhians; Gandhi as Disciple and Mentor; Nonviolent Intervention Across Borders;* and *On the Salt March.*

John P. Synott is a teacher and scholar in peace education, the sociology of globalisation and Korean studies. His publications include *Quality Education: Global Perspectives for Australian Schools* (2009), *Global and International Studies* (2009/2004), *Teacher Unions, Social Movements and the Politics of Education in South Korea, Taiwan and the Philippines* (2002) as well as many journal articles and book chapters on topics such as peace education, sociology of development in East Asia and the rights of indigenous peoples. He was the editor of the *Journal of Peace Education* (2004–2009) and on the editorial group of *Social Alternatives* for two decades. He has also been a member of the International Peace Research Association, where he has held several positions since 1992 and was Secretary General of the Asia-Pacific Peace Research Association (2006–2010). A long-time faculty member of QUT in Australia, he is now Adjunct Professor at the Centre for Peace and Conflict Studies, University of Sydney.

Ravi P. Bhatia is an independent educationist and peace researcher based in Delhi. Trained as a physicist in the universities of Delhi (India) and Massachusetts (USA), he now works in the areas of Gandhian studies, higher education, environmental issues and human rights. He is the Convenor of the Religion and Peace Commission and Council Member of IPRA and also a member of the Research Committee on Education of the Centre for Global Nonkilling.

Chaiwat Satha-Anand is Professor of Political Science at Thammasat University in Bangkok, Thailand. His latest publications include *Essays on the Three Prophets: Forgiveness, Murder and Nonviolence* (Dunedin: Abrahamic Interfaith Group, University of Otago, 2011). He is also the guest editor of *Peace and Policy 17* on protecting sacred spaces from violence (forthcoming, 2012).

Janjira Sombatpoonsiri has just completed her Ph.D at La Trobe University, Australia. Her dissertation explores the use of humour as a vehicle for non-violent struggle. She is currently holding lectureship at the Faculty of Political Science, Thammasat University in Bangkok. Her ongoing research focuses on the impact of the principle of responsibility to protect non-violent protests.

Jularat Damrongwithitham is currently working as a Programme Officer at The Asia Foundation, Thailand. Her award winning MA thesis analyses memories of people who had gone through traumatic experiences during the communist violent suppression period in Thailand, a part from this is also being published as a book chapter from Palgrave (forthcoming).

Chanchai Chaisukkosol is a Lecturer at Institute of Human Rights and Peace Studies, Mahidol University, Thailand. His latest published articles include: The Internet and Nonviolent Struggle: The Anti-government Movement in Thailand 2005–06 (*Social

Alternatives, Issue 3, September 2010); A New Social Contract: The Way Out for Thailand's Political Transformation Crisis (supported by Friedrich-Ebert-Stiftung, 2012).

Senthan Selvarajah is a freelance journalist and researcher. He holds an MA in Global Journalism from Orebro University in Sweden and is currently completing his M.Phil on the Viability of Peace Journalism in the Global South at Swansea University in the United Kingdom. He has worked for the Centre for the Study of Human Rights, Faculty of Law, University of Colombo as a Research and Publications Officer as well as the Foundation for Coexistence, Sri Lanka, as a Researcher. He is the author of *War vs. Peace Discourse: The Press and the Peace Process in Sri Lanka.*

Liu Cheng is Professor of History at Nanjing University, China. In addition to his research and teaching on modern history, he is one of the pioneers who have introduced peace studies as an academic discipline into Chinese universities. He was a visiting scholar at Coventry University's Centre for Peace and Reconciliation Studies in 2003. He organised major international conferences on peace studies in China in 2005, 2011 and 2012. Recently, he translated the works of Johan Galtung, Andrew Rigby, David Barash and Charles Webel.

Tatsushi Arai is an Associate Professor of Peace Building and Conflict Transformation at the School for International Training, Graduate Institute in Vermont, USA. He is also a visiting scholar at George Mason University's School for Conflict Analysis and Resolution in Virginia and a research fellow at the Toda Institute for Global Peace and Policy Research in Hawaii. Previously, also taught international relations at the National University of Rwanda in the aftermath of the 1994 genocide. As a trainer, mediator and dialogue facilitator, he has organised a number of conflict resolution workshops for civil society leaders, diplomats, military personnel, and representatives of international organisations in different parts of the world, including South Asia, East Asia, the Middle East, the African Great Lakes, and North America. His publications include *Creativity and Conflict Resolution: Alternative Pathways to Peace* (2012, Routledge).

Part I
Introduction

1

Introduction

New Paradigms of Peace Research

AKIHIKO KIMIJIMA

This book is a product of the Asia-Pacific Peace Research Association (APPRA). Founded in Yokohama, Japan, in 1980, APPRA is an association of peace researchers in the Asia-Pacific affiliated to the International Peace Research Association (IPRA). APPRA has held conferences at various places in the Asia-Pacific roughly every two years, including one in 2011 at Ritsumeikan University in Kyoto, Japan. Most of the chapters of this book are based on the presentations at the APPRA Conference (2011). We are glad that some authors have contributed the latest results of their research, and that Thomas Weber has demonstrated his friendship with us by contributing his new research on Gandhi and the idea of a non-violent constitution. I believe that the collective efforts of the contributors of this book have broken new ground and present a new paradigms of peace research.

Francis Daehoon Lee's chapter, "Teaching Peace Studies: Implications from Critical Security Studies," proposes the new paradigms of peace research in a broad, fundamental way. Lee reviews the concept of security in detail and points out that the "proliferation of security concepts" in the post-Cold War period, such as common security, comprehensive security, environmental security, and human security, is problematic. He thinks that (1) security is an essentially contested concept; (2) security demands uniform nation-state identity and loyalty; and (3) security discourse obscures and marginalises individual and human dignity and rights. After he follows the recent development of critical security studies, securitisation-desecuritisation studies, and feminist critique to security studies, he argues that the nation-centric, state-centric, security-centric, and male-oriented paradigm of international relations, "the holy trinity in international relations" – the strong solidarity of men, state and war – should be replaced by a critical, new paradigm of peace research. It will de-securitise a security phenomenon, dismantle security politics, and provide frameworks of thinking, analysing, and action for emancipation.

The impacts of the 3/11 disaster on peace research – the earthquakes, tsunami, and particularly the Fukushima nuclear power plant accident – are deep. "The Meaning of Fukushima for Humanity," the chapter by Dr Ikuro Anzai, is originally the keynote speech at the Asia-Pacific Peace Research Association Conference (2011) which impressed the audience very much. APPRA Conference took place seven months later since the 3/11 disaster in Japan and Dr Anzai's speech described the history of nuclear power development in Japan and located the Fukushima nuclear power plant accident – a man-made disaster – in it. Dr Anzai has been critical of the Japanese government's nuclear power policy since the late 1960s and because of this he has been harassed by the people in the Japanese government, the industry and academia. From his own experiences and the 3/11 disaster, he suggests several agenda for future peace research.

"The Criminality of Nuclear Weapons and Nuclear Energy: From Hiroshima to Fukushima," by Kenji Urata, is another important scholarly response to the 3/11 nuclear power plant accident. As a law professor and vice-president of the International Association of Lawyers Against Nuclear Arms (IALANA), he has played an important role in legal struggles – both domestically and internationally – to outlaw nuclear weapons. After 3/11, his understanding of illegality and criminality has developed to include not only the illegality and criminality of nuclear weapons but also those of nuclear power generation in general. That understanding is shared by Judge C.G. Weeramantry and Dr Francis A. Boyle. Although at the moment "nuclear energy for peaceful purposes" is legal and not criminal under the Japanese and international laws, Urata argues that we can start our efforts to change the situation.

Theories and practices of non-violence, and those of Gandhi, have always been very important in peace research, and there were many presentations on these topics at APPRA Conference. Of these, this book includes those by Vidya Jain, John P. Synott, Ravi Bhatia and four Thai researchers – Chaiwat Satha-Anand, Janjira Sombatpoonsiri, Jularat Damrongwithitham, and Chanchai Chaisukkosol. Thomas Weber also contributed a chapter on Gandhi and the idea of a non-violent constitution. These contributions are cutting-edge research in this field.

Vidya Jain in her chapter titled "Swadeshi: Creative Alternative of Globalisation" discusses the concept of Swadeshi (local self-reliance) as a source of inspiration and innovation to defend our freedoms and beliefs in local knowledge systems. She argues that corporate-driven globalisation is a project to extinguish all freedoms of people through the total control of trade, technology and rights. Swadeshi, for Gandhi, was central for creating peace, harmony and sustainable development. Swadeshi or self-organisation in economic affairs is the basis of economic freedom, without which there can be no political freedom or self-rule. Swadeshi is Swaraj (self-rule).

Thomas Weber in his scholarly discourse deliberates on a very important and less discussed subject. What were Gandhi's ideas of democracy and governance? What were Gandhi's views on defence, security and international relations? It would be interesting to examine that how a Gandhian constitution may have looked like (if at all there would have been one) and how the political organisation of his ideal state could have worked and what lessons can be drawn from it for the creation of a more secure and less violent world. Gandhi was quite clear in his belief that non-violence was not limited to use by individuals. It is an attitude of society and could be practised by nations. Dr Weber concludes: "It is still possible that some other fathers/mothers of nations, somewhere, sometime, may have a grand vision and the courage and power to carry it through when they are involved in drafting the governing document of their new country."

John Synott in his chapter "The Educational Legacies of Mahatma Gandhi for Peace Education" discusses the educational principles and experiments of Mahatma Gandhi. Gandhi understood the importance of education for the creation of "new man" and "new world". The centrality of spirituality and moral values in Gandhi's vision is well established. Synott tries to place Gandhi's scheme of education vis-à-vis today's broader context of peace education. However, Synott believes that in spite of his broad perspective Gandhi was a nationalist and his orientations were towards Indian identity, history and circumstances. The final part of the chapter discusses some implications of Gandhi's views on education for peace researchers and teachers. It provides an impetus for a more activist approach to peace research that works towards social change and the transition of international culture towards a culture of peace.

Ravi P. Bhatia in his essay "Dealing with Disasters: Natural and Man-made" warns us to different kinds of disasters in our lives. Some of them are tornadoes, hurricanes, volcanic eruptions and most recent, tsunami. There are other disasters which occur due to human intervention like nuclear disasters. Dr Bhatia offers Gandhian solutions to combat both kinds of disasters. He discusses Gandhian philosophy as well as environmental movements inspired by Gandhi. He concludes by saying that a shift in development paradigm is needed where excessive exploitation of physical resources can be avoided by leading simpler lives and sustaining our environment and different forms of life. Gandhian approach of simple living, moral lifestyles, sustaining environment and bridging the gap between the poor and the rich has to be highlighted.

As Dr Bhatia's chapter shows, one of the issues highlighted by the Fukushima nuclear power plant accident is the necessity of change from a civilisation with high-energy consumption to one that is more decent and modest, and respects being at peace with nature. In this sense, it is natural that Japanese people have rediscovered the writings of Shozo Tanaka (1841–1913), a political activist, environmentalist and organic intellectual, who once served as Member of Parliament in prewar Japan.[1] In 1912, Tanaka wrote, "True civilization does not devastate mountains, or rivers, or villages; nor does it kill humans." This book echoes this sentiment.

The chapter "Humour, Witnessing and Cyber Non-violent Action: Current Research on Innovative Tactical Non-violent Actions Against Tyranny, Ethnic Violence and Hatred" by four Thai peace researchers – Chaiwat Satha-Anand, Janjira Sombatpoonsiri, Jularat Damrongwithitham and Chanchai Chaisukkosol – is an example of innovative peace research and has also shown us the possible direction of future peace research. The authors focus on three tactical nonviolent actions – the use of humour, peace witnessing, and cyber nonviolent actions – and show us their potentials of preventing and overcoming violence. Firstly, as the Otpor (Resistance) Movement in Serbia in the late 1990s demonstrated, the humour in protests helps prevent protests from turning into violence and thus facilitate peaceful change. Secondly, the Peace Witness Volunteer Group has played an important role in preventing and reducing violence in southern Thailand where there have been tensions between the Malay Muslim population and the Thai authorities. The presence of the Peace Witness Volunteer Group in the region and the information-sharing among the larger Thai public have helped prevent the tensions from becoming violent. Thirdly, as in the real world, in the cyberspace too, there are a lot of hate speeches and they may induce hatred, antagonism, and violence. In order to prevent this, not government censorship but actions like "electronic civil disobedience" (e.g., "virtual sit-in") are possible tactical nonviolent actions. They conclude that these "small acts" can be powerful because at their hearts, humour, peace witnessing and electronic civil disobedience are vintage nonviolent actions since they empower ordinary people and into the course of creative actions it will eventually help foster a less violent world.

Conflict transformation is another important field of peace research, and there are many conflicts in the Asia-Pacific region. Many of these were discussed, analysed, and diagnosed at the APPRA Conference. In terms of this area, this book has chapters on the Sinhalese-Tamil conflict by Senthan Selvarajah, on China-Japan relations by Liu Cheng, and on Mainland China and Taiwan relations by Tatsushi Arai.

Senthan Selvarajah, in his chapter "The Transitional Approach between Wars to Peace in Sri Lanka: A Qualitative Conceptual GNH Review," treats the conflict between Sinhalese and Tamils in Sri Lanka. This conflict came to an end by the Sinhalese government's military victory over the Liberation Tigers of Tamil Eelam (LTTE). Post-conflict reconstruction, rehabilitation and reconciliation are the urgent issues in Sri Lanka. The author examines the process using the concept of Gross National Happiness (GNH). GNH is a concept introduced by King of

Bhutan, Jigme Singya WangChuck in 1972 and now attracts wider attention. It is considered a better index of measurement of a country's development than the Gross Domestic Product (GDP). Selvarajah thinks that evaluating the post-conflict reconstruction process by GNH is appropriate because a failure of fulfilling GNH standards – psychological well-being, time use, community vitality, culture, health, education, environmental diversity, living standards and governance – will result in a recurrence to violent conflicts. Based on GNH standards, he thinks, the Sri Lankan government's post-conflict reconstruction process has many problems. The Sri Lankan government's honest and genuine efforts of reconstruction and reconciliation for Tamil people are lacking. At the end of the chapter, the author concludes that the UN and the international community should act in order to establish an international assistance mechanism to provide relief and assistance to the war-affected people in the North and the East.

Liu Cheng's chapter, "Sino-Japanese Reconciliation from a Peace Studies Perspective," is about the fifteen years' war between China and Japan (1931–1945) and how to overcome the antagonism between them. According to him, the atrocities committed by the Imperial Japanese Army in the fifteen years' war are at the centre of the issue. That "national experiences" and their memories lead to the rise of Chinese nationalism and Japan's failure to honestly face its past makes matters worse. To admit the authenticity of other people's history paves the way for seeking common grounds. The author thinks that people will recover from painful memories, get over anger, forgive the former enemy or place hope in the future only when they believe that the evils of the past will never reoccur. He concludes that the Japanese government's and the Japanese people's actions of facing the past honestly should come first.

Tatsushi Arai discusses in his chapter, "Strait Talk: Activating Peace Potential in Youth-led Civil Society Dialogues Across the Taiwan Strait," the conflict between Mainland China and Taiwan. He has facilitated annual week-long dialogues between young civil society delegates from Mainland China, Taiwan, and the United States. These dialogues, "Strait Talk," started as a student-conceptualised event and they have been held at Brown University and the University of California at Berkeley. In this chapter, the author explores lessons learned from them. At the heart of this historical conflict is the Mainland Chinese search for coherent nationhood and territorial integrity, on the one hand, and the Taiwanese desire to determine their own political future and to give full expressions to their diverse and distinct communal identities without Chinese interference, on the other. Strait Talk has offered a unique opportunity of highly interactive, experiential learning to young generations of both sides of the Taiwan Strait. From the experiences of facilitating the dialogues, Arai has observed four trends: (1) both sides view the conflict as a relatively contemporary phenomenon, not to be mythologised; (2) both sides are ready and able to unpack the seemingly non-negotiable nature of sovereignty; (3) contrary to these two trends, however, the young delegates also carry with them strong emotional attachments to their large-group identities; and (4) young delegates of both sides are also ready and able to extend deep empathy with one another, even to the point of crossing the boundaries of their political correctness. Based on these observations, he concludes that time is ripe to start making concerted strategic efforts across the Strait to create robust, self-adaptive, and sustainable mechanisms of civil society interactions that deepen interdependence and make war unthinkable.

Reflections on these conflicts and practices aimed at reconciliation are important contributions in efforts towards peaceful change in the Asia-Pacific. I believe that these efforts are examples of people bearing "peace responsibility," a concept proposed in 2000 by Shinji Takahashi, a philosopher in Nagasaki.[2] Japan's younger generations are unable to understand why they are expected to bear war responsibility, but they do understand that they have "peace responsibility." What "peace responsibility" entails is still in the process of development, but the idea that everyone has "peace responsibility" and must bear this is persuasive.

Notes

1. See, for example, Kenneth Strong, *Ox Against the Storm: A Biography of Tanaka Shozo: Japan's Conservationist Pioneer*, Routledge, 1995.
2. See, for example, Shinji Takahashi, *The A-Bomb Experience and Our Responsibility for Peace: A Philosopher's View*, http://www.hiroshima-cu.ac.jp/modules/peace_e/content0177.html.

2

Teaching Peace Studies

Implications from Critical Security Studies

FRANCIS DAEHOON LEE

This article is to identify some of the key arguments in critical security studies (CSS) and draw meaningful implications for improving peace studies and peace teaching, especially the peace studies related with international studies. The key arguments in critical security studies are drawn from a few works in this field and I added recent contributions from feminist studies. The main motivation comes from the felt need to address the gap between peace studies and these critical views that I sometimes find in my own practice and observations of various learning sites and designs of peace studies. This is also related to my concern for the urgent need for peace studies and teaching to develop meaningful frames that reflect and incorporate critical, epistemological and ontological underpinnings of such critiques, critiques towards the nation-centric, state-centric, security-centric, and therefore, male-oriented and non-critical traditions and discourses in international relations (IR) studies.

Early Critique of Security Studies and Expansion of Security Concepts

There has been a critique that security studies have been an American invention and world-look. It is well known that national security has become a key notion in US foreign policies since George F. Kennan's post-war design. As such security studies took the central stage in the post-war IR studies.

In this light, David Cambell argued on the link between state identity (of the US) and security politics in his study of the US foreign policies.[1] Security politics is not just a part of the overall politics of a state, but an essential part of it because state's identity is constituted through existence of alternative mode of being by the other states, in which identity recognition is a life-and-death struggle.

"Then, danger to a state is not an objective condition, but something which exists in close relation to those to whom it may become a threat. While identity is an inescapable dimension of being and is constituted in relation to difference, difference is also constituted in relation to identity. But neither is fixed by nature, given by God, or planned by intentional behaviour. "Identity of any particular state should be understood as 'tenuously constituted in time ... through a stylized repetition of acts,' and achieved, 'not [through] a founding act, but rather a regulated process of repetition'."[2]

Cambell's study brings security researchers to the importance of domestic politics involved in the formulation or change of state identity (from a developmentalist to a welfare state for example). Moreover, security studies would necessarily focus on the roles of various political and social actors in the sense that they act and react differently to identity formulation or change, because the constitution of identity is achieved through the inscription of boundaries which serve to demarcate an 'inside' from an 'outside,' a 'self' from an 'other', a 'domestic' from a 'foreign'.

Cambell shifts what is given from outside in realist outlook of the world to what is socially constituted, thus, inviting enquirers to ask who constitute the socially constructed identities and how. In this sense, bringing identity question into security analysis is similar to re-establishing the whole approach to security issues. This demystified state.

Post-Cold War security discourses have significantly expanded, to meet the demand, that is, the rising concerns in all areas for safety and livelihood along with growing awareness in human dignity and human rights. New languages of security have emerged such as common security, comprehensive security, cooperative security, food security, environmental security, community security, human security and women's security. Along with it, more metaphors of security have developed: stability, balance, war on drugs, war on poverty, war on illiteracy, war on terror, immigrants as threat, threat of climate change, security controls, community watch, security walls, secure communities, CCTVs, etc. A culmination of this post-Cold War expansionist trend is also found in the conceptualisation of human security in its effort to combine freedom from want and freedom from fear to place itself at the foundation of more traditional security such as national security.

This development or trend can be taken as diverse global/local reactions to the military-strategist domination of this policy area and the realist influence over its studies. It can also be understood as a legitimate reflection on diversifying areas of concerns that go beyond state interest. On the other hand, however, conceptual expansion of this sort is destined to stop before it reaches the state of agenda black hole. Everything may become a security, thus losing what it stands for.

Simon Dalby, for example, demonstrates what is obscured by a security approach and argues security as essentially contested notion. The obscurity of security is because there is an inherent dilemma in the security approaches to social issues that in the process of providing various forms of security, insecurities are also reproduced, often in ways that either actually undermine the initial production of security.[3]

According to Fierke and other similar discussion, the critiques to the proliferation of security concepts are summarised as (1) 'security' being used as an obscure, confusing, not-definable concept (security as essentially contested concept), (2) security as a call for uniform nation-state identity and loyalty, (3) security as ethnocentric concept and language reflecting the interest of the Western nation-state, and (4) security as state discourse to obscure or marginalise the discourse of individual and human dignity and rights.[4]

Ken Booth's Outline of the Development of CSS

Critical Security Studies: Concepts and Cases, edited by Keith Krause and Michael C. Williams, comes as a milestone in synthesising these discussions into a school of thought. Even though the authors here do not explicitly define a "critical" approach of their own, the chapters here represent a comprehensive critique to the neorealist security studies. However, the book was received as a set of mutually incoherent critiques, not fully meeting the sense of Coxian notion of 'critical'.[5]

Reviewing such initial works on CSS, Ken Booth identifies two major roads to CSS, critical theory tradition in social theory and radical tradition in international relations theory, which should converge.[6]

According to Booth, the critical theory tradition draws its critique from the works of the Frankfurt School, Antonio Gramsci, the Marxian tradition, and some critical international relations theory that examine relationships among community, democracy, force and law (such as David Held). Booth draws four core themes from the critical theory tradition in social theory: (1) all knowledge is a social process; (2) traditional theory promotes the flaws of naturalism and reductionism; (3) critical theory offers a basis for political and social progress; and (4) the test of theory is emancipation.[7]

For the second source of the tradition, he finds five schools of thoughts that contribute to the radical international relations tradition, namely, the philosophical tradition of social idealism, the peace studies tradition, the world society or world order school, feminist theorising, historical sociology. Similarly, he outlines that (1) human society is its own invention, (2) regressive theories have dominated politics among nations, (3) the state and other institutions must be de-naturalised, and (4) progressive world order values should inform the means and ends of an international politics committed to enhancing world security.[8]

Booth's tentative proposal for a more critical CSS is as follows:

> "Critical security theory is both a theoretical commitment and a political orientation. As a theoretical commitment it embraces a set of ideas engaging in a critical and permanent exploration of the ontology, epistemology, and praxis of security, community, and emancipation in world politics. As a political orientation it is informed by the aim of enhancing security through emancipatory politics and networks of community at all levels, including the potential community of communities – common humanity."[9]

To this, Tara McCormack adds that unless CSS breaks away from liberal traditions such in human security and call for better security, it fails its promise of becoming an emancipatory project.[10]

Securitisation-Desecuritisation Studies

Securitisation studies is a framework of security analysis advocated by the so-called Copenhagen School led by Barry Buzan and Ole Waever. Here, security is articulated a purposeful language rather than an objective reflection of a reality, or is intrinsically linked with *performative* constitution of identity, is perhaps the best structured into research frame in the Ole Waever's securitisation thesis, which is based on speech act theory. In his often-quoted words:

> "With the help of language theory, we can regard 'security' as a *speech act*. In this usage, security is not of interest as a sign that refers to something more 'real'; it is the utterance *itself* that is the act. By saying it, something is done (as in betting, giving a promise, naming a ship). By uttering 'security,' a state-representative moves a particular development into a specific area, and thereby claims a special right to use whatever means are necessary to block it."[11]

Ole Waever's speech act theory of security studies is informed by language theories that focus on the nature of social act of a spoken language. In the light of Wittgenstein, language is part of social games, and not simply a medium of transferring meanings of language users. Spoken languages play certain social roles by performing certain social acts. There are no 'false' meanings – meanings are all only in use. This is how they perform a certain social act. Most utterances, if not all, are *performative*.

Within the internal construction of state, as Buzan points the direction of our attention to, language of security is an act, a speech act in particular, that engages the uttering and listening actors into that process of mutual constitution. However, security is a particular form of speech acts. It has a logic of excluding something that is considered to be a threat to securing 'we'. It is basically boundary-drawing language that constitutes actual boundary-drawings in perceptions and policies.

As such security is a discriminatory language, because the uttering actor purports to prioritise itself over other actors. The objective of this prioritising is to justify its right to use emergency measures for identified problems. This objective can only be realised if the security speech succeeds in arousing perception of extreme gravity of a problem. Security is also a constitutive language in that what it designates as a possible threat would be a threat by the very speech act itself. These characteristics mark the particular nature of speech act involving security language.

Understanding the constitutive nature of speech act involved in the political nature of security brings us to Waever's securitisation approach to security studies.

> "(I)t follows that a major focus of 'security studies' should be the *process* of securitization and de-securitization: When, why and how elites label issues and developments as 'security' problems; when, why and how they succeed and fail in such endeavours; what attempts are made by other groups to put securitization on the agenda; and whether we can point to efforts to keep issues *off* security agenda, or even to de-securitize issues that have become securitized?"[12]

This perspective makes it obvious that the expansion of security notion in the practice of 'redefining' security leaves the core of meaning of 'security' as uncontested, pushing instead in the direction of securitising still larger areas of social life.[13] Securitisation approach, therefore, radically departs from the expansionist trend in that it directs enquiries to the centre of contestation – who securitises an issue, why and how.

Michael Dillon on Politics of Security

Dillon provides a thorough and fundamental critique to security studies in his book *Politics of Security* in relation to one of the main problems of it, ethnocentric nature of security studies, that is the link between the Western world and security studies.

Dillon makes a key argument that security informs and forms politics and vice versa, and security in international relations is a testing ground for its out-living in or from modernity:

> "The history of security is not the pursuit of a universal value by pre-formed subjects, individual or collective. Given the foundational significance of security to all established formulations of politics, throughout the political tradition of the West, the history

> of security is a history of the changing problematisation of what it is to be a political subject and to be politically subject."
>
> "International Relations is a discipline concerned with observing how the political project of *living-out* the modern emerged, and how it continues to operate globally. I am concerned with how we might *out-live* the modern politically. I think of *out-living* here as surpassing the modern political imagination, not merely surviving its dereliction."
>
> "That it (security) has, in fact, always been concerned with securing the very grounds of what the political itself is; specifying what the essence of politics is thought to be."

This is to ask the frequently un-asked question: "Must we secure security? (This is) The critical conjunction of the philosophical and the political." This is a critical conjunction of the philosophical and the political also in the sense of inheritance of sovereignty from Church to State in the West: "… *extra ecclesiam nulla salus* (no salvation outside the Church) … Salvation was the ultimate form of spiritual security, and now in an obvious connection the dictum goes 'no security outside State,'" because State knows it all.

What this brings to the politics can be called security politics which is much more than security encompasses in about the traditional and expansionist security approaches. It is bout truths, power and subject, calculative reason, ultimate knowledge, and eschatology.

> "What truths about the human condition … are thought to be secreted in security?
> What work does securing security do for and upon us?
> What power-effects issue out of the regimes of truth of security?
> If the truth of security compels us to secure security, why, how and where is that grounding compulsion grounded?
>
> How was it that seeking security became such an insistent and relentless (inter)national preoccupation for humankind?
>
> What sort of project is the pursuit of security, and how does it relate to other modern human concerns and enterprises, such as seeking freedom and knowledge through representative-calculative thought, technology and subjectification? … A terminal paradox …"

> "The philosopher therefore spoke as a security expert. A security expert not merely in respect of what the substantial values were, but increasingly only in terms of how they were to be secured ..."

> "(Inter)national politics of security are, therefore, essentially a form of eschatology; politics thought in the light of the last things, the limit situation as a determinable and determining terminus. But because eschatology is ineluctably linked also, through diverse idioms (essence, cause, *telos* and revelation) to the beginning of things .... Specifying the end (the limit condition as the terminal and not the liminal), politics of security claim also to have to discern the advent of the political."

A few selected quotations listed above point to the following implications: (1) security lies at the centre of the Western idea of the political, (2) security is a doctrine defining all the basics of modern politics especially the authority, loyalty, belonging, knowledge hierarchy, safety, protection, state, etc., (3) security by state has a parallel with salvation by church, (4) threat-knowing has link with death and life of a state, and a parallel with the end of the world (eschatology), and (5) this is related with the security expertise in parallel with the old church clergy class. This is to mention just a few points from Dillon's work.

Feminist Critique to Security Studies and Emancipation

Ann Tickner's critique to realist and neorealist tradition in international relations studies represents a basic critique from gender perspective.[14] Along with Betty Reardon and others, the authors of this approach argue that IR studies without gender is deeply problematic, and actually sustains the holy trinity in IR studies that Jacqie True once called to our attention, the strong solidarity of men, state and war. True identifies this as the main objective of critique to international relations studies from feminist perspectives.[15]

The journal *Security Studies* highlighted in 2009 key critique of feminist studies towards international relations studies:

> "Liberal feminist work calls attention to the subordinate position of women in global politics and argues that gender oppression can be remedied by including women in the existing structures of global politics. Critical feminism explores the ideational and material manifestations of gendered identity and gendered power

in world politics. Feminist constructivism focuses on the ways that ideas about gender shape and are shaped by global politics. Feminist poststructuralism focuses on how gendered linguistic manifestations of meaning, particularly strong/weak, rational/emotional, and public/private dichotomies, serve to empower the masculine, marginalize the feminine, and constitute global politics. Postcolonial feminists, while sharing many of the epistemological assumptions of poststructural feminists, focus on the ways that colonial relations of domination and subordination established under imperialism are reflected in gender relations, and even relations between feminists, in global politics and academic work."[16]

Feminists do offer alternatives to the traditional concepts of peace and security, peace as absence of war and security as maximum self-defence. They argue that peace entails social justice and economic equality, in similar way as Johan Galtung does. This means theorising women's concerns in the notion of structural violence, but with a strong feminist focus on relationships, needs and empathy (rather than institutions, organisations and goal maximisation).[17]

However, contrary to such common views that call for better or alternative security, as in Tickner's and Reardon's proposals for human security, genuine security, global security (which are also popularly known and used in many peace studies), recent feminist scholar's focus on dismantling the security politics and discourse from a more fundamentally critical way.

Jonathan D. Wadley looks into how a state is perceived as a personified actor using Judith Butler's theory of performativity.[18] Wadley argues, not only that the silence toward gender is more obvious in the field of international security than in any others, the gendered reification of states are possible through projecting themselves as stable and masculine protector of all, i.e., through performances of security. States are too often presented as persons having feelings such as fear and anger, intentions of emotions and reason, and actions with purposes and calculations in international relations. Personified states take the image of a human body, in which the brain thinks and feels, the body being diseased or wounded, the limbs taking actions, the soul having an identity and continuity. This body has a blood, flesh and skin, a clear inside and outside, and therefore, experiencing infection from outside and bleeding to outside. Thus, a territorial-familial sovereign state arises as a human (actually masculine) body, and the contest is whether or not this body is the protector of security.

Interestingly, this is well connected with the discussion of state performativity in Waever's discussion of securitisation. Her key arguments are: (1) personification of state is essential in drawing the boundary between the international and domestic and this is a gendered process, (2) security studies totally delete gender in the state's personification and acting as security provider, (3) states reify themselves through performances of security, (4) such identity of state is performatively constituted by the very 'expressions' that are said to be its results, and (5) duality of male gender is copied by personified state (calculatively rational and tough outside, and protection disguised as care inside.)

Christine Sylvester has for long argued that IR is highly gendered, stuffed and bristling with male decision-makers, failing to take into account women as agents of knowledge and theory.[19] Recently, she has been theorising on the fear, how it formulates and is used in gendered politics.[20] This fear is at the basis of security politics (actually in many of the peace studies as well), but the fear in modern times is a reflection of desire to have maximum (gendered) uniformity. In other words, fear is gendered, and fear is the political field where gendered relations are produced in relation to the authority of state. Fear sidelines and silences people and organises authority. Sylvester invites our attention to the invisible, silenced actualities of security politics, how fear creates and engenders authority, emphasising that security is not something to be improved within the gendered state, but to be dismantled and replaced by a fundamentally different attitude and theorising towards fear. This also has great implications to the debates of the current state of state authority and the post-authority international relations such as discussed by Ronnie D. Lipschutz.[21]

Implications to Peace Studies

Peace studies and teaching usually start and centre on the understanding of violence and how to limit or eradicate it. When security stands for the most modern imagination of safety and protection linked with modern nation-state system, there should be a close linkage between peace studies' concern on violence and the way modern states are thought to provide security.

Where there has been substantial development in critical thinking in security studies, its implications to peace studies and teaching have not been fully explored. Here, I tentatively draw a few implications below:

- That all knowledge is a social process implies that knowledge on security-related fields such as fear, safety, protection and force involves social processes that are particular to a society, and that the way state-men-war-security have been constructed in relation to these fields of knowledge should be revealed more actively in peace studies.
- Security lies at the heart of the modern political studies including international studies. Peace studies need to face and address this in a serious way by focussing on the questions of blurring borders of inside-outside including the border between foreign and domestic, and relate this question to how violence is created and justified in the image of protecting the borders (various borders at the same time).
- Traditional theories on security and IR promote the flaws of naturalism and reductionism: this implies that peace studies should progress to be more critical on naturalistic and reductionist arguments concerning violence, safety, identity, gender, territoriality and other similar topics. This critique should employ an active inquiry into various discourses and grammars of naturalism found in discourses of peace in different societies, and connect the findings of inquiry to formulation of alternative grammar and language of peace.
- If critical studies is to provide frameworks of thinking, analysing, and action for emancipation, peace studies should also be so. Peace studies about and for emancipation and emancipation from what can be developed more rigorously. In this regard, there should be more intense exchange between two schools, both in research and teaching.
- In order to grasp recent debates in IR and security studies as well and feminist IR studies and border studies, peace studies

should become more a critical studies, with the focus on engaging in the immediate realities with critical and committed exploration, new epistemology, and new praxis of security, community, and emancipation in world politics.

- Security analysis in peace studies can be better placed as part of critique to political process of making something a security issue and making something not (securitisation). It is better to regard and use the term security in an un-natural way, and pay more attention to how and why people and power mobilise that language. This will open a new field in peace studies towards how and why we need to de-securitise a security phenomenon, i.e., re-interpret the phenomenon, give silence a meaning, find suppressed subjects, bring their stories and languages to the stage and deconstruct the power relations and other effects of security approach. Through de-securitisation, another possible political process, the study of civil society, democracy, human rights, and NGOs can be well connected, especially asking what their roles are in dismantling security politics.
- This will lead to re-examination of the security expertise, or security epistemic communities, which is a necessary step to create an alternative epistemic community of peace. This will create an effect of changing the hierarchy given to security expertise, which is an integral part of the hegemony of security politics in modern life.
- Neglect of gender in IR and silence on the masculine personification of states are at the foundation of the alliance between men and security. Thus, state and security studies should be more strongly and critically raised in peace studies. Feminism should be an integral part of peace studies and teaching, especially with the view to the feminist claim that the gendered nature of IR is centred on the trinity of state-men-war (or security). Gender-informed de-securitisation, therefore, can be a fatal severance to this trinity.
- The feminist critique on the gendered nature of personification of state in particular should be seriously taken into account, so as to develop alternative language and discourses in analysing state behaviour. This is because silence has been too prevailing on this subject in peace studies, and in actual

studies and education for peace there is an obvious lack of alternative languages other than personified state languages.

- Analysis of state behaviour and international relations among states can be better looked at by focussing on the performativity of them, especially in security matters. The concept of performativity will play a crucial role in de-naturalising the realist storytelling on violence and authority that permeates across cultures from international affairs to daily stories. The performativity approach can enhance peace studies and teaching in countering realist paradigm (the world as it has been, and the natural as the real).
- Studies of fear, fear perception, threat, threat-perception, threat-identity-ethics connection, should be actively incorporated in peace studies, especially developing critical thinking and theories towards the tradition of treating threat as a given reality (positivist idea of threat).

Notes

1. Cambell.
2. Ibid., pp. 3–9.
3. Dalby, p. 13, 22.
4. Fierke, pp. 33–52.
5. Cox.
6. Booth.
7. Ibid., pp. 261–64.
8. Ibid., pp. 264–68.
9. Ibid., p. 268.
10. McCormack, pp. 139–42.
11. Waever, p. 55.
12. Ibid., pp. 57–58.
13. Ibid., p. 47.
14. Tickner.
15. Sjoberg, pp. 183–213.
16. Ibid.
17. Terriff et al., p. 95.
18. Wadley.

19. Terriff et al., pp. 94–95.
20. Sylvester.
21. Lipschutz.

References

Barash, David P. and Charles P. Webel, *Peace and Conflict Studies*, Thousand Oaks: Sage, 2002.

Booth, Ken (ed.), *Critical Security Studies and World Politics*, London: Lynne Rienner, 2005.

Buzan, Barry, Ole Waever and Jaap de Wilde, *Security: A New Framework for Analysis*, Boulder: Lynne Rienner, 1998.

Cambell, David, *Writing Security: United States Foreign Policies and Politics of Identity*, Minneapolis: University of Minnesota Press, 1998.

Cox, Robert W., "Social Forces, States and World Orders: Beyond International Relations Theory", in Robert O. Keohane (ed.), *Neorealism and Its Critics,* New York: Columbia University Press, 1986.

Dillon, Michael, *Politics of Security: Towards a Political Philosophy of Continental Thought*, London: Routledge, 1996.

Fierke, K.M., *Critical Approaches to International Security*, Cambridge: Polity, 2007.

Krause, Keith and Michael C. Williams (eds.), *Critical Security Studies: Concepts and Cases,* London: UCL Press, 1997.

Lipschutz, Ronnie D., *After Authority: War, Peace, and Global Politics in the 21st Century*, Albany: State University of New York Press, 2000.

McCormack, Tara, *Critique, Security and Power: The Political Limits to Emancipatory Approach*, New York: Routledge, 2010.

McSweeney, Bill, *Security, Identity and Interests: A Sociology of International Relations*, Cambridge: Cambridge University Press, 1999.

Sjoberg, Laura (ed.), *Gender and International Security: Feminist Perspectives*, London: Routledge, 2010.

——, "Introduction to Security Studies: Feminist Contributions", *Security Studies*, 18: 183–213, 2009.

Sylvester, Christine, "War, Sense, and Security", in Laura Sjoberg (ed.), *Gender and International Security: Feminist Perspectives*, London: Routledge, 2010.

Terriff, Terry et al., *Security Studies Today*, Cambridge: Polity, 1999.

Tickner, Ann J., *Gender in International Relations: Feminist Perspectives on Achieving Global Security*, New York: Columbia University, 1992.

Vaughan-Williams, Nick, *Border Politics: The Limits of Sovereign Power*, Edinburgh: Edinburgh University Press, 2009.

Wadley, Jonathan D., "Gendering the State: Peformativity and Protection in International Security", in Laura Sjoberg (ed.), *Gender and International Security: Feminist Perspectives*, London: Routledge, 2010.

Waever, Ole, "Securitization and Desecuritization", in Ronnie D. Lipschutz (ed.), *On Security*, New York: Columbia University Press, 1995.

Part II

Revisiting the Post-Fukushima Nuclear Age

3

The Meaning of Fukushima for Humanity

IKURO ANZAI

At 14:46 on 11 March 2011, a tremendously destructive earthquake occurred in the north-east part of mainland Japan, depriving approximately 20,000 people of their lives. More than 300,000 people took refuge from the quake, the following *tsunami*, and radiations originating from damaged nuclear power stations in the area. The magnitude of the quake was estimated to be 9, the biggest in the modern history of Japan. The earthquake was named "The Great East Japan Earthquake", which was more than 11,000 times greater than the New Zealand earthquake in Christchurch on 22 February 2011, and 45 times as great as the 1923 Great Kanto earthquake in the Tokyo area which killed approximately 140,000 people.

When I was told about the occurrence of the serious nuclear accident for the first time that evening, I felt very sorry for not having been able to prevent such a catastrophe, although I am a specialist in radiation protection who has been strictly criticising governmental nuclear power policy for more than 40 years since

This is a revised version of author's keynote speech given at the APPRA Conference held at Ritsumeikan University, Kyoto, on 14 October 2011 under the title of "Agenda for Peace Research after 3/11".

late 1960s. As a scientist who has been involved in the field of nuclear science and technology, I was ashamed of my incapacity for not having been successful in persuading our government and the people of Japan about the risks of nuclear power generation tragically demonstrated in Fukushima.

I originally graduated from the University of Tokyo in 1964 as one of the first students of the Department of Nuclear Engineering in Japan. My graduation paper 48 years ago was on the investigation into preventive measures against severe nuclear accidents, although there were no nuclear power plants in Japan at that time. As is well known among Japanese people, the 1960s began with the revision of the US-Japan Security Treaty. This agreement deeply involved Japan in the Vietnam War by offering many military bases throughout the nation to the US, especially in Okinawa. In addition to various new types of weapons such as the pineapple bomb, the ball bomb, the nail bomb, and defoliants, the US military force even had a plan to use B43 hydrogen bombs in Vietnam. One of the mock-up B43 bombs used for training in Iejima Island, Okinawa, is now exhibited at The Kyoto Museum for World Peace, Ritsumeikan University.

The 1960s was also the period when the Japanese government was promoting a so-called "income-doubling policy" of rapid economic growth, which resulted in incidences of serious environmental pollution, industrial accidents, poisoning of mass-produced medical drugs, etc. Many people including workers, teachers, researchers, engineers, mothers and students were beginning to become aware of the importance of the social responsibility of corporations, technologists and scientists. In 1965, a scientists' organisation named the Japan Scientists Association was established for the development of science based on the principles of independence, democracy and harmony. The association was affiliated with individual researchers and educationalists in the fields of not only natural science but also social and human science. I joined the association in 1966, and became one of the board members responsible for the activities of watching governmental nuclear power policy. I learnt much more comprehensively about nuclear issues, not only about the scientific and technological aspects but also the political, economical, social and cultural aspects of nuclear power policy. I was also deeply educated by people in the local communities who invited me to their lecture meetings about nuclear safety issues, and threw varieties of questions at me that were far outside my scientific field but vitally important for the life of their community. These questions were extremely difficult for me to answer, which inevitably drove me to learn broader aspects of nuclear power.

Proposing Six Check Points of Nuclear Policy

A first and very significant opportunity came to me in 1972, when I was requested to make a keynote speech at the first symposium on nuclear power generation organised by the Science Council of Japan (JSC) which is sometimes referred to as the parliament of Japanese scientists. JSC was substantially the official representative organisation of Japanese scientists, and 210 members of JSC, 30 scientists in seven different academic fields, were elected by a direct vote of about 300,000 scientists all over Japan. I was as young as 32 years old at that time, and it was very exceptional for a young scientist like me to have such an opportunity to make a keynote address in JSC about such an important issue.

I proposed six fundamental check points about the healthiness or unhealthiness of Japanese nuclear power policy, which were: (1) the independence of a national energy policy, (2) development not for economic growth but for safety first, (3) a national nuclear power policy that would not devastate the development policies of local communities, (4) the prevention of military use of nuclear energy, (5) safety assurances for the lives of nuclear power plant workers and residents, and proven safety measures against severe accidents, and (6) democracy of nuclear power administration. These check points were crystallised through the social activities of the Japan Scientists Association since its establishment, and functioned for some time as leading principles for anti-nuclear power movement in Japan in 1970s.

The next year, in 1973, I was invited to the National Diet as one of ten scientists in the field of nuclear science and technology who were requested to state their opinions and viewpoints about national nuclear power policy. I took this opportunity to sharply criticise governmental policy. I was then an assistant lecturer working for the Department of Radiological Health, in the Faculty of Medicine of the University of Tokyo, which is a national university. I was a national government employee who nevertheless strictly criticised national nuclear policy, which resulted in my experiencing a variety of harassments in my academic life as introduced later.

Experience in Fukushima

In September 1973, I became deeply involved in anti-nuclear power movement in Fukushima together with the people residing in the vicinity of the nuclear power plants. The government held a public hearing regarding Fukushima Nuclear Power Plant 2, which was the first official public hearing about nuclear power generation ever organised in Japan. But it was a typical example of so-called "*Yarase*" in Japanese, which means a fake or insincere meeting. The majority of speakers and the audience of the public hearing were intentionally chosen from among the people who agreed with inviting nuclear power plants to Fukushima. Nevertheless, I collaborated with other scientists, lawyers and the people in the local community to send our delegates to the public hearing to raise questions about risks of nuclear power and to clarify the unhealthiness of the national nuclear policy. I myself had a chance to make a speech there by the efforts of the anti-nuclear residents who nominated me as a delegate speaking for them. However, the most astonishing thing I experienced there was a speech made by a pro-nuclear woman who was sent from the local community in the vicinity of Fukushima Nuclear Power Plants which are now in crisis. She said, "We need not fear bad effects of nuclear radiation, because, in the 1973 National High School Baseball Tournament, the championship was gained by the high school baseball team from Hiroshima, the A-bombed city, where, it was once said, no grass or trees would grow for 75 years." She seemed to have an intention to hint that radiation is not so harmful as actually feared by referring to the remarkable vitality of the young people who had grown up even in an area devastated by a nuclear weapon. Although it was very sad for me to witness such kinds of unscientific storytelling, unfortunately it seemed to have some effects on the formation of the public acceptance of nuclear power in Japan.

Brief History of Nuclear Power Development in Japan

Now, let me introduce a brief history of nuclear power development in Japan.

Immediately after the end of the Pacific War, electric power in Japan was dominantly generated by hydraulic power plants, and there was only one electric power company named "Japan Electric Power Generation and Supply Company". Japan was virtually ruled by the US Occupation Army, and the US adopted an administrative policy to rule Japan not directly but indirectly through the Japanese government with Emperor Hirohito as a nominal symbol of the unity of the Japanese people. In 1951, the US dismantled the Japan Electric Power Generation and Supply Company into nine regional power companies, i.e., Hokkaido Electric Power Company, Tohoku Electric Power Company, Hokuriku Electric Power Company, Tokyo Electric Power Company, Chubu Electric Power Company, Kansai Electric Power Company, Chugoku Electric Power Company, Shikoku Electric Power Company and Kyushu Electric Power Company. It was done in the name of the democratisation of Japan's economic system by disorganising the so-called *"Zaibatsu"*, which means intensive financial combines. But the real strategic intention of the US was to make Japanese electric power production dependent upon the US. For instance, Kansai Electric Power Company was limited to serve the Kansai area covering big cities such as Osaka, Kobe and Kyoto. These cities needed vast amount of electric power in the process of reconstruction in the postwar period, but Kansai Electric Power Company did not possess enough hydraulic power resources within its territory which inevitably made the company dependent upon thermal power plants, which can be built near an area which consumes much electric power. In the earlier stage, considerable amount of coal produced in Japan was used for thermal power generation, but the fuel was gradually switched to petroleum which drastically and rapidly rendered Japan dependent on the US energy strategy. Nuclear power development in Japan was fundamentally characterised along this same line by accepting the offer of nuclear technology from the US and introducing nuclear power plants originally developed in the US.

On the other hand, Japan is the only nation that has experienced nuclear holocausts by the US atomic bombing on Hiroshima and Nagasaki in 1945. More than 300,000 people were driven to death by the use of these classical nuclear weapons. But, the international community could not have an opportunity to know the terrible damage and aftereffects of the atomic bombings, because the US forbade writing reports and sending photos about the tragedy by press code or news censorship, and restarted nuclear testing from 1 July 1946. But three years later in 1949, the USSR succeeded in developing a plutonium bomb, which motivated the US towards the development of a hydrogen bomb.

On March 1, 1954, a Japanese tuna fishing boat named "Lucky Dragon" was exposed to lethal levels of radioactive fallout produced by a US hydrogen bomb test carried out on the Bikini Atolls, the detonation yield of which was 15 megatons, five times as great as the total yield of bombs used throughout World War II, including the two atomic bombs dropped on Hiroshima and Nagasaki. Seven years later in 1961, the USSR conducted a hydrogen bomb test nicknamed "Tsari Bomba" of 50 megatons, 17 times greater than World War II. Thus the 1950s and '60s were periods when the US and USSR were in the midst of a nuclear arms race based on the strategic policy of nuclear deterrence and the acquisition of a balance of power, which finally resulted in a policy known as "Mutually Assured Destruction" abbreviated as MAD.

The Japanese people activated an anti-nuclear movement in 1954 which was ignited by a US hydrogen bomb test "Bravo" in Bikini Atolls on March 1. Two days after that, Japanese conservative parties, with the initiative of Yasuhiro Nakasone, later Prime Minister of Japan, hastily passed in the Diet a budget of 235 million yen for building a nuclear reactor. The figure 235 came from uranium-235. One year before, Nakasone took part in an international seminar at Harvard University led by Professor Henry Kissinger and had an idea to promote an "Atoms for Peace" project in Japan in cooperation with the US Then, Matsutaro Shoriki, owner of the Yomiuri Newspaper Company, launched a series of travelling expositions to popularise the possibility of the peaceful uses of nuclear energy. I myself had a chance to see one of these expositions in Tokyo in 1959, where a genuine nuclear reactor was exhibited in the middle of the Tokyo Metropolis.

But it is significant to know that the first practical nuclear power plant of 5,000 kW was built and went into operation in 1954 not by the US but by the USSR in Obnisk near Moscow. At that time, the US Atomic Energy Act was prohibiting private enterprises from taking part in nuclear energy exploitation until its revision two months after the Soviet success in practical nuclear power generation. The US hastily developed nuclear power plant by making use of a nuclear reactor system developed for strategic submarines, and managed to operate the Shippingport Nuclear Power Plant in 1958. A year before, a report named WASH-740 (Brookhaven Report) titled "Theoretical Possibilities and Consequences of Major Accidents in Large Nuclear Power Plants" indicated possible effects of "maximum credible accident" as 3,400 deaths, 43,000 injuries and property damage of 7 billion dollars, more than double that of Japan's national budget in those days, which seemed to be too serious for a private electric power company to cope with such a situation. About half a year later, The Price-Anderson Nuclear Industries Indemnity Act, usually referred to as the "Price-Anderson Act", was legislated by which private companies can be indemnified for any claims above approximately 12.6 billion dollars (as of 2011). This Act was considered necessary to create an incentive for private nuclear power production. Four years later, a similar act named "Act on Contract for Indemnification of Nuclear Damage Compensation" was legislated in Japan. It is obvious that nuclear power industry cannot survive such catastrophic situations without the aid of the nation.

In Japan, this connection between the government and the electric power companies was further strengthened by involving local governments by legislating the "Act on Tax for Promotion of Power Resources Development" in 1973 which brought an annual subsidy of greater than 10 million dollars to the local government that accepts a plan to build an electric power plant. Every electric power consumer automatically became a taxpayer by paying about 5 dollars per 1,000 kW-h of power consumption, which creates about 50 billion dollars of national tax income every year. The local community can be blessed with a special subsidy for three years, but infrastructures constructed during the period require persistent funds for maintenance, thereby more nuclear power plants are apt to be invited.

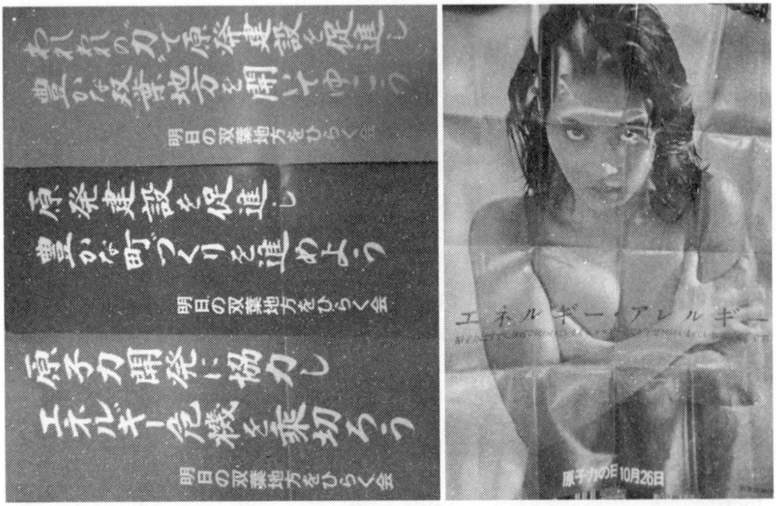

Posters put up by a pro-nuclear residents' organisation in Fukushima are appealing for the promotion of nuclear power. A semi-nude poster on the right was used by the Science and Technology Agency in 1970s, which criticises anti-nuclear people as having "energy allergy".

In addition, residents in the local community concerned were also mobilised to invite nuclear power plants. For example, in Futaba District, Fukushima Prefecture, where a nuclear disaster is going on, a residents' group named "Organization for Building a Bright Futaba District" was formed in early 1970s, which even put up a poster saying "Let's Promote Construction of Nuclear Power Plants by Our 'Power' and Open a Way to Build an Affluent Futaba District". People in the local communities concerned were thus involved in a national mobilisation structure for nuclear power.

Needless to say, many specialists in the field of nuclear engineering were officially requested to authorise the governmental judgment about the safety of nuclear power generation. Journalism could not play a sufficient role for criticism, and rather functioned as disseminators of illusions and mythical fallacies that nuclear power generation is safe and economical.

It is sometimes said that nuclear power generation in Japan has been promoted by a "pentagon" consisting of the central government, the nuclear power industry, local governments, specialists and journalists. I personally feel that residents' organisations inviting nuclear power plants to local communities should be added to this "pentagon", thereby forming a "hexagon", which is akin to the national mobilisation structure that was constructed in war time. This hexagon forms a so-called "nuclear village" which is unusually closed, exclusive and ungenerous. I myself started my student life as a member of this "nuclear village" in early 1960s, but I was ruthlessly ejected from the village in 1970s when I was identified as a harmful criticiser of its policies.

Personal Experience of Academic Harassment

Since I began to openly criticise the governmental nuclear power policy in early 1970s, I experienced extraordinary harassment in my academic life at the University of Tokyo. I was excluded from the education system, and my research budget was completely cut. My lecture tours to various parts of Japan were often tailed by a power company staff in charge of watching me. A medical trainee sent from Tokyo Electric Power Company sat next to me at the laboratory to spy out my ideas about the anti-nuclear movement. Nobody was permitted to talk to me from morning till evening. I experienced different types of obstruction or interference in the process of applications for a professorship at other colleges or universities. I was personally told by my boss not to make academic presentations without his permission, but, based on my belief in academic freedom, I arbitrarily made theoretical publications of my research work which can be carried out without much fund. I was therefore supported by young researchers to a considerable extent, and was often elected a member of board of directors of Japan Health Physics Association, an academic society in the field of radiation protection. I even served as the general secretary of the society in mid-1970s. One day after the board meeting, a member sent from Tokyo Electric Power Company invited me to dinner at a horseflesh restaurant in the old downtown Tokyo, and requested me to study abroad to the US for three years, which I cordially declined.

I could narrowly survive this very difficult time, firstly by my own personal belief in life with dignity, secondly in solidarity with understanding people in the fields of science and public movements, and thirdly, maybe most importantly, through the support of my partner. Very interestingly, the human relationship

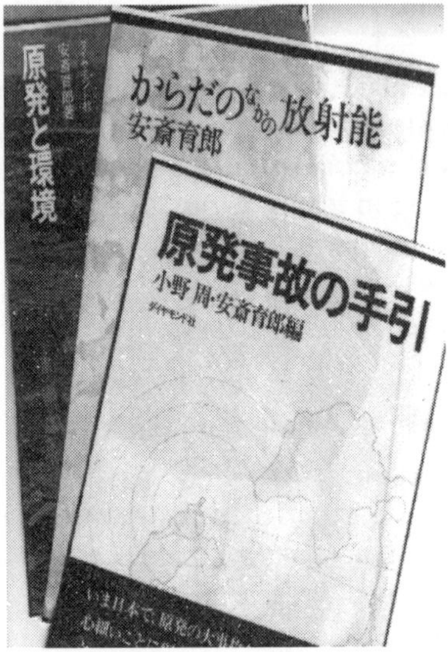

Anzai authored a number of books on nuclear power in 1970s and ’80s, including “Nuclear Power Generation in Japan” (Shin-Nihon Shuppansha, 1974), “Nuclear Power and Environment” (Diamondsha, 1975), “Radioactivity in Human Body” (Godo Shuppan, 1979), “Handbook of a Nuclear Power Plant Accident”

Anzai urgently published “Fukushima Nuclear Power Plant Accident” (Kamogowa Shuppan) April 2011.

between my boss and myself was ironically improved to an extent after a severe nuclear accident in the US that took place at Three Mile Island in March 1979. He seemed to have understood that my warnings about the risks of nuclear power generation were not entirely false. But my position was frozen to an assistant lecturer for 17 years until 1986, when I moved from the University of Tokyo to Ritsumeikan University, which was a great happiness for me.

I must relate this unconstitutional suppression of freedom, which I personally experienced, in the background of nuclear power exploitation in Japan. This seems to be one of the significant elements that have endangered Japanese society.

What Happened in Fukushima?

Now I would like to make some comments about the situation in the radiation disaster area of Fukushima. I visited the area three times (mid-April, early May, and early August) after the accident of March 11. The purposes of my visit were firstly to visit my friends who I have been co-working for a nuclear-risk-free community for about 40 years, secondly to make several lectures for teachers, citizens, workers, young mothers and specialists, thirdly to offer advice on radiation protection to the people who need me, and fourthly to measure radiation levels and to sample soils contaminated with radioactive substances.

The radiation levels have been and still are high in the nearby areas and within so-called hot-spots, even in the city of Fukushima populated by about 280,000 residents some 60 km distance from the nuclear power plant. I made a radiation survey between Iwaki city and Namie town, about 80 km apart, the result of which is shown below. Radiation exposure rate was about 0.5 ìSv/h in Iwaki, but it gradually rose up to 20, 30, or even to 50 ìSv/h in the northwest area of nuclear power plant.

The major cause of external radiation exposure is radioactive cesium-137 deposited on the ground. The total amount of cesium-137 released from the Fukushima Nuclear Power Plants has been estimated to be about 168 times greater than that released by Hiroshima A-bomb, according to the evaluation by the Ministry of Economics, Trade and Industry. But some of the scientists in international community estimate that the amount was more than three times greater than that. The most of these radioactive substances

Ikuro Anzai sampling contaminated soil near Fukushima Nuclear Power Plant on his 71st birthday (16 April 2011)

Ikuro Anzai measuring radiation levels in a cowshed in Namie-machi, 30 km from the Fukushima Nuclear Power Plant (16 April 2011). The level of radiation was as high as 30 ìSv/h, approximately 400 times greater than the normal level in Tokyo.

Lecture meeting in Fukushima (16 April 2011)

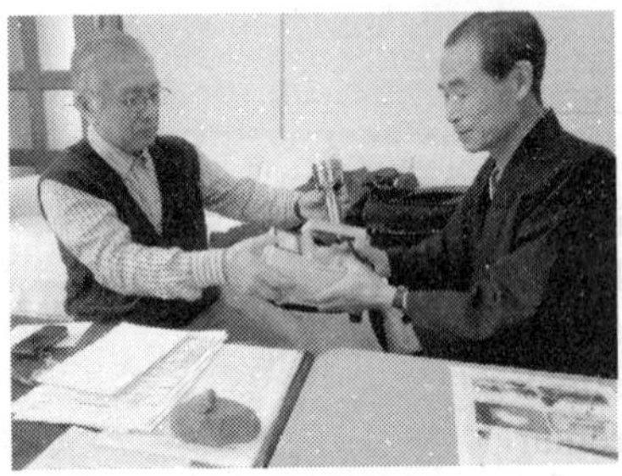

Donating a survey metre to an NGO (7 May 2011)

now deposited on the ground were mainly released during the first week after the hydrogen gas explosions in the plant. It is noteworthy to recognise that radioactive cesium is very tightly caught by the several centimetres of surface soil layer, and I myself verified in cooperation with Ms Yoshiko Tanigawa that cesium-137 is not easily dissolved in water, even if we wash the contaminated soil by large quantities of water. This property is peculiar to the clay-like soil in Fukushima. This soil quality is the main reason why the levels of radioactive contamination of rice cropped in last autumn in Fukushima were considerably low. It also suggests that rainfall will not easily wash out radioactive cesium and the sunflower may not effectively decontaminate the soil in the Fukushima case.

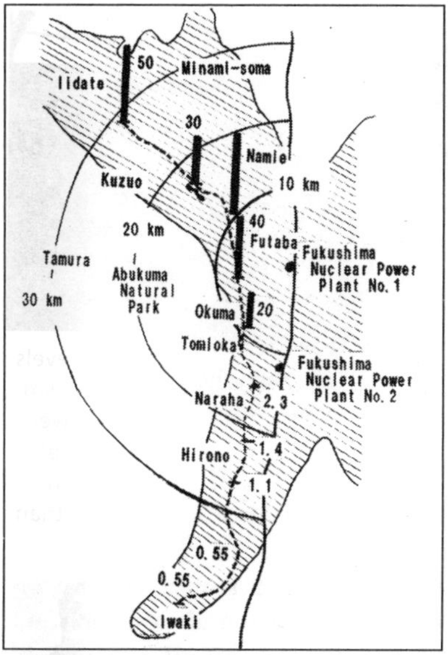

Radiation levels in different locations in Fukushima. Figures are radiation exposure rates expressed in micro-Sieverts per hour. Ordinary level in Tokyo is 0.06~0.07 micro-Sievert per hour. Shaded portion signifies the area where internal radiation dose of thyroid gland between 6 a.m. (March 12) and 0 a.m. (March 24) may have reached 100 milli-Sievert according to an estimation by the System for Prediction of Environment Emergency Dose Information (SPEEDI).

Therefore, in order to reduce radiation levels above the ground, it is quite effective to remove several centimetres of surface soil layer. During my second visit to Fukushima in May 2011, I carried out an experiment in a kindergarten in Fukushima City to demonstrate the effectiveness of surface soil clearance. The radiation level was remarkably decreased by removing only 2~3 centimetres of the surface soil layer, and the administrators of the kindergarten made efforts to eliminate the contaminated surface soil thereafter, which enabled them to have an outdoor event for children in early October.

I am convinced that we should earnestly endeavour to carry out every possible measure to protect people, especially young children, from harmful ionising radiations due to serious accident of nuclear power plants upon which our generation has been

Ms Yoshiko Tanigawa experimenting with the decontamination of surface soil which was sampled by Dr Ikuro Anzai at Shirakawa City in Fukushima Prefecture in early August (photo taken at Anzai Science & Peace Office).

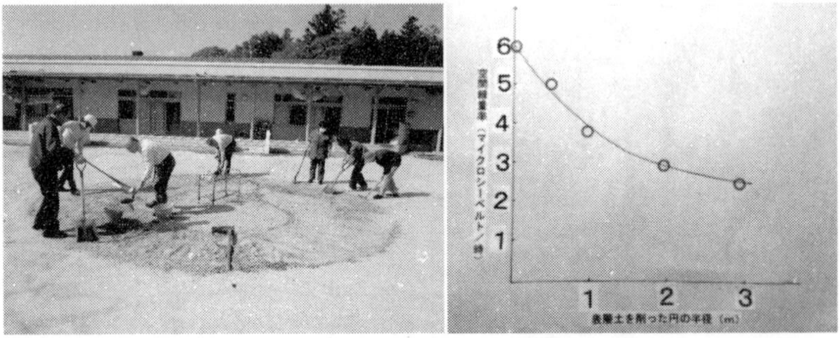

Anzai removing surface soil in a kindergarten. The graph shows a drastic reduction in radiation exposure rate by soil clearance (horizontal axis: radius in metre).

dependent to an extent. Here in Kyoto, we are now unconsciously enjoying electric power generated by nuclear power plants only 60 kilometres from this conference venue. There are 14 nuclear power plants in Fukui Prefecture just adjacent to Kyoto, and vast amount of high-level radioactive waste has already been accumulated, which is to be taken care of by the future generations. Future generations to come after us have to manage to isolate such dangerous nuclear waste from civil life for thousands of years. They must expend huge resources for disposal of nuclear waste which will not produce any value for them. We, people of today, are enjoying nuclear power, and are going to leave a tremendous "negative fortune" to our children, grandchildren, and future generations over tens of thousands of year. We must ask ourselves whether or not it is ethically justifiable.

Agenda for Peace Research After 3/11

Now, as is expected by Professor Akihiko Kimijima, the organiser of this APPRA Conference, I think I must conclude my speech by raising several agenda for peace researchers after 3/11. Based on my personal experience as a nuclear scientist specialising in radiation protection for over 45 years and also as a peace researcher who has been confronting these unprecedented difficulties, I would like to suggest following five points:

1. Regarding the definition of peace, I fundamentally agree with Dr Johan Galtung, and understand peace not only as an "absence of war" but also as an "absence of violence" which can be categorised into direct violence, structural violence and

cultural violence. Although the enormous scale of the earthquake itself and the accompanying tsunami were of natural origin, we still observed a number of incidents of structural and cultural violence which aggravated the damage and pain of the sufferers in the devastated areas. It is the role of peace researchers to make investigations to explain how the effects of an original natural disaster are further aggravated by interconnections of structural and/or cultural violence.

2. An urgent agenda for several decades to come is to construct a comprehensive aid system for the people in disaster areas by integrating useful potentiality in the fields of politics, administration, economics, science, technology, and culture, including preserving efforts for decontamination of the living environment, adequate control of radioactive contamination of foods, dissemination of literacy about radiation and radioactivity for eradicating social discrimination and prejudice against sufferers in an abyss of despair, and the establishment of a health check system to find out and treat stochastic effects of radiation such as cancers and leukemia in the earliest stages. In order to integrate individual effort into a most effective total system, a peace-minded general coordination system must be established.
3. An agenda for peace research suggested from my own personal experience in academic life is to develop a method to sense dangerous social signs in the earliest stage, including signs in the fields of structural and/or cultural violence such as academic harassment, irrational policy execution without sincere attitude toward science, emasculation of democracy, etc. It may be of some help if we will be able to develop some indicators such as the Global Peace Index which was developed by Institute for Economics and Peace (UK), or the Universal Human Rights Index by UN Office of the High Commissioner for Human Rights. Such an indicator, if possible, may be able to function to an extent for warning people to this latent danger in society.
4. Another agenda for the peace researcher is to elucidate the whole story of the Fukushima tragedy not only from the short-term point of view but also from a long-term point of view in world history. Efforts should be made to totally clarify

安斎育郎・立命館大教授が明かす

東大助手「ガラスの檻」に幽閉17年

だれも口きかず孤立無援の日々

A magazine "Weekly Asahi" reported that Anzai had been confined in "an academic glass cage" for 17 years (October 1992).

the direct and indirect reasons why such a catastrophic nuclear disaster occurred in Japan by comprehensively analysing and synthesising historical facts in the light of, for example, subordination of Japan's politics to US strategy in the postwar period, a quite Japanese way of old-fashioned politics symbolised by the combination of the taxation system for promoting nuclear power and *"Yarase"* culture, i.e., faking people's opinion favourable to nuclear power. Lessons from such research, when combined with sincere efforts of educationalists and journalists, may become crucially important for the Japanese people to choose a more peaceful and safer future.

5. Finally I will add an agenda for peace of future generations. This is the agenda in connection with the point I already referred to as the long-lived radioactive waste disposal. How can we deal with the consensus building about the acceptability of technologies which may leave immeasurable potential risk as a "negative legacy", such as the very long-lived nuclear waste which will be tremendously costly but will never produce any value for future generations. Peace researchers are expected to answer the question: Is it ethically acceptable for us to enjoy nuclear energy for our life while leaving behind hard to estimate risks to future generations with no possibility of obtaining their consent?

4

The Criminality of Nuclear Weapons and Nuclear Energy

From Hiroshima to Fukushima

KENJI URATA

The Two Sides of a Damoclean Sword

Szczecin, Poland is one hour by car from Berlin's Tegel Airport, and it is also a stone's throw from the Baltic. This June (2011), the General Assembly of the International Association of Lawyers Against Nuclear Arms (IALANA) was held at the University of Szczecin. The current IALANA president is Justice C.G. Weeramantry, who is also the former vice-president of the International Court of Justice (ICJ). In the advisory opinion on the use of nuclear weapons, Weeramantry wrote a dissenting opinion that "the use or threat of use of nuclear weapons is illegal in any circumstances whatsoever." He is already world-famous for this.

In his keynote speech at the General Assembly on June 19, 2011, Weeramantry said: "Nuclear weapons and nuclear energy are the two sides of a Damoclean sword .... The fibers of the threat by which the sword is suspended are being cut one by one through the increasing number of nuclear states, the availability on the

This paper was originally published on the website of the University for Peace, Peace and Conflict Monitor, October 5th, 2011, and it was republished on the website of Lawyers Committee on Nuclear Policy, in which you can have a look IALANA NEWS, No.1, February 2012, pp. 27–30.

internet of knowledge regarding nuclear weapons construction, the availability of materials from the waste of nuclear reactors, and the activities of terrorist organisations who would love to acquire a bomb. The sword of Damocles is being made more dangerous every day."[1]

Weeramantry's argument firmly pushes aside the prevailing dichotomy that nuclear arms are different from the energy of nuclear reactors. Weeramantry perceives nuclear weapons and nuclear energy – the two pillars of the nuclear age – as being connected, and calls upon people to squarely face the grave problems common to both.

What should form the nucleus of our thinking in our approach to this situation called "from Hiroshima to Fukushima"? After considering this I concluded that it is the concept of the criminality of nuclear weapons and nuclear energy. But one cannot find the concept of nuclear energy criminality in Japan. For example, even the Japan Confederation of A- and H-Bomb Sufferers (Hidankyo) has appealed only to the criminality of nuclear weapons.

The Criminality of Possessing and Deploying Nuclear Weapons

Just after the Berlin Wall fell, the IALANA German office held a convention of experts in Berlin. I too was invited and attended. Francis A. Boyle, a US professor of international law, delivered an address at this meeting, where he advocated his theory that, under the Nuremberg Charter, the atomic bombings of Hiroshima and Nagasaki are war crimes and crimes against humanity.[2]

In fact, prior to that time Boyle had already asserted the criminality of not only nuclear weapons use, but also possession. In 1986 he had published his paper "The Relevance of International Law to the 'Paradox' of Nuclear Deterrence."[3] The controversy had always been presented in terms of whether it is legal for states to possess nuclear weapons, but we must note here that nuclear states do not possess nuclear weapons alone. Boyle reframed the issue in the following way. These states "have actively deployed nuclear weapons in enormous numbers and varieties by attaching them to delivery vehicles that are interconnected with sophisticated command, control, communications, and intelligence (C3I) networks. Such nuclear weapons systems are ready for almost instantaneous launch upon immediate notice. Hence, the only meaningful question concerns the legality of modern nuclear weapons system as they are currently deployed and programmed for use."[4]

He responded to this question as follows: "The nuclear weapons systems maintained by all the world's nuclear weapons states, and especially by the two superpowers, are far beyond this stage of mere possession, and have been at the point of deployment and preparation for immediate use in a thermonuclear war for quite some time. As pointed out earlier in this chapter, under the Nuremberg Principles, such planning, preparation and conspiracy to commit crimes against peace, crimes against humanity, war crimes, and genocide, inter alia, constitute international crimes in their own right."[5]

He continued: "Indeed, any international agreement purporting to legalise the possession and deployment of nuclear weapons and their related systems would violate a peremptory norm of international law and thus be void in accordance with article 53 of the 1969 Vienna Convention on the Law of Treaties. If piracy, slavery, armed aggression, crimes against peace, crimes against humanity, war crimes, and genocide are universally considered to violate jus cogens, then a fortiori the threat by the two nuclear superpowers to exterminate the entire human race, coupled with their imminent capacity to do so, must likewise do the same."[6]

His serious doubt is also directed at those who back the abstract proposition that nuclear deterrence is legal. He argues that the US doctrine of nuclear deterrence is illegal, and that its illegality has the effect of encouraging military antagonism by other countries.

The Criminality of the Continued Existence and Proliferation of Nuclear Power

It was Weeramantry who wasted no time in discussing the Fukushima issue from the perspective of criminality. On March 14, three days after the Fukushima Daiichi accident on March 11, he sent an open letter to the environmental ministers of various countries, stating that the continuance and proliferation of nuclear power not only violate all principles of international law, but also are crimes against future generations.[7]

Weeramantry says that each citizen holds the environment in trust. In this respect, those in charge of nuclear power for governments have a special responsibility. The frightening consequences of nuclear power will bring catastrophic damage to future generations. But that's not all. Even though photovoltaic power and other renewables can supply all the energy the world needs, these are to be ignored. Nuclear reactors are terrorist targets. Although the total amount of waste produced by nuclear reactors is immeasurable, there is no way to treat it safely. To continue and expand nuclear power while knowing these things is to continue violating the environmental trust, and to abandon our responsibility to our children and grandchildren. This cannot be justified in the light of any standards of morality or the law. Nuclear power violates all principles of humanitarian law, international law, environmental law, and also international law related to sustainable development. This means that unless government authorities take immediate action to stop the construction of new nuclear power plants, they are committing crimes against future generations while being aware of the danger.

Weeramantry appealed to environmental ministers of all countries to take immediate action.

I was deeply impressed by his view, and moved by his wisdom and courage. I myself advanced the argument that the continued existence and proliferation of nuclear power is also a crime against the current generation.[8] I submit that the Japanese government and Tokyo Electric have committed a grave attack against the human dignity of the general public living in the Fukushima area, thereby reducing their quality of life in the extreme and otherwise committing inhumane acts against them. Although they may try to exonerate themselves by claiming they had no such intent, intent is not a constitutive requisite to establish a crime against humanity.

In that human dignity has been attacked, the suffering of those exposed to radiation in a nuclear accident qualitatively holds something in common with this hibakusha of Hiroshima and Nagasaki. Moreover, the number of nuclear accident victims is far higher – so high that even now it is uncertain. At Fukushima, low-dose exposure including internal exposure in reality threatens the lives, health, and safety of on-site workers, children, and

Fukushima Daiiachi 2/14/2011

regional residents. What is more, it is recognised that the harmful impacts of the radioactive substances emitted extend to the global environment including the atmosphere and oceans, lead to ecosystem damage, and impinge on the survival of humanity.

Meanwhile, Boyle too was quick to point out the criminality of the nuclear power industry. His March 20 letter can be summed up as follows. Japan's nuclear energy (nuclear power) industry continues crimes against humanity as defined by Article 7 of the Rome Statute of the International Criminal Court, of which Japan too is a party. The same can be said also for the nuclear energy (nuclear power) industries throughout the world, not just that of Japan. The people of Japan should use this legal conclusion to get Japan's nuclear energy industry to stop its crimes against humanity. The same should be done for the nuclear energy (nuclear power) industries all over the world, not just that of Japan. MOX in particular contains plutonium, the deadliest substance known to humanity. Furthermore, Fukushima Daiichi's unit three uses MOX/plutonium, and an explosion has already occurred there. Japan's government should continue hitting the nuclear energy industry with demands for information disclosure.[9] This opinion gave me some ideas.

Nuclear Disarmament, Nuclear Power Phaseout and Quest for Peace

IALANA's June 19 Szczecin Declaration includes the following two elements: Bring about a start of preparatory work for the conclusion of a nuclear disarmament convention, and call for the worldwide abolition of nuclear energy. In relation to the second, IALANA took a resolution by the May 26 directors' meeting of the Japan Association of Lawyers Against Nuclear Arms (JALANA) as a call to abolish nuclear energy, and supported it. The declaration also stated that what is needed is a complete switch to renewable energy and to democratising energy production.

Let's take a retrospective look at the background and characteristics of this year's General Assembly. The main point of the IALANA resolution adopted in June 2009 was the outlook on the Non-Proliferation Treaty (NPT) conference to follow in May 2010. It says that to make a reality of the future vision of a world without nuclear weapons, it is necessary to have a convention which would attain total and permanent nuclear disarmament.

IALANA stated that it had expectations for demands from the NPT Review Conference to quickly start negotiations aimed at concluding such a convention. But IALANA saw this expectation as having ended in failure, and therefore decided that instead of gradualism, it would itself work toward a means to "make a leap" toward a world without nuclear weapons. At this point the dichotomy that "nuclear weapons are different from the nuclear energy that drives reactors" was still pervasive.

But in response to the March 11 Fukushima Daiichi accident, IALANA was suddenly faced with the question of whether to conduct activities to bring about a world without nuclear energy. Also, April of this year was the 25th anniversary of the Chernobyl accident. I should mention in passing that the International Physicians for the Prevention of Nuclear War have issued a new critical opinion stating that the perception held by the International Atomic Energy Agency and other parties underestimates accident damage.[10] IALANA also questions whether claims can be made for a clean energy revolution through the global proliferation of nuclear power.

This brings the new achievements of this General Assembly into clear view: Twenty-three years from its founding, IALANA has advanced to the quest for peace from the abolition of nuclear arms, and has decided to position a worldwide nuclear power phaseout under these two objectives, and to tackle this challenge in its capacity as legal specialists. Seen from a different vantage point, one could say that IALANA has decided to see nuclear disarmament, nuclear power phaseout, and the quest for peace as a trinity, and to work toward achieving it.

When we become aware of this stance and tackle the challenge of phasing out nuclear power in our capacity as legal specialists, there are any number of examples. There is the legal system under nuclear power treaties, with the Statute of the International Atomic Energy Agency at its pinnacle. In Japan there is the legal system under the Atomic Energy Basic Law. So, what approach should be taken? For example, how do we deal with the "inalienable right" granted under Article IV of the NPT? The current treaty text establishes "the inalienable right of all the Parties to the Treaty to develop research, production and use of nuclear energy for peaceful purposes." Therefore, we should address the situation by assuming this can be changed. Even if nearly all UN members are parties to the NPT, action is taken in line with the procedures for international legislation. If these efforts conform to the advance of the renewable energy revolution, a solid outlook will present itself.

Notes

1. IALANA, Schützenstr. 6a, 10117, Berlin, Final Declaration of the General Assembly of IALANA, Szczecin, 19th of June 2011, http://ialana.net/uploads/media/Szczecin_Final_DeclarationVers.4_01.pdf.
2. Francis A. Boyle, "The Criminality of Nuclear Deterrence." This article is the record of an address delivered on September 4, 2010 at a conference in Feldkirch, Austria. The conference was the XVIII Conference "Mut Zur Ethic": Direct Democracy.
3. Francis A. Boyle, "The Relevance of International Law to the 'Paradox' of Nuclear Deterrence," *Northwestern University Law Review*, Vol. 80, No. 6, pp. 1407ff, Summer 1986.
4. Ibid., p. 1444.
5. Ibid.
6. Ibid., p. 1446.

7. "Nuclear Reactor Catastrophe in Japan" (Translated by Kenji Urata), *Nihon no Kagakusha*, July 2011 (in Japanese).
8. Kenji Urata, "Nuclear Power Accidents: Nuclear Power and Nuclear Weapons Present the Same Threat," a "Word from the Wise" column distributed by Kyodo News in newspapers including the *Akita Sakigake* (June 10) and *Shinano Mainichi Shimbun* (June 22) (in Japanese).
9. Nuclear Power Industry is a Crime Against Humanity! http://mwcnews.net/focus/letters-to-editors/9423–nuclear-power-industry-is-a-crime-against-humanity.html, Sunday, March 20 2011, 09:11.
10. The surprising difference between the IPPNW's new report "Health effects of Chernobyl" and the document "A Comparison with the Chernobyl Accident" from the Japan Prime Minister's Office. Peace Philosophy Centre, http://peacephilosophy.blogspot.com/, April 18, 2011.

Part III

Non-violence: Gandhi and Beyond

5

Swadeshi

Creative Alternative of Globalisation

VIDYA JAIN

The twentieth century was a strange and contradictory century. It was the bloodiest century in history with two world wars and a number of bitter and endless conflicts. The last decades have put the world on the path of globalisation where phenomena of intolerance, terrorism and war are inherent. It we look at the balance sheet of development and human well-being, of achievement and deficits, of profit and people, of power and poverty, of universalism and particularism, of totalitarianism and democracy, of homogenisation and pluralism, of hegemony and equiliria, of masculinity and feminity and above all of global village and fractured civilisation, a disastrous picture of new world (dis)order emerges. The basic nature of world cosmos (truth, beauty and goodness) is shattered. Globalisation is an extension of liberal ideology. The liberal ideology and its concomitant policies of liberalisation and globalisation are not devoid of contradictions, particularly when implanted in an alien land and when it overlooks the historical – cultural roots and conditions. Culture and traditions in reality give to every political principal its distinguishing colour and discriminating effect.

The main contribution of liberalism is its libertarian ontology by virtue of which it makes individual initiative, his liberty and rights and a constitutionally limited government essential components of its theory.

In liberal theory human nature is based on self-interest or the enlightened self-interest. The individual in particular is the consumer of material goods. To borrow some phrases of Macpherson, the individual of liberalism is "an infinite appropriator" and an infinite consumer of utilities; it is this "possessive" individual who satisfies his self-interest by exerting power over and exacting their capacities.[1] "A point to be noted here is that when liberal democracy was established in Western countries during seventeenth to nineteenth centuries, it had an enormous liberalising force. It revolutionised not only the economic order but the entire social set-up. Instead of a society based on custom, on status, and on authoritarian allocation of values and politics, there emerged a society based on individual choices and mobility, impersonal market-relations and contract. But, by nineteenth century the reality floated on the surface – that it is only the "haves" who have choices to choose, while the "have-nots" have no choices to choose from.

It is true that this liberal individualistic substance of liberal democracy as reflected in its infancy in the theories of Locke was modified into a sort of communitarianism in the nineteenth century because of situational compulsions and it laid the foundations of the twentieth century welfare state. It was then that its ultra-hedonistic concept of human nature was dropped to enable it to accept a positive view of liberty, a positive view of state and a positive link between the individual and the state. Nevertheless, its basic essence, self-interest, remained the same.

Kant undertook to show that the essence of every human being is his free moral will. This moral will is essentially rational and autonomous; and individual freedom consists in obeying the commands of his own "moral will". The Kantian conception of the "autonomy of will" was touched upon by J.S. Mill, and adopted by T.H. Green. Mill, although made the Benthamite philosophy palatable by making happiness qualitative, yet failed to situate logically his concept of liberty with the autonomy of moral will. Green was more successful. He established a direct link between individual moral (rational) will and the general will; and this link was manifested in this concept of "the common consciousness of the common good."

The liberal-democratic ontology, thus conceived, reached its climax in Benthamite Utilitarianism via the Philosophical Radicals. Bentham's Utilitarianism was the philosophy of egoistic-psychological hedonism. He took an atomistic view of society and conceived of individuals in the society as "free floating" entities.

Nonetheless, sociability entered into the ontology of liberalism in the nineteenth century. This imparted a humanist and an ethical touch to the libertarian ontology of liberal democracy. Thus, from "possessive individualism" to a sort of communitarianism was a big leap forward. Today, Western liberalism and its concomitant process liberalisation is spreading fast and many non-Western nations, including India, have come under its sway. In recent times significant contributions were made in the liberal democratic theory by John Rawls, Robert Nozick, Carole Pateman, etc., by their emphasis on social cooperation and participation. But their theories failed to develop the ideology of liberalism in tune with the philosophy of the above-mentioned twin norms. These norms could not be assimilated in the practice of liberalisation.

John Rawls, through contractarian theory, refers not only to political liberty but also emphasises on economic equality within the framework of distributive justice. Justice as fairness, according to him, entails two principles. The first principle emphasises on equal basic liberties. The second principle entails difference principle ... it means equality of opportunity followed by a justification of inequality in distribution of social and economic goods to the extent that such inequality works to the benefit of the least advantaged.

But a few questions arise here: Are these non-Western nations marching towards real development? Are they not being tied to the apron-strings of the West? Are they independent in the real sense of the term?

One cannot but endorse the anxiety of Edward W. Said who giving a critique of the dominating influence of Western imperialism and liberalism on global culture, says, "We must not condemn ourselves to repeat the imperial experience. How, in the redefined and yet very close contemporary relationship between culture and imperialism, a relationship that enables disquieting forms of domination, can we sustain the liberating energies released by the great decolonising resistance movements and the mass uprisings of the 1980s? Can these energies elude the homogenising processes of modern life, hold in abeyance the interventions of the new imperial centrality?"[2]

The requirements of social cooperation. The reason for this failure was that it had no philosophy (with the exception of T.H. Green's philosophy) to prove that the "self" is a "social self" and the good of the "self" is conducive to the common good. The alternative socialist theories of the West did emphasise on social cooperation and equality, but they completely submerged the "individual" to the needs of the community. These two countervailing theories that dominated the early twentieth century Western thought thus presented a stark choice between what appeared to be irreconcilable values of "individuality" and "sociability".

Globalisation is not a simple but a complex set of processes, which operates at multiple levels of political, economic, cultural and ideological. It is a social process in which the constraints of geography on social and cultural arrangements recede and in which actually people are receding. By catching hold of economy, West in general and America in particular wishes to have a cognitive and ideological superiority over the rest of the world. The charming concepts of global village, etc., are fake and illusionary and it is nothing else than concentration of wealth, power and knowledge in the hands of America.

Globalisation has generated widespread social, economic and cultural insecurity. It is not the cross-cultural interaction of diverse societies but an imposition of a particular culture on all others. It is the predation of one class, one race, one nation and often one gender. In "global" the dominant "local" seeks global control. The global is not universal human interest, it represents a particular interest and culture which has been globalised through its reach and control.[3]

The liberalisation of trade has led the way to enslavement of people. The industrial technological development, military supremacy, cultural hegemony, arrogance of English language, dehumanising competition, commodification and commercialisation have endangered the very existence of human souls and mother nature. The world is "composed of autonomous individuals and market is not the world that anyone lives in – not even the free enterprises or welfare liberal ideologies. This world is a world without families. It is also a world without neighbourhoods, ethnic communities, churches, cities and towns, even nations (as opposed to states)".[4]

Swadeshi (Local Self-Reliance): The Creative Alternative

According to Gandhi, Indian society is far more alienated than any other because of the crippling poverty of its people, and also because of the serious inroads that values of the alienated West have made into our society by creating an irresponsible power elite. Therefore, Gandhi propounded the principle of trusteeship and Swadeshi. In trusteeship it expresses the inherent responsibility of the privileged, the educated and those with money, knowledge and skills to the community and in particular to the poorest.

On the principle of Swadeshi, Gandhi believed that the necessary determination and fervour could be marshalled only on the basis of patriotic commitment. National economic self-determination is as national political self-determination. Swadeshi has a rich cultural philosophical heritage, although this heritage was eclipsed for centuries because of the foreign domination. The Indian Renaissance that occurred in the nineteenth century awakened consciousness of her glorious past. It also accelerated the urge for national independence. Incidentally, the Renaissance and the Reformation in India coincided with the revision of liberalism in West. Indian moderates believed in the postulates of restructuring polity and economy by means of self-governance (swa-shashan). Swa-shashan is Swaraj, and Swaraj entails both Swadesh and Swadeshi.

Swadeshi is a complete philosophy, it stands for a distinctive attitude towards politics and society. It is not a creed. It is a particular standpoint, it is a philosophy of life and a code of conduct. The essence of liberalism is self-preference, its practice thereby is exploitative in nature. It is exploitative of the village by city, of man by machine and of nature by science and technology. Swadeshi is an anti-colonial concept. It refers to the structures of power which colonise both externally and internally. It is a search for our own identities. Like individuals, communities and nations too have their own identity. Global economy has no concern for the local identities, the contexuality, the ecology, style of life, experience and indigenous skills.

Swadeshi is the key concept in Gandhi's philosophy. It is not merely an economic doctrine but also has ideological implications, In Swadeshi, Gandhi not only envisaged economic salvation of India but also found an answer to psychological and political problems. According to Gandhi, "that economics stands for social justice, it promotes the good of all equally, including the weakest, and is indispensable for decent life".[5]

Since two of the main attributes of Swadeshi, self-sufficiency and self-reliance, involve "doership," it becomes the philosophy of praxis, of action. The essence of praxis is reverence for and performance of duty. Duty is dharma. In Indian philosophy dharma does not have an ordinary connotation meaning "religion." It is not that. It is something more. It is a composite word having four components: first, righteousness; second, right as against wrong; third, rights in the sense of rightful claims; and fourth, a spirit of obedience to law. Rights and duties in this context are, thus, correlative and are basic ingredients of dharma. Action in pursuance of dharma leads to self-development and self-realisation, and concomitantly to the development of the community. This is real freedom. Thus, if "freedom" is the definition of "duty", no less is "duty" the definition of freedom. This double law – on the one hand expanding freedom into duty, and on the other hand controlling freedom by duty – has a binding force under the aegis of dharma.

It is evident then that Swadeshi, like liberalism, emphasises on individual freedom, but with an entirely different connotation. Freedom which is inherent in Swadeshi entails a sense of vocation. In the ideology of liberalism and liberalisation there is an evasion or dilution of the content of vocation; and it is this evasion/dilution that has made the modern man (under the spell of liberalisation) isolated and an instrument in the hands of forces over which he has no control. Such a bewildered and insecure individual has become a pawn in the hands of the monopolistic capital.[6]

Swadeshi is the search for our nation's identity.[7] Gandhi says, "My nationalism is as broad as my Swadeshi. I want India's rise so that the whole world may benefit. I do not want India to rise on the ruin of other nations."[8] He says further, "No nation on earth has risen without adopting Swadeshi as the principle of life."[9] For Gandhi, Swadeshi was a positive concept based on building what a community has in terms of resources, institutions and structures. Imposed resources, institution and structures leave people unfree and non-sustainable. Swadeshi for Gandhi was central to the creation of peace, freedom and sustainable development. Swadeshi or self-organisation in economic affairs is the basis of economic freedom, without which there can be no political freedom or self-rule. Swadeshi is Swaraj.

For Gandhi, Swaraj and Swadeshi are complementary. For true Swaraj, Swadeshi was an important imperative to be followed. Swaraj is my birthright. Swaraj is the birthright of all people. Gandhi's Swaraj does not imply governance by a centralised state but decentralised self-governance by local communities. In period of injustice and external domination when people are denied economic and political freedom, it requires peaceful non-cooperation with unjust laws and regimes which Gandhi realised and stated in Hind Swaraj. "As long as the superstition that people should obey unjust laws exists, so long will slavery exist."[10] And a non-violent resistance can remove such a superstition. The word 'Swadeshi', however, was not coined by Gandhi himself. It was in vogue in the national movement even before his emergence on the political scene. Dadabhai Naoroji Sri Aurobindo, Tilak, Gokhale, Ranade and others propounded the doctrine of Swadeshi.

Swadeshi is people-centred and not government-centred. It refers to self-reliance and self-control ranging from individual to society. Gandhi was concerned with the value and dignity for every man. Gandhi's respect for the individual arises from his faith in God. God is impartial and selfless. So by following the path of God we follow the path of truth and non-violence. Empowering individual opens the way to socio-economic justice.[11]

Swadeshi extends to all aspects of institutionalised life: economic, political, religious and cultural. Ramashray Roy discusses Gandhi's concept of Swadeshi in terms of Gandhi's

General Sociological Theory of self and society.[12] Basically, Gandhi was opposed to excessively rapid capitalist development and disruption of local communities. He anticipated the modern notion of appropriate technology.[13] He emphasised the importance of local people's knowledge to solve local problems.

Swadeshi is a basic aspect of Gandhi's self-reliant village. Spinning wheel and wearing khadi are symbolic idioms. Basically, he was not against industrialisation and factory production, but he was opposed to the type of proletarianisation that would put people out of work and centralise economic decision-making.

Machine has stolen worker's work. Weaver, blacksmith, carpenter all have been substituted by the machine. In the sphere of machines, Swadeshi means use of local raw material, exchange in the local market and control of the local territory as well as social community. The knowledge basis also ought to be local which means that local knowledge system ought to have primacy over the recognised universal knowledge systems. Further, the technical practice and its conception belong to a worldview whose inseparable other parts are the rituals, forms of worship and beliefs of the practicing community, and the bigger world to which it belongs. The Swadeshi movement is not just a technical alternative. It involves a belief that truth and non-violence shall be the ultimate victors. It is not a belief in some distant goal. It is a regulative belief, a basis for the incorporation of human values within the body of science and technical practice.

The idea of Swadeshi is as old as national consciousness.[14] Arising spontaneously and mostly in an unorganised and isolated manner, the Swadeshi movement in the early phase gathered widespread support from the vernacular press and the local efforts of innumerable faceless men. It created a patriotic sentiment which served as moral force to boycott foreign goods. The ideology of Gandhi regarding his deep interest, support and propaganda for Swadeshi had deep linkages with the economic problems of unemployment amongst our people and advised them through his speeches. He encouraged men and women to ply charkha, spin khadi and boycott foreign goods. It promoted a deep sense of love for goods manufactured in India and their use generated the spirit of selfless sacrifice amongst the masses.[15]

Swadeshi is not against science and technology; it is against its monopolistic use, and against the cult of hatred, death and destruction that it sometimes generates. In fact, it would be an ideal situation if India could import the know-how of science and technology from the West, and in return could export her philosophy of Swadeshi. If that could be possible, Gods would descend on the Earth and there would be Eternal Peace! This, of course, is a utopian ideal. But the logic of expressing this ideal at this point is to emphasise the fact that India has no hesitation in importing "the True, the Good and the Beautiful" from outside, not as a beggar but as a self-reliant nation. India indeed has a composite culture. She has synthesised and weaved into one fabric different cultures and ideas through generations and generations; and more importantly, she has synthesised "faith" with "reason". Einstein had rightly said: "Science without religion is lame, religion without science is blind." The eminent scientist had used the word "religion" in the sense of "faith". It is the synthetic vision of the Indian philosophy and culture enshrined in the concept of Swadeshi that inspires a sense of goodwill, harmony and peace.

Gandhi elucidated his concept of Swadeshi with its religious, moral and spiritual connotations in his address on 14 February 1916, at a missionary conference in Madras. To quote Gandhi, "Swadeshi is that spirit in us, which restricts us to the use and service of our immediate surroundings to the exclusion of the more remote. Thus, as for religion, in order to satisfy the requirements of the definition, I must restrict myself to my ancestral religion. This is the use of my immediate religion surroundings. If I find it defective, I should make use of the indigenous institutions and serve them by curing them of their proved defects. In ... that of economics, I shall use only things that are produced by my immediate neighbours and serve these industries by making them efficient and complete – where they might be found wanting. Such Swadeshi, if reduced to practice will lead to the millennium."[16]

The logic of Swadeshi is (a) if there is any product presently imported of which a domestic substitute could be developed, that substitute must be developed, (b) the domestic substitute developed must be of the labour-intensive type, and (c) if there is no labour-intensive domestic substitute possible, the product must simply be dispensed with. This means at once that the pattern of elitist consumption will become much more restricted and the employment created in order to produce the basket of widely consumed commodities will become much larger. The feasibility of Swadeshi, then, depends on the willingness to accept a fairly massive equalisation of the pattern of consumption. It is clear that Swadeshi economics implies a thorough-going application of import-substitution growth. The substitution is by labour-intensive techniques in the case of consumption goods and to some extent by capital-intensive techniques in the case of capital goods. As Gandhi says, "Industrialization on a mass scale will necessarily lead to passive or active exploitation of the villagers as the problems of competition and marketing come in. Therefore, we have to concentrate on the village being self-contained, manufacturing mainly for use".[17]

The growth tactics of a poor economy employing the Swadeshi strategy can, therefore, be described in terms of the following paradigms. First, there must be a decision to abjure the consumption of any commodity not producible by labour-intensive methods. Second, there must be a plan to build up labour-intensive mass consumption to supply adequate level of goods to the consumption basket. Third, there must be a simultaneous attempt to build up capital/intermediate goods' capacity but only to the extent required by the planned pattern of growth of the mass-employment industries. Fourth, any existing unavoidable import will be gradually dispensed with as domestic output grows. Fifth, as the economy gradually approaches self-reliance, international trade will be gradually reopened in the form of exports of mass-employment goods surpluses and the purchases of manufactured non-producible within the domestic economy.

Swadeshi is not obsolete in today's context. It is the creative alternative to the rule of centralised nation state as well as the rule of global corporations and institutions such as WTO. Economic freedom requires reduced control by the World Bank, IMF, WTO, the G7 and global corporations. It is freedom for the people to have secure livelihoods, to have control over the policies and resources that make their livelihoods.

Swadeshi as conceived by Gandhi was not against either internationalism or universal brotherhood. He wanted India to be a self-dependent unit as only a self-dependent India can support the world. He was of firm belief that a weak unit could neither sustain itself nor help others. According to him, the main aim of Swadeshi was the protection of the home industry. Gandhi did not favour isolation of India from the world. He categorically asserted that his Swadeshi provided for foreign import if it was useful for the country or the people. In his opinion, Swadeshi which excluded the use of everything foreign, no matter how beneficent it may be, was narrow interpretation of Swadeshi.[18] The worldview of Swadeshi cannot go against internationalism or pacifism rooted in love and non-violence automatically becomes its two ideals. These ideals inspire a sense of universal brotherhood and a sense of common consciousness of the common good. Swadeshi synthesises autonomy and self-reliance with universal brotherhood and internationalism. Thus, in Swadeshi, autonomy at micro level is synthesised with the "global world vision" at macro level.

The Swadeshi ideology is not redundant or outmoded. It has scientific value. In fact, no country has risen to heights without paying proper attention to its indigenous institutions and resources. It does not mean that we isolate ourselves from the world or process of liberalisation should be reversed. What we need today is a well conceived, multipronged strategy by which we can realise the economic growth on a sustainable basis.[19] We should put more emphasis on social policies, education, poverty and raising standards of living of people. This can be achieved only by reformulating India's development policy. We have to place greater emphasis on labour intensive sector than on the capital and technology. This type of economic policy would be real Swadeshi.

Gandhi's policies are revolutionary. These follow from Gandhi's personal experience. After all, he gave up all types of privileges by choosing simplicity in his life. His philosophy involves strengthening the individual, family, community and society which in turn by its very nature weakens, fundamentally the hold of the existing market and state framework. No government has promulgated Gandhian policies.[20]

At an individual level, Gandhi's code of voluntary simplicity or poverty offers a sustainable alternative to modern lifestyles. One of the best known aphorisms, that the world has enough for everybody's need but not enough for everybody's greed, is, in effect a one-line environmental ethic. This was an ethic he himself practiced; for resource recycling and the maximisation of needs were integral to his life. His analysis of macro processes of economic development, his prescription for rural reconstruction, and his morals for living, at all these levels is inspirational.

"Gandhi lives on – as a perennial source of inspiration and political innovation to defend our freedoms. Corporate globalization as a project is set to extinguish all freedoms of people through the total control of trade, technology and prosperity rights. It threatens the river to flow and organisms to evolve, of farmers to save seeds and grow crops, of consumers to be free to choose what they eat and know how their food is produced. These fundamental freedoms of all species and ordinary humans are being stolen in the name of 'free trade' and of globalization".[21]

The economic, corporate-driven globalisation is often presented as a process of new interconnections between societies. However, to the extent that it is geographical, it is actually about the global reach of corporations – not about a global joining of hearts of people worldwide. The real project of this globalisation is colonisation and commoditisation of the very resources and processes that gives us life – our biodiversity, our food, our water.

Without the legacy of Gandhi it would be impossible to imagine a response to the totalitarianism built into the project of owning life, owning seeds, owning water. Patents of life and the new biotechnologies are today's tools of imperialism.

It was to regenerate livelihoods in India that Gandhi thought of the charkha (spinning wheel) as a symbol of liberation and a means of generating self-reliant livelihoods. Power-driven mills were the symbol of development in that period of early industrialisation. However, the hunger of mills for raw material and markets destroyed livelihood and caused new poverty.

Gandhi said, "Anything that millions can do together, becomes charged with unique power." The spinning wheel had become a symbol of such power. "The wheel as such is lifeless, but when I invest it with symbolism, it becomes a living thing for me". The spinning wheel symbolised a technology that conserves resources, people's livelihood and people's control over their livelihood. It needed people's hands and minds instead of treating themselves as surplus. This critical mixture of decentredness, livelihood generation, resource conservation and strengthening of self-reliance was essential to undo the waste of centralisation, livelihood destruction, resource depletion and economic and political dependence that had been engendered by the industrialisation associated with colonialism. Gandhi's creative vision of Swadeshi, Swaraj, Satyagraha and Sarvodaya inspires us to build sustainable economics and living democracies. In his legacy we found hope, freedom and creativity. As long as the superstition that people should obey unjust laws exists, so long will slavery exist.

Gandhi's legacy lives on, and gives us hope to shape ever-new instruments to keep life in all its diversity and integrity. Gandhi's legacy carries the seeds for the freedom of humans and all species. Gandhi's legacy is humanity's hope.

The violence of corporate globalisation on the one hand and wars justified on grounds of shallow religious and narrow nationalist identities on the other demand a response that is simultaneously local and universal. It needs to be local in terms of production, both to reduce our ecological footprints and to create more livelihood and job opportunities; local too in terms of our diverse identities, rooted in biological and cultural diversity, in our sense of place and our sense of belonging. It must be universal because we share life with the rest of life, and humanity with all of humanity.

The dominant form of globalisation takes a narrow, highly localised interest and imposes it as 'global', as 'universal'. The imposition involves deep structural violence, but it also creates vicious cycles of violence as identities are threatened, securities eroded, and terrorism emerges. The universal cannot be a globally imposed local interest. It is the emergent quality of all people living by the principle of non-violence; non-violence to human beings as socio-economic justice and to non-human life as ecological sustainability. The universal is the unfolding of the potential of diverse locals acting as self-organised and guided by principle of love and reverence for life. As Tolstoy wrote from his deathbed, it is: "... understanding that welfare for human being is only in their unity, and that unity cannot be attained by violence. Unity can only be reached when each person, not thinking about unity, thinks only about fulfilling the laws of life, only this supreme law of love, alike for all humans, unifies humanity".

When the self is perceived as being at war with nature and society, rather than part of nature and society, alienation and violence become natural to being. Peace and recovery of our ecological selves requires that we re-embed ourselves in the web of life and in the web of social relationships.

The need today is to resuscitate a positive, an inclusive, a generous Swadeshi, to build and renew confidence in our abilities and skills in our people and knowledge system. Above all, to be willing to learn, to change, to adapt, to keep our doors and windows open and not be swept off our feet.

Notes

1. For details, see C.B. Macpherson, *The Political Theory of Possessive Individualism:* Hobbes and Locke, 1962; *The Real World of Democracy,* 1965; *Democratic Theory: Essays in Retrieval,* 1973; and *Life and Times of Liberal Democracy,* 1978.
2. See Edward W. Said, *Culture and Imperialism,* London: Chatto and Windus, 1993, p. 401.
3. See, Vandana Shiva, "Arthic Swaraj or Economic Slavery?" *The Observer,* February 3, 1998.
4. Robert N. Bellah, "Community Properly Understood: A Defence of 'Democratic Communitarianism'", in Amitai Etzioni, ed., *The Essential Communitarian Reader,* p. 17.
5. *Harijan,* 9 October, 1937.
6. For details description see, Erich Fromm, *Escape from Freedom,* New York, Holt, Reinhart, and Winston, 1941.
7. Erik Erikson, *Gandhi's Truth: On the Origin of Militant Non-Violence* New York, W.E. Morton, 1993.
8. M.K. Gandhi, *An Autobiography: The Story of My Experiments with Truth,* Ahmedabad, Navjivan Publishing House, 1940.
9. *Collected Works of Mahatma Gandhi,* Publication Division, Govt. of India, New Delhi 1958, Vol. XV, p. 379.
10. M.K. Gandhi, *Hind Swaraj,* Ahmedabad: Navjivan Publishing House, 1938, p. 29.
11. For details see, G.S. Herbert, "Gandhiji on Poverty" *Sarvodaya,* Vol. XXII, February, 1973.

12. Ramashray Roy, *Self and Society: A Study in Gandhian Thought,* Sage Publications, New Delhi, in collaboration with the United Nations University, 1985.
13. See, Robert J. Mitchell (ed.) *Experience in Appropriate Technology,* Ottawa: The Canadian Hunger Foundation, 1980.
14. See, S.R. Bakshi, *Gandhi and Ideology of Swadeshi,* New Delhi: Reliance Publishing House, 1987.
15. *Young India,* 17 June, 1926, p. 218.
16. M.K. Gandhi, *India of My Dreams,* Ahmedabad: Navijivan Publishing House, 1927 p. 412.
17. *Harijan*, 29 August 1936.
18. K.P. Karunakaran, *Gandhi: Interpretations,* New Delhi: Gitanjali Publishing House, 1985.
19. S. Gurumurthy, "Swadeshi and Nationalism" *Seminar,* No. 469, New Delhi, September 1998.
20. See Ramesh Diwan, "Mahatma Gandhi, Amartya Sen and Poverty". *Gandhi Marg,* Vol. 20, No.4, January–March, 1999.
21. For details see, Vandana Shiva, The practice of earth democracy: Looking ahead – Experiments from 30 years of participatory research and community action in *Development Dialogue,* Uppsala, Sweden, no. 52, August 2009.

6

Gandhi and the Idea of a Non-violent Constitution

THOMAS WEBER

The British had ruled India for their own gain for around 150 years. When India became independent it did so following a lengthy, basically non-violent, struggle to achieve freedom and emerged with history's greatest non-violent activist as its "father of the nation". On the gaining of independence, one of the first tasks of a new state is to write a constitution to determine its political organisation and powers and duties, to regulate the relationship between the state, public authorities and the citizens. Although Gandhi was dead by the time the Indian Constitution was promulgated, he had given more than clues or hints as to how he envisaged the governance of a free India. Some writers claim that the resultant document, with its heavy dependence on the British Government of India Act of 1935 and the US Constitution, and with its reliance on centralisation, was anathema to Gandhi's thinking about constitutional issues. Others have argued that to dichotomise the outcome as a victory for the modernist Nehru/Ambedkar model over a traditionalist Gandhian one is too simplistic a view. They argue that the two visions were in fact complimentary and that Gandhi understood this. Still others have taken the debate far from an argument about centralisation versus decentralisation, about the importance that should be placed on the village, and about whether the document should have placed more emphasis on a bottom up rather than a top down organisational model. Some, like Douglass Lummis, point out that here was a unique chance for something completely different to emerge. Here was the possibility for the first time in history for the materialisation of a non-violent state, nothing less. But it was a possibility that was squandered with India taking its place in the ranks of other more or less ordinary states of the international community. It can be questioned whether such an opportunity (if there indeed was one) will ever come again, nevertheless it may be of some benefit to examine what a Gandhian constitution may have looked like and how the political organisation of his ideal state could have worked and what lessons can be drawn from it for the creation of a more secure and less violent world.

Gandhi's Views Regarding Governance and Democracy

Gandhi warned that by political independence he did not mean imitation of the British or any other parliament. He wanted a political system suited to the Indian people and this he described as *Ramraj*, "the sovereignty of the people based on pure moral authority."[1] He noted that while no mere transference of political power in India would satisfy him, he did concede that such transference was a vital necessity for India.[2] But the transference of power was to go to the village rather than a central government. Gandhi envisaged the independent country as being made up of "ever-widening, never ascending circles" of communities. He saw society as an "oceanic circle whose centre will be the individual, always ready to perish for the village, the latter ready to perish for the circle of villages, till at last the whole becomes one life composed of individuals never aggressive in their arrogance, but ever humble, sharing the majesty of the oceanic circle of which they are integral units."[3]

The villages were to be independent republics that as far as possible supplied their own vital needs. They would grow their own food and cotton for clothing, would have schools, a public hall and theatre, and their own clean water supply. Caste would disappear and there would be no "untouchability". The government of the village would be maintained by a *panchayat* of five persons, annually elected by the adult villagers. The panchayat would be "the legislature, judiciary and executive combined to operate for its year of office." Gandhi believed that such a system would provide a perfect democracy based upon individual freedom. In saying this, he conceded that "I have not examined here the question of relations with the neighbouring villages and the centre if any."[4]

If national life was perfect, it would be self-regulating and there would not be any need for national representatives and the people would live in a state of enlightened anarchy. Of course ideals are never reached and Gandhi realised there had to be some sort of state, but a state which governs the least.[5] If the people did not allow this minimalist state to do its work by taking the law into their own hands, social order would end and the state would cease to exist in a way that would lead to destructive rather than enlightened anarchy. During the mass rioting that accompanied independence, Gandhi asked the populace to allow the government to carry out its tasks.[6]

Gandhi noted that while democracy could not work as long as there is a "wide gulf between the rich and the hungry millions",[7] it could not be worked by "twenty men sitting at the centre. It has to be worked from below by the people of every village."[8] What can we make of these seemingly contradictory threads in Gandhi's views? It would appear that a state, even a coercive and soulless state, was unavoidable. And, as independence got ever closer and Gandhi had to deal in practicalities, his views on the state mellowed and he started to see it as a vehicle for change that could combat deep-seated injustices such as the institution of untouchability and even as the setting for large industries.[9] However, these tasks were minimal and, as Terchek points out, Gandhi's "discussion of an enlarged state is usually tied to eliminating untouchability, encouraging employment, and providing an equitable distribution of land for peasants."[10] In other words, according to Parekh, Gandhi now realised that the state was more complex than he had imagined and that it had the potential for both good and evil.[11] Nevertheless, he continued to stress decentralisation and the day before his death even released a draft constitution of sorts (commonly known as his "last will and testament") in which he asked the Congress Party to dissolve itself and for its members to become servants of the people[12] in order to address local problems in a way that more or less sidestepped the state, forming "complementary and mutually regulating institutions of the state and the *Loka Sevak Sangh* [people's service association]".[13]

Ramraj, the ideal system of government, according to Gandhi was a perfect democracy in which inequalities based on possession and non-possession, colour, race or creed or sex vanish. In it land and state belong to the people, justice is prompt, perfect and cheap and, therefore, there is freedom of worship, and of speech and the press – all this because of the reign of the self-imposed law of moral restraint. Such a state must be based on truth and non-violence and must consist of prosperous, happy and self-contained villages and village communities.[14]

A document by Wardha (a town near Gandhi's Sevagram Ashram) college Principal Shriman Narayan Agarwal, titled *Gandhian Constitution for Free India*[15] was published in 1946 with a foreword by the Mahatma himself. The small book proposed to spell out how Gandhi's vision could be turned into a workable constitution. Agarwal noted that Gandhi had been kind enough to twice go through drafts of his book, suggesting several amendments before writing the foreword. In that foreword, Gandhi warned the reader not to make the mistake to assume that the writing accorded with his views in "every detail." After all he could not "undertake to check every thought and every word of it." However, he also added that "nothing in it has … jarred on me as inconsistent with what I would like to stand for", and that the document was "a thoughtful contribution to the many attempts at presenting India with constitutions. The merit of this attempt consists in the fact he has done what for want of time I have failed to do." In other words, with Gandhi's caveat in mind, this is as useful a guide to the Mahatma's idealistic constitutional thinking a few years before the actual task of sitting down to produce the constitution may have forced certain compromises.

This ghost-written constitution spells out how a decentralised Gandhian polity may work. First, the villagers would elect a panchayat and the elected panchayat presidents of a certain number (somewhere around twenty depending on population) of villages would constitute a local panchayat. All the presidents of the local panchayats would constitute the district panchayat. "The functions of these higher bodies shall be *advisory* and not *mandatory*; they shall guide, advise and supervise, and not command the lower Panchayats."[16] These panchayats, in turn, would send their presidents to the provincial panchayat which would co-ordinate and audit the accounts of the lower level of panchayats, be prepared for emergencies, administer universities, organise transport and provide irrigation facilities and manage key industries. The same process is repeated to provide the All-India Panchayat, the only central legislature. It would focus on defence and security, currency, foreign policy and industries of key national importance. The head of the central panchayat would be the head of the national government. By way of summary, Agarwal noted that for Gandhi, such an ideal constitution "must be based on the organisation of well-knit and coordinated Village Communities with their positive and direct democracy, non-violent cottage economy and human contacts."[17] Gandhi was far more concerned with the freedom and happiness of the citizen than of the state and the panchayat system was the way to ensure Ramraj.

Although, while speaking in the Constituent Assembly, India's first Prime Minister Jawaharlal Nehru called Gandhi the architect of the Assembly and the "Father of our Nation", noting that "his great spirit hovers over this place and blesses our undertaking",[18] about a month before Gandhi's assassination, Agarwal expressed his regret to the Mahatma that the Draft Constitution made no reference to the notion of decentralised democracy. In his newspaper, Gandhi responded that this was an "omission calling for immediate attention if our independence is to reflect the people's voice. The greater the power of the panchayats, the better for the people."[19] Agarwal requested an answer to the question: "Will the nation respect Mahatma Gandhiji's plea for decentralisation of political power among the numerous village communities?" Then he demanded that "The wish of the Father of the Nation who was also the Architect of our Freedom, must be respected!"[20]

The Indian Constitution

In August 1947, Dalit ("Untouchable") leader and Law Minister of the Government of India, Dr Bhimrao Ramji Ambedkar was elected by the government to chair its committee which was to draft the independent country's new constitution. Three weeks after Gandhi's assassination, the Draft Constitution was submitted to the President of the Assembly. It contained no mention at all of panchayats or any political institutions based on Gandhian ideology. Dr Ambedkar had no truck with Gandhi's idealised system of governance through village republics. He saw in the villages prejudice, communalism, ignorance, narrow-mindedness, and filth. They were places where Hindus exploited the untouchables. In the Constituent Assembly he claimed forcefully that "village republics have been the ruination of India" and that he was glad "that the Draft Constitution has discarded the village and adopted the individual as its unit."[21]

Although Ambedkar had condemned the idea of panchayats as the basis for the Constitution, by way of compromise to the Gandhians who demanded panchayati raj as a necessary component of the Mahatma's vision, Ambedkar offered Article 31–A (which became Article 40 in the final document). The Article appeared in Part IV of the Constitution: the non-enforceable section on Directive Principles of State Policy rather than as a basis of the political structure of the country. It reads, "The State shall take steps to organise village panchayats and endow them with such powers and authority as may be necessary to enable them to function as units of self-government."[22]

The Constitution of India was passed by the Constituent Assembly on 26 November 1949. The document, which became operational on 26 January 1950, was based on the principles of western constitutionalism, proclaimed a secular republic with the goals of securing justice (social, political and economic), liberty (of thought, expression and faith), equality (of status and opportunity), and fraternity (to ensure the dignity of the individual and the unity of the nation). The central government maintained total responsibility for defence, foreign affairs, railways, airlines, shipping, the post and currency. The states maintained control of police forces, the administration of justice, health, education, agriculture, fisheries and local government.

While Gandhi desired a decentralised government with directly elected village panchayats which in turn indirectly elected higher levels of government, the Indian Constitution delivered "a centralised, direct elected parliamentary-democratic government"[23] with a weak Gandhi-inspired Article 40. However, it also abolished untouchability and sanctioned an adult franchise, provided for minority rights, personal freedoms, civil liberties, freedom of speech and association, all within a secular state. In its directive principles, the document also contained such Gandhian touches as the desire to prohibit cow slaughter and intoxicating drinks, and to promote cottage industries.[24]

So, did India end up with a Gandhian constitution? Agarwal complained that the constitution was "not based on the essential indigenous traditions and culture."[25] He believed that administrative systems could not be transplanted; they had to reflect the "soul" of a nation. In this vein, others have claimed that the current document is entirely alien because it was borrowed from Western constitutions and "sits uneasily with the cultural ethos of the Indian people",[26] and that it is an alternative to a Gandhian constitution.[27] Others thought that given India's then current circumstances, Gandhi's constitutional ideas were not only anachronistic but totally impractical.[28] Still others suggested that idea of a Gandhian constitution is an oxymoron,[29] after all, according to Gandhi, genuine Swaraj (freedom) is achieved "when we learn to rule ourselves" and "such Swaraj has to be experienced, by each one for himself"[30] and, on the other hand, Parel notes that while "Gandhi did not participate in the deliberations of the Constituent Assembly that drew up the Constitution of India", nevertheless "the idea of India that underlies the Constitution is virtually Gandhian" because it is "his philosophy of nationalism" that is "the intellectual glue that holds independent India together."[31]

The panchayat system was important for Gandhi because his aim was to bring about a society based on non-violence. And for him the centralised state epitomised violence even in its attempts to do good.[32] Of course constitutions are not merely about government institutions, forms of representation, democracy or power. They are also about state security and defence. Gandhi's constitutional ideas also encompassed this aspect of governance.

Gandhi's Views on Defence and Security

The framers of the Indian Constitution knew Gandhi's views on defence and security. During the debates over the peace sections of the constitution, it was recalled that at the 1931 London Round Table Conference on India's future, "Gandhi declared that if he got swaraj, if the Congress was master in this country, one of the first things he would advice it to do would be to disband the army and police, and anything else which savoured of violence in the organization of the Indian State."[33] In fact, Gandhi said that, "Since we shall be at peace with all the rest of the world, neither exploiting nor being exploited, we should have the smallest army imaginable."[34] Nevertheless, in the final document, Article 51 of the Constitution (again in the section on directive principles without enforcement capability) enshrined India's endeavours to promote international peace and security in a way that any constitution could have done.[35] This was as far as the Gandhian insistence on non-violence went and it was only enacted after much deliberation.[36]

In 1942, Gandhi had told his biographer Louis Fischer that he "did not think that a free India will function like the other countries of the world. We have our own forms to contribute."[37] A few years later he still had the highest hopes for India: "Nowhere in the world does a State without government exist. If at all it could ever come into being, it should be in India; for, ours is the only country where the attempt has, at any rate, been made."[38] While Gandhi understood that many of his colleagues were not interested in his vision of a decentralised system of village republics, he also knew "on the contrary that many would have India become a first-class military power and wish for India to have a strong centre and build the whole structure round it."[39] He, however, had no vision of great power status for India.[40]

Gandhi saw decentralisation as being necessary for a non-violent society, because violence is inherent in a centralised state which needs adequate force for self-defence.[41] For Gandhi, "The State represents violence in a concentrated and organised form. The individual has a soul but the State is a soulless machine, it can never be weaned away from violence to which it owes its very existence."[42] But how can such a self-regulated society of enlightened anarchism, where every person "is his own ruler"[43] be established? Even Gandhi observed that such a completely non-violent society might never be established because every individual "might not reach the requisite level of moral development."[44] While he believed sufficient non-violence could be cultivated to allow for the eschewing of an army, a small police force ("wholly different ... from the present day force" in that they would be composed of lightly armed reformers who acted as servants of the people) may be necessary.[45] After all, crime would be minimal in a face-to-face society with no hunger and little disparity in earning. Where crimes did occur, they would be dealt with through the moral pressure of local opinion.[46]

In Gandhi's vision, a decentralised India would not require an army as it could rely on a Shanti Sena (peace army) of "non-violent soldiers" trained in Gandhian non-violence. In such a country there would be no danger of civil war and "no foreign country was likely to invade a polity whose fiercely independent-minded citizens would resist it to the death."[47] India would have no imperial design on any other country and will be self-sufficient in its economy. Without a race to capture foreign markets there will be little chance of international conflict.[48] And very practically,

> Decentralisation and ruralisation are imperative for successful defence against foreign aggression; they alone can defy modern warfare. The centralised industries provide an easy target for air-bombing so that a few bombs can successfully dislocate the whole national economy. Thus, from the strategic point of view a country with its large-scale industries concentrated in a few big towns becomes highly vulnerable.[49]

Under the heading "National Defence", in his *Gandhian Constitution*, Agarwal notes that Gandhi "would like Free India not to maintain any armed defence against foreign aggression. Gandhi wants India to develop disciplined non-violent power to face invasions bravely and successfully."[50] However, adding that Gandhi was a realist, Agarwal notes: "He is fully alive to the limitations of his own country. Although he will be genuinely happy if free India could agree to maintain only a Non-violent Army, he does concede that the ideal would be difficult of immediate realisation"[51] because he was even more afraid of cowardice than violence among his people.

Where defence of the state was thought of as being important, Gandhi recommended civilian, rather than military defence.[52] Civilian defence, unlike conventional warfare, does not aim to defend particular objects such as borders and buildings, but is concerned with the defence of the whole body of society ("our way of life"). A physical taking over of the country would be conceded (perhaps after the invader was invited to walk over the corpses of unarmed citizens blocking invasion routes)[53] and a non-violent political struggle would be substituted for aggressive war where the aggressor becomes akin to a domestic tyrant, and civil disobedience and non-cooperation become the tactics.[54] Such a policy would give individuals a genuine say in their own security, it would not be seen as threatening by neighbours and so give less pretext for invasions and hopefully lessen dangerous arms races.

As news of the Nazi genocide of the Jewish people reached him, Gandhi grappled with the ideal way that large-scale evils should be combated. Speaking of Nazi oppression, he claimed that if ever there could be "a justifiable war in the name of humanity" then the "war against Germany ... would be completely justified. But I do not believe in any war."[55] And, as Japanese forces advanced through Burma threatening India with invasion, Gandhi was forced to clarify his ideas on actions to be taken in times of war. He warned against using violence to meet violence even in the case of national defence, "for the defence has to resort to all the damnable things that the enemy does, and then with greater vigour if it has to succeed."[56] Because Gandhi believed that there should be no yielding to brute force, and property to which there was a just claim should be defended, there could possibly be the occasional need to engage in a "war without weapons". And this had to be done in a positive way, that is with the aim of converting of the opponent rather than the negative way of waging conventional conflict minus the violence.[57] This approach relies on conciliation, unilateral steps towards disarmament and truth seeking, and a non-Machiavellian foreign policy backed up with a programme of civilian defence if an invasion should nevertheless occur.

Gandhi believed that in a "living wall" of unarmed citizens approach to self-defence "there will be no greater loss in men than if forcible resistance was offered; there will be no expenditure in armaments and fortifications."[58] This approach would be most effective if undertaken by a community where everyone was a true satyagrahi.[59] In such a case there would be no need to organise elaborate civilian defence programmes because the most effective nonviolent measures would occur spontaneously. While the discipline required for a living wall approach to the defence of borders is more than a little unlikely to be achieved, Gandhi firmly believed that given proper training and proper leadership such non-violence "can be practiced by masses of mankind."[60]

In an interview, appearing under the title "Can India be Defended?" that Gandhi gave to the American journal *Liberty* in August 1940, he expounded on the actions that a hypothetically free India would undertake in the face of invasion. Gandhi declared that "The representatives of the free Indian State would let the invader in without opposition. But they would tell the invader and all his forces at the frontier that the Indian people would refuse to cooperate in any work in any undertaking. They would refuse to obey orders despite all threats and despite all punishments inflicted upon them."[61]

In his *Gandhian Constitution*, Agarwal notes: "Moreover, if India, under the inspiring guidance of Gandhiji, is able to attain political independence through non-violence (which it more or less did), she will surely release tremendous forces of amity and good-will among the warring nations of the world. As Gandhiji expresses the hope, her Independence and freedom would spell non-aggression and international harmony."[62] The Gandhian President of the Constituent Assembly and first President of the Indian Republic, Rajendra Prasad, made special reference to what he saw as a Gandhian Article 51, stating that "While a world torn with conflicts was still depending on armaments to establish peace and goodwill, India was destined to play a great part, if she proved true to the teachings of Gandhi and gave effect to this directive principle of the Constitution."[63] Given all that Gandhi had said in the subject, all that he tried to teach his beloved countrymen, could India have played a part far greater than the one envisaged by Prasad, one more similar to Gandhi's vision as noted by Agarwal?

A Chance Squandered?

It needs to be remembered that during the framing of the constitution, India had already fought a war with Pakistan, and for many a highly decentralised system of government was not seen as conducive to national defence. Further, the political upheaval threatened the country with famine and the interim government needed to be mindful of thoughtful food distribution, while the Kashmir dispute raised questions about national integration. The low level of economic development of the country, with its need for efficient communications and transport, electric power and heavy industries, was also viewed by many in power as not best achieved through a substantially decentralised governmental system.

All the above may be true, however a recent article raises the question about whether something fundamentally important, and perhaps possible, was squandered. And, sadly, possibly it was a once in history opportunity. C. Douglas Lummis points out that Western democracy in practice amounts to little more than "the right to participate in periodic elections."[64] In contrast, the Gandhian constitution, as spelled out in Agarwal's book, "gives popular sovereignty a different structure by placing it not with that vague entity 'the people' but by clearly locating it in a multiplicity of specific organisations: the villages." And this means that sovereignty is concrete rather than a myth that can all too easily slip out of people's hands: "it is right there in the village where the people live, and where they can hold on to it." And none of these village republics would have a violent arm. Gandhi dreamed of, and later his followers Vinoba Bhave and Jayaprakash Narayan to some degree brought into existence, a system of volunteer shanti sainiks (soldiers of peace) undertaking non-violent peacekeeping work in self-governing villages.[65] Even if the panchayat system and volunteer peacekeepers could not take the place of the state and army, they could perhaps have been introduced within the state framework. Unfortunately this experiment vanished when the centralised state, in the form of Prime Minister Indira Gandhi's declared "state of emergency", assumed dictatorial control of the country.[66]

Still, Lummis wonders why the Gandhian proposal is not as well known as many other utopian works, and concludes that the works of other utopian writers are read for theoretical interest only. Their plans do not need to be dismissed as "unrealistic" simply because they are non-threatening and there is, in any case, no agency to actualise them. Gandhi, on the other hand, did not write out of theoretical interest and for at least a brief moment there was the possibility of an actualising agency: Gandhi and his Congress and public supporters.

> For it had already been proved to the world many times over that, for reasons no one has ever been able fully to explain, this combination of The Congress of India with Gandhi at its head had the power to transform manifest impossibilities into possibilities, and then into accomplished facts. ... Under his leadership, phenomena hitherto dismissed as impossible in the political world were brought into being ... [and] surely that is why his proposal inspires a feeling of unease that other utopian proposals do not. For while it is difficult to imagine his constitution being realized in India today ... it was a possibility then, or would have been had the leaders of The Congress not deserted Gandhi and opted for an ordinary (violent) state.

Lummis is certainly right that such a constitution coming into force "is hardly imaginable now". However, given this, he further asks why the thought of it still makes us uncomfortable. His answer it interesting:

> The very fact that it was a manifest possibility in the recent past upsets an axiom of our political belief: that the (violent) nation state is inevitable and necessary; that it is not to be doubted; that it has no alternative; that the establishment of the state, including the Indian state, was not a human choice, but a Destiny .... The Gandhian Constitution forces one to realize that, at that time, it was a choice. It is poignant to think that this [Agarwal's] shabby, ignored little used book ... outlines India's Road Not Taken.

We are invited to ask, What if? Had the government carried out Gandhi's plan, it would have been an unprecedented event, a revolution of "not the people at the bottom rising up and seizing the state, but the people who have just seized the state, walking away from it and joining the people at the bottom." Of course it was not going to happen. By this time in his life Gandhi had been more or less sidelined by those negotiating independence and they were not about to take the Mahatma's advice and become humble village workers. They wanted to engage in the task of shaping the new India as government officials. Gandhi complained that he was no longer being listened to. He lost his oft-repeated desire to live to the age of 125 in order to render service to his people, and seemed to be preparing himself for death. It is difficult to imagine what would have become of Gandhi had he not been assassinated soon after India had gained her independence. In any case, his death was perhaps his greatest and most important sacrifice: to a large degree it shocked the still turbulent country into peace.

Gandhi could now become a "Father of the Nation" that India could be more proud of than any other country of their own heroic founder. He had given India great respect in the world. Towards the end of his paper, Lummis takes up this point, noting that the government could now engage in *realpolitik* and arm itself without the criticism of Bapu ("father" as Gandhi was often called) and in fact utter phrases such as "in keeping with the ideals of Gandhiji", when, to anyone who cared to notice, they were in keeping with anything but.

Conclusion: Other Possibilities

Lummis was right; even if there had been a chance of a Gandhian peace constitution, the opportunity was squandered. However, this does not mean that all possibility along these lines is irrevocably lost.[67] There are over a dozen countries without armies,[68] and, although there are attempts to roll it back, Article 9 (where the Japanese people renounce war and the use of force to settle disputes as a sovereign right) is still in Japan's constitution, and there has been a recent upsurge in the viewing of the meaning of security through different lenses, including non-violent ones.

Many international relations theorists have realised that, in a state system, the security of one state is tied up with the security of others. The idea here is that the proponents of "common security" say that a zero-sum approach, where the gain of one automatically means the loss for another, is no longer adequate. In other words, that the emphasis must be on security for everyone rather than national defence, and that this security must be more than merely military security. A more radical idea, "comprehensive security", goes back to the fundamentals by asking what exactly it is that we are talking about when we talk of security. Security for whom? The answer has to be for people, not states or governments. State security must only be a means to an end; the real measure is how people feel. And security for people must encompass all security threats that people feel, and these need not be, and in fact are not, restricted to military security threats that can possibly be guarded against through a build-up of weapons. As Gandhi well knew, the state can be quite secure from invasion while much of the population feels insecure. Further, there are now those who are talking in terms that could well have come straight from the Mahatma. A growing number of theorists are talking about civilian defence, very similar to Gandhi's "living wall" approach to defence, and shanti sena-like organisations such as Peace Brigades International are protecting human rights campaigners, especially in the Third World, where the police do not or cannot.[69]

Part of the arguments for these newer views of security and defence is that the people have a genuine say in their own security because it is not taken out of their hands. It would be far cheaper for a state to forego the need to have a standing army, and this would mean more money left over to take care of other areas of insecurity such as the fear of joblessness, or inadequate health care and education. Further, if it is adopted, it would end the security dilemma – the country would be less likely to be invaded because neighbours would no longer see it as a threat, making the rationalisations for an attack less plausible in the international arena, and curtailing the need for costly and in the end self-defeating arms races. Sounds like Gandhi?[70]

Power pointed out that Gandhi may not have adequately grasped many crucial issues which need to be faced in international politics; he may not have devised an effective method to end war, and did not construct a new theory of international affairs.[71] Lummis and some of the newer defence theorists would beg to differ, claiming that Gandhi's vision was simply too far ahead of its time and too radical for those of us with less vision. Nevertheless Gandhi's active achievements and his example have changed the life of many. And through his achievements and the achievements of those he influenced, the world has also been changed. Gandhi's philosophy of conflict and his insistence on justice go to the heart of the struggle for a better system of international relations. Gandhi was quite clear in his belief that non-violence was not limited to use by individuals. He claimed that it could be an attitude of society and could be practiced by nations.[72] And it is still possible that some other "fathers/mothers of nations", somewhere, sometime, may have a grand vision and the courage and power to carry it through when they are involved in drafting the governing document of their new country.

Notes

1. "Speech at Exhibition Ground, Faizpur", *Harijan*, 2 January 1937.
2. "What of the West?", *Young India*, 3 September 1925.
3. "Independence", *Harijan*, 28 July 1946.
4. "Question Box: Village Swaraj", *Harijan*, 26 July 1942.
5. "Power Not an End", *Young India*, 2 July 1931.
6. "Speech at Prayer Meeting", *CWMG*, LXXXIX, 17 September 1947, 195–97.
7. M.K. Gandhi, *Constructive Programme: Its Meaning and Place*, Ahmedabad: Navajivan, 1941, p. 24.
8. *Harijan*, 18 January 1948, quoted in Ronald J. Terchek, *Gandhi: Struggling for Autonomy*, Lanham: Rowman & Littlefield, 1998, p. 173.
9. Bhikhu Parekh, *Gandhi's Political Philosophy: A Critical Examination*, Delhi: Ajanta, 1995, pp. 117–21.
10. Terchek, *Gandhi*, p. 166.
11. Parekh, *Gandhi's Political Philosophy*, p. 119.
12. "Draft Constitution of Congress", *Harijan*, 15 February 1948.
13. Parekh, *Gandhi's Political Philosophy*, p. 122.
14. "Two Posers", *The Hindu*, 22 June 1945.
15. Narayan Agarwal, *Gandhian Constitution for Free India*, Allahabad: Kitabistan, 1946.
16. Ibid., p. 85.
17. Narayan Agarwal, "Gandhi and Decentralization of Political Power", in Kshitis Roy (ed.), *Gandhi Memorial Peace Number*, Shantiniketan: Visva-Bharati Quarterly, 1949, p. 180.

18. *Constituent Assembly Debates*, Vol. I, New Delhi: Publications Division, Government of India, 1966, p. 60.
19. "Who Should be Provincial Governors?", *Harijan*, 21 December 1947.
20. Agarwal, "Gandhi and Decentralization of Political Power", p. 183.
21. *Constituent Assembly Debates*, Vol. VII, pp. 38–39.
22. Eventually this section of the Constitution was strengthened in 1993 with the Seventy-third Amendment of the Constitution of India. The amendment set out the powers and functions for panchayati raj institutions.
23. Thomas Pantham, "Gandhi and the Constitution: Parliamentary Swaraj and Village Swaraj", in Rajeev Bhargava (ed.), *Politics and Ethics of the Indian Constitution*, New Delhi: Oxford University Press, 2008, p. 60.
24. For a summary of the debates surrounding these issues, see Dilip Kumar Chatterjee, *Gandhi and Constitution Making in India*, New Delhi: Associated Publishing, 1984, pp. 146–52.
25. Agarwal, "Gandhi and Decentralization of Political Power", p. 177.
26. See Rajeev Bhargava, "Introduction: Outline of a Political Theory of the Indian Constitution", in Bhargava (ed.), op. cit., p. 30.
27. Granville Austin, *The Indian Constitution: Cornerstone of a Nation*, Oxford: Oxford University Press, 1966, pp. 31–32.
28. Ibid., pp. 39–49.
29. See Bhargava, "Introduction", p. 8; and Peter Ronald de Souza, "Institutional Visions and Sociological Imaginations: The Debate on Panchayati Raj", in Bhargava (ed.) op. cit., p. 82.
30. M.K. Gandhi, *Hind Swaraj or Indian Home Rule*, Ahmedabad: Navajivan, 1939, p. 65.
31. Anthony Parel, "Gandhi in Independent India", in Judith M. Brown and Anthony Parel (eds.), *The Cambridge Companion to Gandhi*, Cambridge: Cambridge University Press, 2011, p. 221. On this, see also O.P. Minocha, "The Impact of Gandhian Ideology on the Indian Constitution", in Verinder Grover (ed.), *Gandhi and Politics in India*, New Delhi: Deep & Deep, 1996, pp. 151–77; and S.N. Ray and D.K. Chatterjee, "Gandhi and the Making of the Indian Constitution", in V.T. Patil (ed.), *Studies on Gandhi*, New Delhi: Sterling, 1983, pp. 61–82.
32. "If the State suppressed capitalism by violence, it will be caught in the coils of violence itself and fail to develop non-violence at any time." And "I look upon an increase in the power of the State with the greatest fear because although while apparently doing good by minimizing exploitation, it does the greatest harm to mankind by destroying individuality

which lies at the root of all progress." "Interview to Nirmal Kumar Bose", *The Hindustan Times*, 17 October 1935.

33. See arguments by K.T. Shah, *Constituent Assembly Debates*, 1966, Vol. VII, p. 598. For a good summary of the debates over Article 51 of the Constitution and Gandhi's influence on their drafting see: Dilip Kumar Chatterjee, *Gandhi and Constitution Making in India*, New Delhi: Associated Publishing, 1984, pp. 152–54.
34. "Statement to Reuters", *The Hindustan Times*, 5 September 1931.
35. Article 51 stipulated that "The state shall endeavour to: (a) promote international peace and security; (b) maintain just and honourable relations between nations; (c) foster respect for international law and treaty obligations in the dealings of organised peoples with one another; and (d) encourage settlement of international disputes by arbitration.
36. See *Constituent Assembly Debates*, Vol. VII, pp. 595–603.
37. Louis Fischer, *A Week with Gandhi*, London: Allen & Unwin, 1943, p. 57.
38. Quoted in Anand T. Hingorani and Ganga A. Hingorani, *The Encyclopaedia of Gandhian Thoughts*, New Delhi: AICCI(I), 1985, p. 325.
39. "Independence", *Harijan*, 28 July 1946.
40. Austin, *The Indian Constitution*, p. 37.
41. See "Hand-Spun as a Measure of Value", *Harijan*, 18 January 1942 and "Spinning-Wheels vs. Mills", *Harijan*, 30 December 1939.
42. "Interview to Nirmal Kumar Bose", *The Hindustan Times*, 17 October 1935.
43. "Power Not an End", *Young India*, 2 July 1931.
44. See Jayaprakash Narayan, "Gandhi and the Politics of Decentralisation", in Sibnarayan Ray (ed.), *Gandhi, India and the World: An International Symposium*, Melbourne: The Hawthorn Press, 1970, p. 240.
45. "My Idea of a Police Force", *Harijan*, 1 September 1940.
46. For more on this see, Unto Tähtinen, *Non-Violent Theories of Punishment: Indian and Western*, Delhi: Motilal Banarsidass, 1983, pp. 47–50.
47. Parekh, *Gandhi's Political Philosophy*, p. 115.
48. Ibid., p. 112.
49. Agarwal, *Gandhian Constitution*, pp. 63–64.
50. Ibid., p. 109.
51. Ibid., p. 110.

52. See Thomas Weber, "Gandhi's 'Living Wall' and Maude Royden's 'Peace Army'", *Gandhi Marg*, Vol. 10, no. 4, 1988, pp. 199–212.
53. "Letter from Europe", *Young India*, 13 December 1931.
54. See T.K. Mahadevan, Adam Roberts and Gene Sharp (eds.), *Civilian Defence: An Introduction*, New Delhi: Gandhi Peace Foundation, 1967; and Adam Roberts (ed.), *The Strategy of Civilian Defence: Non-Violent Resistance to Aggression*, London: Faber, 1967.
55. "The Jews", *Harijan*, 26 November 1938.
56. "On its Trial", *Harijan*, 15 March 1942; and see also "How to Combat Hitlerism", *Harijan*, 22 June 1940.
57. Anders Boserup and Andrew Mack, *War Without Weapons: Non-Violence in National Defense*, New York: Schocken, 1974, pp. 21–36.
58. "Two Questions from America", *Harijan*, 13 April 1940.
59. That is, one versed in satyagraha, Gandhi's truth-seeking method of non-violent activism.
60. "Some Questions Answered", *Harijan*, 17 December 1938
61. Pyarelal, *Mahatma Gandhi, Volume X: The Last Phase, Part II*, Ahmedabad: Navajivan, 1958, p. 814.
62. Agarwal, *Gandhian Constitution*, p. 112.
63. *Constituent Assembly Debates*, Vol. XI, pp. 992–93.
64. C. Douglas, Lummis, "The Smallest Army Imaginable: Gandhi's Constitutional Proposal for India and Japan's Peace Constitution", *The Asia-Pacific Journal: Japan Focus*, January 18, 2010, available at *http://japanfocus.org/C_Douglas-Kynnus/3288*
65. During the heady days of the 1960s to the mid-1970s, Gandhi's chief disciples were again looking at the issues concerning police and armed forces, village republics, political parties and elections, and on building democracy from below through "organic communities" which could select their own candidates. See Thomas Weber, *Gandhi's Peace Army: The Shanti Sena and Unarmed Peacekeeping*, Syracuse: Syracuse University Press, 1996; and Thomas Weber, *The Shanti Sena: Philosophy, History and Action*, New Delhi: Orient BlackSwan, 2009.
66. While the 1993 Seventy-third Amendment of the Constitution of India formalised panchayati raj institutions, the Shanti Sena faded away.
67. Reactions to Glenn Paige's advocacy for a "nonkilling society" seem to be that while it is not currently possible it is possible to become possible. See Glenn D. Paige, *Nonkilling Global Political Science*, New Delhi: Gandhi Media Centre, 2002, p. 20.

68. However, it must be admitted that almost all of the about one dozen armyless states (it depends on what degree of forces and alliances are included), with the exception of Costa Rica and Panama, are tiny.
69. See Yeshua Moser-Puangsuwan and Thomas Weber (eds.), *Nonviolent Intervention Across Borders: A Recurrent Vision*, Honolulu: Spark M. Matsunaga Institute for Peace, 2000.
70. See Thomas Weber, "Gandhi and World Politics", in Siddharth Mallavarapu and B.S. Cimni (eds.), *Handbook on International Relations*, Delhi: Pearson Longman (forthcoming).
71. Paul Power, *Gandhi on World Affairs*, London: Allen & Unwin, 1961, pp. 135–36.
72. "Equal Distribution", *Harijan*, 25 August 1940; and "Discussion with Abdul Gaffar Khan", *Harijan*, 12 November 1938.

References

Agarwal, Narayan, "Gandhi and Decentralization of Political Power", in Kshitis Roy (ed.), *Gandhi Memorial Peace Number*, Shantiniketan: Visva-Bharati Quarterly, 1949, pp. 177–83.

——, *Gandhian Constitution for Free India*, Allahabad: Kitabistan, 1946.

Austin, Granville, *The Indian Constitution: Cornerstone of a Nation*, Oxford: Oxford University Press, 1966.

Bhargava, Rajeev (ed.), *Politics and Ethics of the Indian Constitution*, New Delhi: Oxford University Press, 2008.

——, "Introduction: Outline of a Political Theory of the Indian Constitution", in Bhargava (ed.), pp. 1–40.

Boserup, Anders and Andrew Mack, *War Without Weapons: Non-Violence in National Defense*, New York: Schocken, 1974.

Chatterjee, Dilip Kumar, *Gandhi and Constitution Making in India*, New Delhi: Associated Publishing, 1984.

Constituent Assembly Debates, New Delhi: Publications Division, Government of India, 1966.

de Souza, Peter Ronald, "Institutional Visions and Sociological Imaginations: The Debate on Panchayati Raj", in Bhargava (ed.), op. cit., pp. 79–91.

Fischer, Louis, *A Week with Gandhi*, London: Allen & Unwin, 1943.

Gandhi, M.K., *Collected Works of Mahatma Gandhi* (*CWMG*), vols. 1–100, New Delhi: Publications Division, Government of India, 1958–1991; and revised CD-ROM version, New Delhi: Publications Division, Government of India, 1999.

——, *Constructive Programme: Its Meaning and Place*, Ahmedabad: Navajivan, 1941.

——, *Hind Swaraj or Indian Home Rule*, Ahmedabad: Navajivan, 1939.

Hingorani, Anand T. and Ganga A. Hingorani, *The Encyclopaedia of Gandhian Thoughts*, New Delhi: AICCI(I), 1985.

Lummis, C. Douglass, "The Smallest Army Imaginable: Gandhi's Constitutional Proposal for India and Japan's Peace Constitution", *The Asia-Pacific Journal: Japan Focus*, January 18, 2010, available at *http://japanfocus.org/C_Douglas-Kynnus/3288.*

Mahadevan, T.K., Adam Roberts and Gene Sharp (eds.), *Civilian Defence: An Introduction*, New Delhi: Gandhi Peace Foundation, 1967.

Minocha, O.P., "The Impact of Gandhian Ideology on the Indian Constitution", in Verinder Grover (ed.), *Gandhi and Politics in India*, New Delhi: Deep & Deep, 1996, pp. 151–77.

Moser-Puangsuwan, Yeshua and Thomas Weber (eds.), *Nonviolent Intervention Across Borders: A Recurrent Vision*, Honolulu: Spark M. Matsunaga Institute for Peace, 2000.

Narayan, Jayaprakash, "Gandhi and the Politics of Decentralisation", in Sibnarayan Ray (ed.), *Gandhi, India and the World: An International Symposium*, Melbourne: The Hawthorn Press, 1970, pp. 237–50.

Paige, Glenn D., *Nonkilling Global Political Science*, New Delhi: Gandhi Media Centre, 2002.

Pantham, Thomas, "Gandhi and the Constitution: Parliamentary Swaraj and Village Swaraj", in Bhargava (ed.), op. cit., pp. 59–78.

Parekh, Bhikhu, *Gandhi's Political Philosophy: A Critical Examination*, Delhi: Ajanta, 1995.

Parel, Anthony, "Gandhi in Independent India", in Judith M. Brown and Anthony Parel (eds.), *The Cambridge Companion to Gandhi*, Cambridge: Cambridge University Press, 2011, pp. 219–38.

Power, Paul F., *Gandhi on World Affairs*, London: Allen & Unwin, 1961.

Pyarelal, *Mahatma Gandhi, volume X: The Last Phase, Part-II*, Ahmedabad: Navajivan, 1958.

Ray, S.N. and D.K. Chatterjee, "Gandhi and the Making of the Indian Constitution", in V.T. Patil (ed.), *Studies on Gandhi*, New Delhi: Sterling, 1983, pp. 61–82.

Roberts, Adam (ed.), *The Strategy of Civilian Defence: Non-Violent Resistance to Aggression*, London: Faber, 1967.

Tähtinen, Unto, *Non-Violent Theories of Punishment: Indian and Western*, Delhi: Motilal Banarsidass, 1983.

Terchek, Ronald J., *Gandhi: Struggling for Autonomy*, Lanham: Rowman & Littlefield, 1998.

Weber, Thomas, "Gandhi and World Politics", in Siddharth Mallavarapu and B.S. Cimni (eds.), *Handbook on International Relations*, Delhi: Pearson Longman (forthcoming).

——, "Gandhi's 'Living Wall' and Maude Royden's 'Peace Army'", *Gandhi Marg*, Vol. 10, no. 4, 1988, pp. 199–212.

——, *Gandhi's Peace Army: The Shanti Sena and Unarmed Peacekeeping*, Syracuse: Syracuse University Press, 1996.

——, *The Shanti Sena: Philosophy, History and Action*, New Delhi: Orient BlackSwan, 2009.

7

The Educational Legacies of Mahatma Gandhi for Peace Education

JOHN P. SYNOTT

Introduction: Principled Non-violence as the Basis of Social Action

Throughout his leadership of the struggles for freedom, justice and independence for Indians in South Africa and India, Mohandas Karamchand Gandhi maintained that the values which most inspired him were his beliefs in the truth of the spiritual nature of every person and the unity of all human life. He wrote and spoke of these beliefs on many occasions. For instance, while speaking to students in Mysore in 1927, he said, "Whatever I have been doing is done with a sense of my duty to God. And this I consider to be the right thing. God is not seated in the skies, in the heavens, or elsewhere. He is enshrined in the heart of everyone – be he a Hindu, Mohammedan, Christian or Jew, man or woman" cited in *The Hindu,* 21 July 1927 (*CW* 34, pp. 203–4). This belief in the spiritual unity of all people was the foundation of his strategy of *Satyagraha* which means The Pursuit of Truth (Kumar, 2009: 17). Eminent Gandhian scholar Ravindra Kumar quotes Gandhi's description of *Satyagraha* as:

> a Dharmayuddha, one of the most powerful methods of direct action; it is a force that works silently and apparently slowly in reality; there is no force in the world that is so direct or so swift in working; it excludes every form of violence, veiled or unveiled, and whether in thought, word or deed. (*Harijan*, 15 April 1933, quoted in Kumar, 2009: 18)

Widely recognised among Gandhi followers and peace studies scholars is that the central means of *Satyagraha* is *Ahimsa* (non-violence) (Ramachandran and Mahadevan, online; Kumar, 2009). Referring to these two qualities, Gandhi said, "it is impossible to disentangle and separate them. They are ... rather of a smooth unstamped metallic disk. Who can say which is the obverse and which is the reverse? Nevertheless, ahimsa is the means; truth is the end." (Gandhi, In Search of the Supreme, 27; quoted in Kumar, 2009: 19).

There have been many commentaries on Gandhi's use of these insights in pursuing political goals in South Africa and India and in his vision of an ideal society (e.g., Bhana and Vadeh, online). Subsequently, Gandhi's model has been acknowledged as the inspiration for non-violent social and political action in a range of contexts. As well-known examples, Dr Martin Luther King acknowledged Gandhi's influence on his campaign for civil rights for African-Americans (King, 1958), Bishop Desmond Tutu acknowledged the inspiration of Gandhi in his role in the struggle to remove the apartheid regime in South Africa and Mrs Aung San Suu Kyi has been inspired by Gandhi in her non-violent resistance to the military rule in Myanmar. Peace studies scholar Nagler (1999) described Gandhi as the most articulate and complete representative of this approach of principled non-violence and added: "Gandhi, master of both the content (non-violence) and the most effective form (concrete, especially constructive action) of a peace culture, is proposed as the 'culture hero' of the next millennium" (Nagler, 1999: 237).

Nagler contrasts Gandhi's approach of principled non-violence to that of strategic non-violence in which one acts without violence as a means to an end but is not based on the spiritual principles of human unity such as Gandhi espoused. Nagler (1999) observed that the transition from communist rule to democracies in Eastern Europe and the overthrow of other authoritarian regimes around the world were achieved largely through strategic non-violence, without following the *Satyagraha* path. The case of the so-called Arab Spring in 2012 during which non-violent popular uprisings led to the overthrow of autocrats in Egypt, Tunisia and Yemen, is a current example of strategic non-violence. Of course, in the case of recent uprisings in the Middle East, this principle has been sorely tested. In Libya a bloody civil war developed after initially non-violent protests, and Syria has moved in this direction after use of extreme force by the entrenched Assad family led by the dictator president. The use of 'people power' against authoritarian regimes has been widely and successfully used but it does not necessarily represent the dawn of a new culture of peace or a new value system and worldview. As Nagler comments:

> to see the dawn of a new culture we need a new value system and worldview, and these can only come from the nonviolence that is based on active, self-sacrificing love or 'soul force'. A new culture, in other words one that does not generate so much abrasive conflict in the first place, must take root from a new cultural idea – specifically, a new idea of the person and the kind of power and influence persons can exert on each other. In this sense strategic nonviolence ... is not radically different from the general matrix of the industrial-colonial worldview. (1999: 244)

Beyond the context of the immediate struggles in which he participated, Gandhi considered the ways in which to transform existing societies to embrace the principles of *Satyagraha* and recognise the mutual dependence of man's activities on one another and the unity of human life. In particular he saw an important role for education. He wrote: Education must be of a new type for the sake of the creation of a new world (Gandhi, *Harijan*, 19 January 1947).

Dichotomies in Peace Education

The distinction between principled non-violence and strategic non-violence presents a useful perspective in understanding contemporary social and political upheavals. It is useful in the analysis of non-violent positions in international relations, political economy, and social relations.

The dichotomy is also useful in the analysis of different approaches in education and, particularly, peace education. Education is the key traditional social mechanism for the transmission of culture. Formal education emerged from traditions of cultural teaching, including religious and political indoctrination. In modern nation-states educational institutions are a strategic means for implementing state policies. Modern nations are focussed on education that will enhance the nation's international economic strength in the global economy. Education also serves as a vehicle for social cohesion, transmission of national values, and patriotic loyalty in independent nations. This extends to situations where education systems serve as vehicles for consolidating religious authoritarianism, as in modern Iran, as well as secular dictatorships such as the Assad tyranny in Syria or the Kim regime in North Korea. Such approaches in education are strategic and aimed towards the continued legitimacy and continuity of power of the doctrine or group in the country.

Within the broad scope of educational practices peace education performs a range of important roles. In societies with significant conflicts or post-conflict societies peace education works to halt, transform and reconcile conflicting forces and establish peaceful conditions (Salomon and Nevo, 2002). In other contexts, peace educators engage in critical analysis of the mainstream system, and work to identify practices oppressive of human rights and remove them. In other instances, aspects of peace education have been 'mainstreamed' into the system in curriculum areas as values education, human rights education and environmental education. Practices associated with peace education, such as conflict resolution, have been incorporated into school processes (Johnson and Johnson, 2006). It would be fair to claim that peace education has a greater presence in Western schools at the present time than at any previous time in educational history.

Peace education provides a particularly important area of education where non-violent behaviour is promoted as a core principle. There are many valuable conceptualisations of peace education in the peace education literature (e.g., Harris and Morrison, 2003; Synott, 2005). There are holistic models such as Danesh (2002) and Wenden (2004). Similarly, there are many examples of peace education in practice across different educational contexts. For instance, programmes of peace education in conflict and post-conflict societies are recognised as important features of any progress towards removing conflict and establishing peaceful societies (Schulz, 2008; Harris and Lewer, 2008).

Likewise, there are approaches to peace education in societies that are not engaged in major conflicts but where there are forms of social violence which manifest in schools. These include mass killings in schools, bullying and inter-group conflicts (e.g., Rigby, 2006; Hughes and Donnelly, 2006; Synott, 2009). Much of the peace education work in this area revolves around the critical examination of structural violence in specific societies and the advocacy of ways to remove such practices. Peace education that seeks to remove racism or other forms of discrimination revolves around this approach. Non-violent conflict resolution, promoting peaceful school cultures and teaching individual peacefulness are ways school programmes use peace education approaches to build secure environments and prevent conflicts. The *Journal of Peace Education* with its foundations in IPRA provides a wide range of perspectives and examples of peace education theory and practice. The publications of Harris (2004), Reardon (1986), Toh and Floresca-Cawagas (1987), Navarro-Castro and Nario-Galace (2008) are just a few excellent works in an area whose scholarship is increasing constantly.

In a broader context peace education has set one of its goals as the promotion of a world culture of peace. The educational mission of UNESCO and coalitions such as The Hague Campaign for a World Culture of Peace represent international educational organisations that aspire towards this ideal and goal. Such a notion of a world culture of peace is espoused in other statements of global change such as The Earth Charter. Many of these approaches to peace education have evolved from the basic principles of human rights as espoused in the Universal Declaration of Human Rights.

There are, then, many different approaches towards peace education and it is evident that they are not all the same and, indeed, are conceived and practised from different foundational concepts and principles. Nevertheless the doctrine of non-violence is common across all approaches in peace education and can be said to distinguish peace education from all other approaches to education. However, as discussed previously, non-violence can emerge from the different conceptual platforms of principled non-violence or strategic non-violence.

In modern history Gandhi was the foremost advocate and greatly identified with the doctrine of principled non-violence. He also had some strong practical engagements with education. Therefore, it can be useful in sustaining approaches in the expanding field of peace education to continually study the concepts and approaches of Gandhi in their application to education. Such an undertaking is not a straight-forward procedure, for there are limitations presented when we undertake that study. These are historical and contextual factors particular to Gandhi's times and circumstances.

Limitations in Analysis of Gandhi's Educational Vision

"I have nothing new to teach the world. Truth and non-violence are as old as the hill" (Gandhi, *Young India Weekly*, 10 October 1931, quoted in Kumar, 2010: 60).

An initial difficulty is that, as in his many other fields of activity, Gandhi did not write or formulate any comprehensive treatise on education. Nevertheless, through the course of his actions, writings and recorded speeches, he made many comments and pronouncements about education. An additional difficulty is that throughout his life Gandhi changed and refined his views on many topics and issues. He acknowledged this and maintained his right to shift his opinion and change his mind. Gandhi commented, "I am not at all concerned with appearing to be consistent. In my search after Truth I have discarded many ideas and learnt many new things" (*Harijan*, 29 April 1933; quoted in Kumar, 2010: 67). His views on education certainly fit this self-characterisation. Gandhi also wrote that his latest views on any topic should be considered as his most complete views since he was continually refining his understanding of issues. He wrote in *Harijan*: "When anybody finds any inconsistency between any two writings of mine, if he still has faith in my sanity, he would do well to choose the later of the two on the same subject" (29 April 1923: 2). Nevertheless, the task requires an identification of key principles, pronouncements and practices throughout the totality of his life and work, for as Gandhi said, "My life is my message" (quoted in Kumar, 2010: 56).

A further recognition for contemporary, internationalised scholars in peace education is that Gandhi's practical orientations were towards Indian identity, history, and circumstances. Although Gandhi had a broad perspective that reached out towards universal unity and freedom, most of his specific statements were directed towards the Indian context. This includes his statements about education. Therefore, some degree of cultural relativity has to be applied in an analysis of Gandhi's statements on education. This approach is intensified by the fact that Gandhi was more than a great nationalist. He held the notion that India would assume a pre-eminent place in world affairs and profoundly influence other countries. Statements such as Gandhi's pronouncement that, "I feel that India's mission is different from that of others. India is fitted for the religious supremacy of the world," display some ingenuousness and probably need to be appreciated in their contexts and as rhetoric to inspire his followers. He made many similar statements on India's singular traditions and destiny. Thus, the search to identify Gandhi's views on education needs to employ some perspectives of comparative education and analysis.

With the cultural differences, there is a time gap in educational practices of a century ago, as compared to modern times. Gandhi's views on education were very much a rebellion against the norm of British colonial education that was fairly consistent across the wide sweep of colonies, including Australia, Canada, Ireland, and Kenya. Lancastrian model teaching, strong discipline, rote learning, views of children as lesser beings needing to be controlled and trained dominated school practices in all English-speaking colonies. Gandhi's educational views challenged the very basis of these approaches. He was against the notion of compulsory schooling that had been the mission of educational reformers in England. Gandhi said, "The foundation that Macauley made of education has enslaved us. I do not suggest that he had any such intention, but that has been the result" (quoted in Kumarappa, 1953; online). Particularly his insistence that education should be non-violent and therefore not imposed on children challenged the paradigm of schooling that had shaped British education since the advent of mass compulsory schooling in the late eighteenth century (Rich, 1989; Sherington et al., 1987).

A further characteristic of Gandhi's views on education is that his views were often different to contemporary twenty-first century standards in education. Perhaps Gandhi's views on sex education are the most obvious of these. Gandhi recognised that sex education was essential for both boys and girls but he proposed that the goal of such education was to empower men and women to resist the constant pressure to "subserve and cater for the sex urge" (*Harijan*, 22 November 1936; quoted in NCTE, 1998). His goal of sex education was to "have for its object the conquest and sublimation of the sex passion" as an important step on the path of self-control and realisation of the spiritual self. In addition, Gandhi insisted that the only person qualified to teach sex education is one who has achieved personal mastery over sexual desire or what he called "the science of sex control," (*Harijan*, 22 November 1936; quoted in NCTE, 1998). Such notions appear unrealistic in the contemporary liberal attitude towards sex education in modern societies, and certainly near-impossible in terms of teacher requirements. Nevertheless, his position rests on a traditional Indian spiritualist and yogic perspective on sex and the practice of *brahmacharya* was espoused by Gandhi as an ideal for himself and his followers. Thus he was consistent in this invocation of Indian spiritualist traditions.

This preliminary discussion has sought to identify some of the difficulties in the analysis of Gandhi's views on education. The following section will present and briefly discuss the key components of Gandhi's educational positions. The writings and recorded speeches of Gandhi I have sourced for this discussion are from two excellent primary sources of Gandhi's documents on education, the excellent *Gandhi on Education* (1998) published by the Indian National Council for Teacher Education (J.S. Rajput, chair) and the equally excellent compilation of Gandhi's writings in education edited by Bharatan Kumarappa, first published in 1953 and now available online (Kumarappa, online).

Critique of Existing Systems of Education

Gandhi's unhappy educational experiences under the educational systems he encountered in India and South Africa provided the foundations for his resolve to explore alternative educational approaches.

His personal experiences of schooling were fairly typical of Indian boys at the time and were shaped by the colonised condition of his country. Although his family was moderately middle-class his experiences of school were at local schools provided by the British-controlled government (Fischer, 1950; Feuerlicht, online). All teaching was in English language. Born in the small state of Porbandar in western India, he first attended school in 1875 at the age of six. Gandhi historian Roberta Feuerlicht (online) commented that Gandhi was a shy student who struggled with mathematics and progressed slowly at the school. When the family moved to the town of Rajkot in the following year, Gandhi's shyness was so intense he would run home from school to avoid ridicule from other boys. He was a high school student when he was married by family arrangement at the age of 13 years and Feuerlicht reports that his scholarship had improved by then, including winning minor academic prizes. He finished high school at the age of eighteen, in the same year his father died. Gandhi briefly attended a small Indian college but did not stay long. His major transition came when he was encouraged to go to England to study. He subsequently left his young wife in Rajkot and travelled to England to study law at University College, London in 1887. His motive in doing so was primarily to follow his father's career as a prime ministerial official working for local Indian princes operating under the control of the British.

In some ways Gandhi's experiences as a student in London pre-figured those of Indian students enrolling in Western universities today. He experienced language difficulties, cultural dislocation and poverty but also interesting engagements with English culture, although he never revelled in it. Yet it was in England where Gandhi was introduced to the seminal writings and principles that were to form the basis of his philosophy. Ironically it was an English colleague who asked Gandhi to study with him the *Bhagavad Gita*, the oldest written epic in the world. Gandhi had not previously read the ancient epic but discovered there the spiritual foundations of Indian traditions and values such as renunciation and noble actions. The Gita had such a strong personal appeal to him that he was to refer to it as his "dictionary of conduct". He also studied the New Testament especially the Sermon on the Mount with its proclamation of non-violence that was to profoundly influence him. Gandhi also discovered the writings of John Ruskin and Leo Tolstoy, whose views on pacifism, the spiritual life and collective communities were to influence him greatly. He returned home immediately after he graduated in 1891 but found employment prospects poor in India because he knew British law but nothing of Hindu or Moslem law that were practiced in local government in India (Feuerlicht, online). Desperate for work Gandhi even tried to become a high school English teacher but was considered unqualified. He was in a difficult situation, trying to support his young family of wife and two sons at the age of twenty-four when the opportunity was offered to him to act on behalf of an Indian law firm in a case in South Africa. He left for South Africa in 1893, initially for a one-year term of employment.

This summary of Gandhi's own educational experiences reveals the general sense of alienation and distorted learning he experienced under the colonial education system of late nineteenth century India. His experiences as a law student in England that resulted in an academic qualification of the colonial power that was effectively useless in his own country prefigured the broader phenomenon called "the diploma disease" (Dore, 1976) that characterised ex-colonial newly independent Third World nations following decolonisation in the 1960s and later. Gandhi regretted his schooling as a period of "half-baked knowledge and indulgence," yet it was his educational experiences that shaped his choice of career and decision to travel to South Africa.

When Gandhi arrived in South Africa he soon experienced discrimination first hand and became familiar with a wide range of legal discriminations, official oppression and general racial prejudice directed against the Indian community in both the British and Dutch (Boer) territories (Bhana and Vadeh, online). Living in the British-controlled territories of Durban and Natal, he decided to challenge discriminations directed at him and became the leader of a campaign to overcome the laws and practices that oppressed Indians.

The situation of colonial education in South Africa was, if possible, more oppressive than in India. One of the laws that controlled the lives of Indians was that Indian children were not permitted to attend government schools but had to attend Christian schools. This was an impossible situation for the Hindu population and led Gandhi to embark on educational activities of his own.

In essence, he regarded the whole process of education for Indians in South Africa and India as an "artificial education" taught in English as a vehicle for colonialism. He knew that "the colonial system will not respond to the needs of the people" and that "the prevailing system of education has made slaves of us; everything belongs to the government," he wrote (quoted in NCTE, 1998).

Gandhi began to formulate his own conception of education that would support the struggle for freedom. He proposed that "the purpose of all educational efforts is to gain freedom" and saw that the choice was between education for freedom or submission. In line with his deepest views he maintained that ultimately education is for the growth of spirit and self-realisation. "Our weapons are spiritual," he said and insisted that education should develop this capacity. It led him to his belief that emancipation would be gained through the miracle not of learning but of character; "not by meeting the government, sword against its shining sword but with peaceful spiritual effort against his aggressive Satanic way."

In his early years of building the resistance Gandhi recognised that students were involved in the forefront of political resistance and revolutions in other places, such as Korea against Japan's colonial regime. Students were at the forefront of the mass demonstrations that supported Korean leaders in the Declaration of Independence in 1919. Gandhi recognised the importance of young people to his mission and sought for ways to build their capacities for pursuing Satyagraha. Moreover, he ensured women would be important to his peaceful revolution and proposed that women's freedom and equality in education should be recognised, although not identical education as men's but appropriate to what he saw as the roles women fulfilled in his culture.

Thus, he began to formulate specific details for a model of schooling. He brought to this his view of the unity of human life. He wrote that "the whole gamut of man's activities ... constitutes an indivisible whole. You cannot divide life, social, economic, political and religious, into separate watertight compartments" (quoted in Kumar, 2010: 65). He therefore regarded the key purpose of education is to build character, and this should maintain a balance of physical, intellectual and religious learning. His view of religious learning was inclusive of different faiths, consistent with his view of a common God across all religions.

He placed priority importance on manual learning and industry over literary learning.

Recognising, from his own experience, the destructive effects of having to learn only in English, Gandhi insisted that education should be in vernacular languages. The issue of language was a particular passion for him, for he believed that "to give English to millions is to enslave them." He elaborated:

> It is worth noting that, by receiving English education, we have enslaved the nation. Hypocrisy, tyranny, etc., have increased; English-knowing Indians have not hesitated to cheat and strike terror into the people. Now, if we are doing anything for the people at all, we are paying only a portion of the debt due to them. It is not a painful thing that, if I want to go to a court of justice, I must employ the English language as a medium; that, when I become a Barrister, I may not speak my mother tongue, and that someone else should have to translate to me from my own language? Is not this absolutely absurd? Is it not a sign of slavery? Am I to blame the English for it or myself? It is we, the English-knowing men, that have enslaved India. The curse of the nation will rest not upon the English but upon us. (quoted in 'English Education', Kumarappa, 1953; online)

Gandhi made insightful analyses into the ideological functions of the colonisers' language long before the writings of Fanon, Said and other scholars who deconstructed the institutionalisation of oppression. He denounced the normalisation of English through its exclusive use in schools and, insisted on the use of vernacular languages in the school communities he formed.

Just as he developed positions on the purpose of schooling, Gandhi also formed views on the roles and identities of teachers. He was a strong advocate that teachers must demonstrate to students character-building by example and be models of the principles and values they were teaching. Gandhi maintained that a training of the spirit in education was only possible through "exercise of the spirit." Therefore, the lives and characters of teachers must be exemplary models. They should show self-discipline and be inspired by a "spirit of service" just as Gandhi was. In the school teachers should share daily life with students, undertaking manual work, cooking and other activities, and they should receive just a living wage for their efforts.

In these ways Gandhi challenged the system that maintained the legitimacy and power of the British government over the colonised Indians. His critiques against the system of control through education were accompanied by various efforts to break away from that system and provide different, liberating forms of education for his family and community. Gandhi's educational experiments were the core of his educational engagements, He was not an educational theorist specifically but a practical strategist needing to develop alternatives models that would work to support his political and social goals rather than deny them. Thus Gandhi's direct involvement in education is important in the context of his struggles for freedom for his people. They also represent interesting educational efforts that place Gandhi in the context of other educational innovators of his time, such as Maria Montessori, Rudolph Steiner and John Dewey. Gandhi wrote that he had "no difficulty in agreeing with the scientific views of Madame Montessori" (quoted in NCTE, 1998) but that they were unsuited to conditions in India. However, there are interesting parallels in his educational activities with all of these educational innovators who were his contemporaries.

Gandhi's Schooling Experiments

Throughout his life Gandhi was presented with circumstances in educational matters that challenged him to apply his views on education in a number of ways. He later commented: "I have tried myself or through others to impose my educational 'fads' on other children too and have seen the results thereof .... But the ultimate result of my experiments is in the womb of the future" (quoted in NCTE, 1998).

Home Education

Circumstances shaped his personal engagements with education. The first instance was when his sons, aged nine and five years old, joined him in South Africa at the end of 1896. There was little in the way of schooling available for the lads and a 10-year-old nephew who travelled with the family from India. Gandhi's decision to provide schooling for them at home under his tutelage was partly an act of resistance against the schools for European children where Indian children could not normally attend, but in which Gandhi was able to enrol his children through his social connections (Feuerlicht, online). The only other school options were the missionary schools for Indian children, that taught largely in English and imposed Christianity on the Hindu children. Again, he objected to this derogatory form of schooling.

Initially, Gandhi employed an English governess to work under his instruction but he found this was not suitable, so he took the task of educating his children onto himself, and his three sons never attended a public school. His eldest son later broke away from his father and attended a high school in India and, later university. Gandhi himself later commented that it may have been in their future career interests to give his children a school education much as his own had been, but that it was a matter of self-respect and principle that he should turn away from the model he knew was derogatory to Indians and explore leaning that would give them "liberty and self-respect" (NCTE, 1998).

The absence of opportunities for schooling his sons and the other Indian children in South Africa, initially, encouraged Gandhi to take up some of the ideas on learning that had been influenced by Ruskin, Tolstoy and other communitarian idealists he had read in England, as well as traditional Indian learning models of ashram education. He decided that the right education was one that involved constant contact with parents and that was grounded in practical experience. So he set about trying to structure a range of educational experiences for his children, while also pursuing his professional activities and his campaign for political rights for Indians.

He saw the type of practical experience that should be learned was that which was important for everyday life. One such activity was the making of bread, for which he installed a heavy wheat grinder in his home and had his sons learning through the process from fresh wheat to baked bread to learn "simplicity, health and economy". Nursing ill members of the household and dealing with the family's sanitation buckets were other tasks for which the children were given responsibility. Certainly there were some similarities in this aspect of Gandhi's notions to those of the American educator John Dewey, who also placed high priority on practical learning.

Gandhi also intended that he would provide some learning about history, literature, and world affairs and planned to discourse to his sons on such matters on their daily walks to and from his office in Johannesburg. However, the journey became dominated by adult colleagues and conversations about politics and campaign strategies, such that Gandhi had scant time for the home schooling he had conceived for his boys. He later wrote that had he been able to give some regular hours to their literary training it would have been adequate but what he ended up providing was a failure, if judged by normal educational outcomes. Yet he had no regrets in that he had acted faithfully to his purpose to build up their characters.

The Tolstoy Farm School

The difficulties Gandhi faced in providing education for his children were shared by other members of the Indian community in South Africa, some sixty-thousand people. Those working with Gandhi regularly in the struggle against racism for Indians were just a couple of hundred people and they shared his principles and struggled to survive against active oppression. Also, by 1909 Gandhi had spent time in jail for his leadership of the campaign. There he studied the writings of Tolstoy especially on non-violent resistance, religion and ideal communities. Gandhi had visited a Trappist monastery near Durban and seen the benefits of an intentional community following a deeply-held ideal. Moreover, the financial resources of the movement were desperate and it was difficult for movement members to earn a living for their families. Deportations, police surveillance and other incursions threatened the activists and their families. With the financial and moral support of his close associate Herman Kallenbach, who in 1910 purchased about one thousand acres of land for the venture in a rural district outside Johannesburg, Gandhi established The Tolstoy Farm. The farm worked to protect the families in the movement as well as build the spiritual and practical ideals of Gandhi's evolving philosophy. The farm was a total community of shared labour, product and values between its families. With an adult population of about 100, there were some 20–30 children at any time.

The resident population was not constant and Gandhi, who styled himself the 'father' of this community, was frequently absent in the peaceful struggle against the British government. This chapter is only concerned with the educational activities at the farm but the school was an integrative activity in the community. The skills necessary for maintaining the community were taught to children through taking on responsibilities and sharing them with teachers and other adults. Children participated in the welfare and conduct of the community.

Some of the activities that the children undertook were cooking, constructing the school buildings, shoe and clothes-making and gardening for the wholly vegetarian community. They were involved in running the school. Gandhi later wrote that "they took delight in the work."

Although predominantly a practical idealist, Gandhi was not anti-intellectual and had a great respect for knowledge and reading. He had learned greatly from his own reading and the farm was named after one of the writers and thinkers who had inspired and taught him. Thus, some portion of each day was put aside for geography, Indian history, arithmetic and writing, basic science and English. Reading was encouraged but discourse and shared experiences from teachers was considered more important than book learning.

The various activities at the school were focussed on the core goals of what Gandhi called "the culture of the heart" that underpinned the building of character. The spiritual and moral qualities that Gandhi aspired to in *Satyagraha* for himself and all his community were the cornerstone of the educational activities of the Tolstoy Farm. Religion was taught through the seminal teachings of the faiths represented at the school, including Hindu, Muslim and

Christian. In Gandhi's view, all religions were responding to the one god.

Education for Satyagraha in India

As he gained momentum in his political campaign in India, Gandhi initiated a boycott of government schools. This action was followed by the formation of the *Satyagraha* Ashram in Kochrab, Ahmedabad, in 1919. Forced to move from the initial location, they relocated to a remote site on the banks of the Sabarmati river. The Sabarmati Ashram became the base for Gandhi and his followers, many of whom had accompanied him from South Africa. The 36–acre site, not far from a British prison, was to become the home from which he launched all his major campaigns. During his time at Sabarmati, Gandhi was imprisoned for six years in the nearby prison and it was there he wrote his famous autobiography, *My Experiments with Truth* (Gandhi, 1954). According to one commentator, the main objectives of Sabarmati Ashram were: education, truth (non-violence and love), celibacy, control of the palate (no liquor or meat), no stealing, use of home-made articles, conquest of fear, and the eradication of untouchability (Manav Sadhna, online). This list includes most of the focussed activities Gandhi pursued and advocated through his life.

The ashram was a live-in school that drew on the traditions of Hindu educational training where students lived with a spiritual teacher and under his guidance pursued the path of spiritual self-realisation. Gandhi adapted the model to his educational concepts and formulated his views in a list of twenty-seven proposals. He noted that his own "perhaps peculiar" views on education "have not been accepted by my colleagues in full" (quoted from "Experiments with Education in India", NCTE, 1998). The focus, as in the Tolstoy Farm experiment, was to develop moral strength and purpose and there was a similar focus on manual work, character and spiritual growth through diverse religious paths. In keeping with the Indian traditions, Gandhi advocated that each child should learn their parents' hereditary craft and through their work in this activity earn money for the school community. He promoted the notion that schooling must be related to the actual conditions of people such as rural peasants so that they could "take charge of their lives" (NCTE, 1998). This was in marked contrast to the alienating textbook model of education imposed on Indians by the British government.

There were rules but no compulsion or punishment in the school and there was a focus on recognising and developing the special aptitudes of each child. Gandhi promoted the notion that learning should not be burdensome but like play.

In the ashram there was more structured learning than in previous activities, with book learning introduced in stages and more emphasis on academic learning in the later years of school. In line with the struggle for Indian independence, there was an emphasis on the history of ancient and modern India, as well as mathematics, science, botany and geography. English was taught and students were expected to know "good, at any rate, correct English" (Gandhi, NCTE, 1998) but native languages Gujarati and Hindi were the main languages of the school.

As in his previous educational activities, Gandhi insisted that teachers should be inspired by a spirit of service to the school community, set high levels of self-discipline, engage in manual work and model training of the spirit through their own "exercise of the spirit".

The ashram succeeded Gandhi. One modern commentator described how it happened in these words:

> On March 12, 1930, directed by his 'inner voice,' Gandhiji embarked on a 240 mile walk with 79 selected followers to break the Salt Tax, imposed by the British. This, known in history as The Dandi Salt March, united the country and set into motion the events that would later free a nation. Gandhi was no longer referred to as Mohandas, but as Mahatma, or 'Great Soul.' Gandhi has said he would never return to Sabarmati until India achieved Independence. He did, though on a sombre note, see India gain Independence on August 15, 1947; but was unable to return to Sabarmati, as he was assassinated by Vinayak N. Godse, a staunch Hindu fanatic, on January 30, 1948. India's Independence had divided its people into two nations; India and Pakistan. It was for this reason Gandhi sought no celebration on August 15th, and it was his avocation of Hindu-Muslim unity that finally ended his life. (Manav Sadhna, online)

Revival of Gandhian Views on Education

Recording his impressions of India in the early decades of post-colonialism, the well-known writer V.S. Naipaul, from Trinidad with an Indian family background, observed ways in which the significance of Gandhi had been appropriated away from the masses and become owned by the powerful. In 1967, Naipaul wrote, as example:

> There is a whole department of the Central Government at work on The Complete Works of Mahatma Gandhi; they have an entry, under that name, in the Delhi telephone directory. But The Hindu newspaper of Madras reported in March that 90 per cent of high-school students in one district knew nothing of Gandhi except that he was a good man who fought for independence. (Naipaul, 2002: 27)

In this essay Naipaul wrote of the widespread belief in the "magical intervention" of Gandhi and other persons raised to the level of sacredness in India and how this simplifying of the world acted to disempower people from engaging in rational analysis of their own conditions and from setting their own goals and actions. Such attachments, he suggests, capture individuals and whole sections of society in dependent and accommodating dispositions that prevent them from seizing the possibilities of a different future.

Moving forward forty years, India has changed in ways inconceivable to Naipaul, but where in contemporary India does Gandhi sit? There are certainly many views on this question.

A recent book on Gandhi titled *Mahatma Gandhi and his Struggle with India,* by Joseph Lelyveld argued that the driving force in Gandhi was his religious asceticism. This is a lifestyle choice quite out of favour in contemporary India. A review of this book in *The New York Times* commented:

> Few figures seem more remote from contemporary India than Mohandas Karamchand Gandhi, the Mahatma, or "Great Soul," who spearheaded the struggle for independence. Gandhi's beloved rural poor figure only intermittently in the consciousness of a country now focused on call centers, software entrepreneurs and movie stars. In the cities the Gandhian ideals of service, self-denial and universal uplift have been drowned out by the

> aggressive nationalism and shiny consumer culture of India's urban boom.
>
> ... In this context, Joseph Lelyveld's judicious and thoughtful new book, "Great Soul: Mahatma Gandhi and His Struggle With India," seems almost eccentric, devoted as it is to explaining the evolution of a social and moral philosophy that, 60 years after the end of the British Raj, has lost the attention of the nation it once enthralled. (Kunzru, 2011)

It may be the case that in the excitement of long-overdue economic development and a growing middle class in India that Gandhi's values of non-possession and frugal lifestyles have been pushed aside. However, there are some indications that his legacy is being revived in education. Whereas Gandhi's educational activities were always outside the government education of his time and remained so in the post-colonial decades, sixty years after his time there are signs that the national government began to recognise the value of incorporating some of Gandhi's educational principles into mainstream schooling. The excellent publication by the National Council for Teacher Education of Gandhi's written and recorded comments on education in 1998 was followed by a reformed National Curriculum Framework (2005) by the National Council for Educational Research and Training.

In the executive summary of this document, the Council repudiated the examination-dominated, competitive model of education for economic development that had been the paradigm of education in India during its development years. It commented, "The fact that learning has become a source of burden and stress on children and their parents is an evidence of a deep distortion in educational aims and quality".

The Council expressed the view that, in order to move towards a new and humane system of learning in India they had sought 'guidance' from the national constitution. Gandhi was the initial author of the first draft of that constitution, which went through various subsequent forms but retained some of the core values espoused by Gandhi. The Council formulating the national curriculum framework identified the identity of India as a "secular, egalitarian and pluralistic society founded on the values of social justice and equality" as stated in the Constitution.

Using this principle as a platform for the new curriculum, the Council advocated a range of new approaches for education in India. They included the following features that incorporate some of Gandhi's key educational proposals:

- Connecting knowledge to life outside the school.
- More emphasis on practical learning.
- Ensuring that learning shifts away from rote methods.
- Enriching the curriculum so it goes way beyond textbooks.
- Making examinations more flexible and integrating them with classroom life.
- Nurturing an overriding identity informed by caring concerns within the democratic polity of the country.

Peace Education in the National Curriculum Framework

Perhaps of most interest to readers of this chapter is the inclusion of Peace Education in the National Curriculum Framework as part of the social science curriculum, but linked into other areas of study. The National Council for Educational Research and Training declared that: "The case for peace education within the framework of the National Curriculum is compellingly clear in the light of escalating trends of, and taste for, violence globally, nationally and locally" (NCERT, 2005, online).

The Council recognised the need for peace education both in teacher training courses and for children in schools. There were several areas where the model of peace education proposed in the National Curriculum Framework sits comfortably with Gandhi's views for *Satyagraha* education:

- The central focus is on moral development. While the new curriculum framework does not explicitly advocate non-violence, it aims for peace education that inculcates "the values, attitudes and skills required for living in harmony with oneself and others including nature." This goal is certainly in the direction of Gandhi's educational views and the recognition of nature is in keeping with his emphasis on non-harm to animals and protection of nature in his schools.
- The new curriculum takes a holistic approach to health education, with recommendations for the practice of traditional Indian yoga in schools and an affirmation of the integral aspects of physical, social, mental and emotional health.

- The Council states in the framework that the new orientation is driven by a "conviction that our strength lies in the presently-deprived three-fourths of our people" (NCERT, 2005). This statement is aligned to Gandhi's position that he was working for the poor and disenfranchised people of India. The statement is emphasised throughout the National Curriculum Framework with comments that assert that the new approach is to strengthen democracy and justice in India, which was certainly a goal of Gandhi's.

It seems that the new curriculum framework for Indian education has done something towards invoking the educational goals and beliefs of Gandhi. The document is an attenuated version of Gandhi's views and does not advocate the powerful activist intentions of Satyagraha education and the commitment students were required to make to pursuing its methods and goals. However there are certainly a number of areas where mainstream education in India is moving to adapt some of Gandhi's ideals and methods. Of particular satisfaction to him would be the new emphasis on the use of vernacular languages in the classroom, an emphasis on manual and practical learning to accompany "book learning" and, of course, the key focus on all of this as a "national values framework."

Perhaps the new approach to Gandhi's educational views in India is an effort to balance the runaway commercialism that has gripped India as it progresses in the global economy. The trend in education may be one aspect of a broader social trend that has emerged as a positive reaction to a new social imbalance that is emerging in India as the gap between 'haves' and 'have nots' grows wider and many educated youth are excluded from benefits of the economic boom. There are indications of movements for human rights, political and environmental issues emerging to challenge the rampant commercialism. One commentator reported that:

> Thousands of young Indians are joining Gandhian youth organisations, or flocking to summer camps at Gandhian ashrams. Teenagers are volunteering to work in slums and poor villages. Not just Gandhi's image, but his principles and the way of life he taught are catching on in India again. (*Creative Minds*, 8 February 2011)

Another commentator in this journal noted that "suddenly Gandhi is an alternative voice in an India that has become obsessed with material wealth and advancement." This writer stated that there are over one hundred and fifty youth organisations dedicated to carrying on Gandhi's work and these members refer to themselves as "the new Gandhians". They advocate austerity and non-violence in a violent and materialistic world.

Gandhi's Educational Views and Contemporary Peace Education

The above developments are heartening for those many teachers and researchers who are interested in peace education in India. They can be seen as positive results of the many years of campaigning for peace education by colleagues in India who dedicate their work to promoting both peace education in its wide understanding and also the values of Gandhi.

The final part of this essay will discuss some implications of Gandhi's views on education for international peace education researchers and teachers. My proposal here is that an assessment of Gandhi's views provides an opportunity to refresh and strengthen peace education. In particular, it provides an impetus for a more activist approach to peace education that works towards social change and the transition of international culture towards a world culture of peace.

Some key areas of Gandhi's approach to education that retain value for contemporary peace education are:

(i) Moral consciousness is the directing force of social organisation and change: The above description of Gandhi and education emphasises that this pure value based on Gandhi's understanding of the interconnectedness of human lives is the central concept from which peace education develops as a theory and practice. It is the rationale for the strategic living of *ahimsa* or the non-violent way. It is manifest in social action against injustice but also in everyday life that includes work, learning, eating, and social relationships. It is the common basis of religious values and the education that derives from them. This notion is the foundation of Gandhi's principled non-violence as compared to strategic non-violence, considered previously.

Gandhi, moreover, emphasised that this moral consciousness is more than the practising of individual values. It is directed towards political action and social change against situations of oppression, whether local or more broadly located. Gandhi saw this as the key purpose of education and this view challenges modern peace educators to firstly aspire towards the ideals themselves, in their own practice, and to be activist in their work as educators.

(ii) The learning of non-violent ways is difficult: Gandhi's educational model reflected his own ascetic practices. In his schools in South Africa and India, Gandhi set up learning experiences from which teachers and students learned self-discipline, community independence, and moral strength through practice. Sparse conditions, physical labour and working for the community were all aspects of Gandhi's approach. This rigorous training of the spirit was for strengthening his followers for social and political action, which was the purpose of the school-based moral training.

Contemporary peace education – including the Indian model described above – places importance on values education. Peace education in conflict and post-conflict situations always emphasises the importance of values education. In schools around the world, values education is used as a strategy to help resolve conflicts in schools, whether it is in intercultural relations or in bullying behaviour.

Gandhi offers these prospects to modern schools involved in values peace education. Firstly, the total environment and practices of the school, including teachers' commitment and characters, are vital in this form of education. It is a whole-school approach and effort that provide the proper learning environment for peace education. Children are very quick to identify hypocrisy in the system, its teachers and educational practices.

Secondly, book and simulated learning are not sufficient to learn *ahimsa*. Gandhi, as discussed above, played down the importance of book learning in favour of experiential learning. Students in his schools learned through their hands, through the real products of their efforts such as gardens, buildings and practical crafts. A computer-mediated learning model is sweeping schools today and the value of computer skills for students is a high priority for education in the digital age. One of the new challenges for peace educators is to engage with this process and find ways to link the new skills to core values of peaceful thinking and action such as non-violence. Gandhi is also challenging schools to move outside sedentary learning models towards physically engaging learning activities.

(iii) Unity of religious belief and tolerance (incl. of atheism): As the basis of religions is regarded as belief in the single deity, Gandhi in his schools and through his life advocated tolerance between different religious groups, cultures and languages. His inter-faith multiculturalism has gained importance in the context of current schisms between Muslims and other faiths. The harmony between Hindu and Muslim Indians was the final struggle of Gandhi's life, which cost him his life. It is appropriate for peace educators to bring Gandhi's principles into current efforts to promote inter-faith understanding and tolerance as ways of addressing the important conflicts between religions taking place in the world today. As over a decade of tragedies around the world show so clearly, the need to resolve the religious basis of conflicts is one of the most important challenges facing the world community.

(iv) Education must attend to the removal of poverty: Gandhi's statement that poverty is a crime is a proposition that challenged economic inequalities of his time and applies these days to the structure of global capitalism which continues to pursue comparative advantage and 'trickle-down' theories of raising standards of living. In India, Gandhi challenged the embedded caste structures that appropriated wealth at the top end and oppressed to abject status those who were born as members of the lowest caste. The great economic and social inequalities exploited in the contemporary global economy present a singular challenge for peace educators to place as a high priority and explore ways to directly contribute to the removal of poverty locally and internationally. This includes recognition of the political, social and educational needs of other groups of subordinated cultures and communities, such as indigenous people. Gandhi's heart was directed towards the aspirations of the disenfranchised peasants in his nation and he was driven by an outlook of compassion and identity as he strove to make his life no more comfortable or privileged than theirs. Of course he was a famous figure but his actions towards his goal

reflected his belief in the moral force of the oppressed. His extended hunger strikes turned the very condition experienced by the poorest people in India into a powerful weapon against oppression.

Moreover, Gandhi practised a strict personal non-materialism and maintained this practice in his schools and for teachers. His efforts remain models for peace educators to embrace in their personal and teaching activities.

In Gandhi's view education is a moral action that follows from the recognition of the interconnectedness of human life and education therefore should be dedicated to the equal welfare of all. In the current context, those involved in peace education have a responsibility to work for the eradication of poverty through their educational efforts. This is a challenging task not just because of its enormity but also because of institutional obstacles. In universities, for instance, little support is provided for research that explores alternative ways of eradicating poverty.

(v) Equality of all should be practised in Education: From a situation in colonial India, where virtually little formal education was available for girls and women were excluded from participation in public life, Gandhi advocated the importance of equal education for girls. While his views were for an education appropriate to the social norm of women's domestically-oriented roles, he was a strong advocate for the rights of women in education.

Similarly, Gandhi's emphasis that education should be available for all social castes and cultural groups, taught in the vernacular, foreshadowed the views of later anti-colonial theorists and the emergent campaigns for educational rights for indigenous people and other subordinated communities.

While the discussion here has focussed on Gandhi's explicit educational views and activities there are many aspects of his broader social perspective that have meaning for twenty-first century peace education. For instance, his critical analysis as to how the British colonial government maintained a range of military, legal, linguistic and institutional structures to facilitate their political dominance and economic exploitation of Indians offers an example of authoritarian models that replicate similar models of structural violence. In another area Gandhi was very suspicious of technological forces, such as mass production which he regarded as destructive to communitarian interests. Gandhi's examples of self-sufficiency, such as spinning the cloth for his clothes and grinding flour for bread, provide models for educational experiences that seek to liberate children and adults from technological obsession and dependence. In another aspect, harmonious living and the maintenance of the natural environment were practised in Gandhi's schools and this was embraced as a moral and practical duty for all members of the community.

Challenges of Gandhi's Educational Views to Peace Educators

In the previous section of this chapter I have attempted to identify a number of ways that Gandhi's views on education in his struggle for India's freedom can be relevant to contemporary peace education. This chapter will conclude with some considerations of ways that Gandhi's views on education continue to challenge peace educators and offer radical approaches for us.

There is a strong focus on personal realisation in Gandhi's educational positions and this sets standards to which contemporary peace educators can aspire. To what extent are (or should be) peace educators change agents engaged in the spiritual/moral quest of *Satyagraha*? In the contemporary world, with its processes of formal accreditation of teachers, can peace educators be seekers of self-realisation, through discipline, dedication to their work, participants in manual labour and focussed on building their own characters through "discipline of the spirit" in order to lead young people down that ideal path of truth? None of this is required to become a teacher in modern school systems.

Similarly, Gandhi's exhortations to teachers raise concerns over the extent to which contemporary peace educators should be accommodating and adjusting their peace education ideals and programmes in order to find a legitimate place in the university and school curriculum and research agenda. Gandhi was always wary of compromise and his educational activities demonstrate his refusal to surrender his principles when under pressure. This was an essential feature of his principled non-violence and it was a central aspect of *Satyagraha* both as practice and goal. It invites peace educators of today to remain committed to principled non-violence as the key ingredient of any peace education program. Such a program will embrace all aspects of schooling. From such a perspective, peace educators will remain as leaders in identifying conflicts and issues in society that are oppressive of human rights and dignity and lead the way through non-violent actions in addressing these issues.

Finally, and most importantly, Gandhi's education was an education for social and political action founded on principled non-violence. Teachers were activists rather than employees in a school. Teachers in Gandhi's schools practised self-discipline, asceticism and other activities for a social purpose, which was the liberation of Indians and India. These views on the role of education and its key actors challenge modern peace educators to be assertive leaders in non-violent struggles against contemporary oppression, obstacles to freedom and the creation of a new world based on a culture of peace. Such obstacles may be wars, political oppression and violent conflicts. They may also be ongoing social problems such as environmental degradation, human health challenges (such as malnutrition and obesity), gender discrimination, and economic injustice. Peace educators, strengthened by their "training of the spirit" and dedicated to service of all, will lead students by example in the practice of *Satyagraha* education. This is the profound legacy of Gandhi's educational views and experiments

Conclusion

In conclusion, the recognition of Gandhi's contribution to peace education is a step towards affirming Gandhi's pre-eminent role in social change towards a better world for all. This recognition asserts the true meaning of Gandhi's work and teachings for humanity across the global society and practical means through education where Gandhi's legacy can be put to work. Such an acceptance of Gandhi's views by those who value the substance of his efforts challenges more recent trends towards a commercialism of Gandhi's name and a crude identification of Gandhi with the emerging 'brand India' that is a growing presence in the global economy.

There certainly have been signs of a contemporary re-imagining of Gandhi as an icon of globalising India. The economic value placed on Gandhi can be measured at one level by the price fetched for a small number of personal belongings of Gandhi – his food-bowl, glasses, sandals and watch – that were auctioned in New York city in March, 2009. Originally expected to fetch $30,000, the effects realised the price of $1.8 million, purchased by a wealthy Indian businessman who thereby established their market value that will continue to be traded.

Around the world there has been a recent trend of erecting Gandhi statues in homage to his status and meaning as an Indian man of peace. The Indian government has been active in funding and promoting these statues in places such as New York, Milwaukee, Belgrade, Switzerland and London. In 2010, a cast-iron bust of Gandhi was constructed at the University of New South Wales, Australia, in the wake of racist attacks on Indian students. Nominated as a symbol of multiculturalism, the statue was more a means to shore up the important Indian student market that was threatened by the attacks. Such statues are meant to serve a world-wide strategy for recognition of 'brand India' and its various products, including the Mahatma.

Gandhi has been recognised as a commercial drawcard in the entertainment industries. The story of Gandhi provided a basic platform for the opera *Satyagraha* by experimental musician Phillip Glass, performed at the New York Metropolitan Opera in 2008. The 1982 Hollywood biographical movie *Gandhi*, directed by Richard Attenborough, was a commercial success while recent Indian movies also characterised Gandhi. In one of these, a comedy titled *Lage Raho Munna Bhai* (2006), Gandhi appears as a light-hearted character promoting 'Gandhigiri', the application of *Satyagraha* to everyday life problems experienced by the Bollywood stars who appear in the main roles. The movie won awards and was commercially successful.

The commercialisation of Gandhi's image and promotion of Gandhi as an avuncular and eccentric figure that stands for quaint and old-world values distorts and trivialises the powerful and visionary messages of Gandhi's life and legacy. Placing Gandhi's principles and methods at the centre of peace education will go some way towards re-claiming Gandhi's rightful place at the forefront of the movement towards a world culture of peace.

References

Bhana, S. and G.H. Vadeh, *The Making of a Social Reformer: Gandhi in South Africa 1893–1914*. Available online at www.mkgandhi-sarvodaya.org/social_reform. Accessed April 13, 2012, n.d.

Danesh, H.B., "Towards an Integrative Theory of Peace Education", *Journal of Peace Education*, Vol. 3, 55–78, 2002.

Dore, G., *The Diploma Disease*, London: Allen & Unwin, 1976.

Feuerlicht, Roberta Strauss (eds.) *Mohandas K. Gandhi 1869–1948: A Concise Biography*. Available online at: www.progress.org/gandhi. Accessed April 4, 2012.

Fischer, L., *The Life of Mahatma Gandhi*, New York: Harper & Bros, 1950.

Gandhi, M.K., *Sathiya Sodhani: The Story of My Experiments with Truth*, trans. from Gujarati by Mahadev Desai. Ahmedabad: Navajivan Publishing House, 1927. Available online at: www.mkgandhi-sarvodaya.org/autobio/autiobio.htm Accessed April 10, 2012.

Harris, I. and M. Morrison, *Peace Education* (2nd edn), Jefferson, NC: Mcfarland & Co., 2003.

Harris, I., "Peace Education Theory", *Journal of Peace Education* Vol. 1, No. 1, 5–20, 2004.

Harris, S. and N. Lewer, "Peace Education in Conflict Zones: Experience from Northern Sri Lanka", *Journal of Peace Education*, Vol. 5, No. 2, 127–40, 2008.

Hughes, J. and C. Donnelly, "Contact as a Policy Mechanism for Promoting Better Relations in Integrated Schools in Northern Ireland and Bilingual/bi-national Schools in Israel", *Journal of Peace Education*, Vol. 3, No. 1, 79–97, 2006.

Indian National Council for Educational Research and Training (2005) National Curriculum Framework. Available online at: www/ncert.nic/rightside/links/pdf/framework/nf2005.pdf

Indian National Council for Teacher Education (NCTE) (1998) *Gandhi on Education* (Charman: J.S. Rajput). New Delhi: NCTE. Available online at: www.ncte-india.org/pub/gandhi/gandhi_o.htm. Accessed March 18, 2012.

Johnson, D.W. and R.T. Johnson, "Peace Education for Consensual Peace: The Essential Role of Conflict Resolution", *Journal of Peace Education*, Vol. 3, No. 2, 147–74, 2006.

King, Martin Luther, *Stride Toward Freedom: The Montgomery Story*, New York: Harper & Bros, 1958.

Kumar, R., *Gandhian Thought: New World, New Dimensions*, New Delhi: Kalpaz Publications, 2009.

——. *India and Mahatma Gandhi*, New Delhi: Kalpaz Publications, 2010.

Kumarappa, Barappan (ed.) *Towards New Education* by M.K. Gandhi, Ahmedabad: Navajivan Publishing House, 1953. Available online at: www.mkgandhi.org/towrds_edu/towrds_edu.htm. Accessed April 13, 2012.

Kunzru, H., "Review of Joseph Lelyveld's *Mahatma Gandhi and his Struggle with India", The New York Times*, March 29, 2011.

Manav Sadhna (ed.) *The Sabarmati Ashram*. Available online at: www.indcast.com/ms/ASHRAM%20History.htm. Accessed April 13, 2012.

Nagler, M.N., "What is Peace Culture?", in Ho-Won Jeong (ed.), *The New Agenda for Peace Research*, Aldershot, UK: Ashgate, 233–60, 1999.

Naipaul, V.S., "A Second Visit (orig. 1967), in Pankaj Mishra (ed.), *The Writer and the World*, London: Picador, 15–34, 2002.

Navarro-Castro, L. and J. Nario-Galace, *Peace Education: A Pathway to a Culture of Peace,* Quezon City, Philippines: Center for Peace Education, Miriam College, 2008.

Ramachandran, G. and T.K. Mahadevan (Eds.) *Gandhi: His Relevance for Our Times*, New Delhi, Gandhi Peace Foundation, 2005. Available online at: www.mkgandhi_sarvodaya.org/_relevance/g_relevance.htm

Reardon, B. (ed.) *Comprehensive Peace Education*, New York: Teachers College Press, 1986.

Rich, P.J., *Elixir of Empire: The English Public Schools, Ritualism, Freemasonry and Imperialism*, London: Regency Press, 1989.

Salomon, G. and B. Nevo (eds.) *Peace Education, the Concepts, Principles and Practices around the World*, Mahwah, NJ: Lawrence Erlbaum Associates Publishers, 2002.

Schulz, M. "Reconciliation Through Education: Experiences from the Israeli-Palestinian Conflict", *Journal of Peace Education*, Vol. 5, No. 1, 17–32, 2008.

Sherington, G. et al., *Learning to Lead: A History of Girls' and Boys' Corporate Schools in Australia*, Sydney: Allen & Unwin, 1987.

Synott, J., "Peace Education as an Educational Paradigm: Review of a Changing Field Using an Old Measure", *Journal of Peace Education*, Vol. 2, No. 1, 3–16, 2005.

——. *Quality Education: Global Perspectives for Australian Schools*, Terrigal: David Barlow Press, 2009.

Wenden, A. (ed.) *Educating for a Culture of Social and Ecological Peace*, Albany: State University of New York Press, 2004.

8

Dealing with Disasters

Natural and Man-made

RAVI P. BHATIA

We are all familiar with both natural disasters and those caused by the intervention and exploitation of the environment by mankind. Here we do not speak of the disasters caused by wars and terrorism where thousands of people are killed or driven away from their homes.

There are several types of natural disasters like tornadoes, hurricanes, volcanic eruptions, earthquakes and lightning, etc., that adversely affect both humans and animals and often cause large-scale damage and deaths. Another relatively new form of natural disaster – tsunami, which causes devastation on a vast scale – has arisen. The latest occurrence of a tsunami was on 11 March 2011 in the north-eastern part of Japan that caused immeasurable havoc in conjunction with a severe earthquake. It also led to lethal radiation being released in the environment due to the breakdown and overheating of the Fukushima nuclear plant.

Earlier, in December 2004, a severe tsunami struck Sri Lanka, Thailand, Indonesia and the southern-eastern parts of India. It is estimated that the tsunami killed more than 5,000 people in Thailand itself and overall resulted in more than two hundred thousand deaths in addition to causing large-scale destruction in these regions. India marked the seventh anniversary of the tsunami by holding peace rallies and offering floral tributes to the victims across the coastal belt where about 12,000 people perished.

On 19th September 2011, a terrible earthquake measuring 6.8 on the Richter scale occurred in the state of Sikkim (north-east part of India) resulting in terrible destruction and deaths in this and a few nearby states and the neighbouring countries Nepal and Bhutan. An officer of Sikkim University, Gangtok, has written a heart-rending account of the quake that was published in *The Hindu* the next day. I reproduce a few lines of this: "It was 6.10 in the evening when I suddenly felt the tremor. Living here we are used to frequent tremors ... but this wasn't the usual earthquake. It felt like a destructive child was frantically shaking her doll's house and we were like helpless dolls inside getting pushed in all directions. We could hear the sound of things hitting the floor. The power was gone. It was pitch dark ..."

At least 100 deaths had been reported in Sikkim itself with several more in the adjoining regions and in Nepal and Bhutan.

Another earthquake measuring 5.9 on the Richter scale rocked the same region as well as Myanmar and Bangladesh on 21 November 2011. The epicentre was located in Myanmar. This region is considered by seismologists to be the sixth most earthquake-prone belt in the world. The region experienced one of the worst earthquakes, measuring 6.9, in 1897 killing more than 1,500 people.

In June of last year a volcano called Dubbi volcano located in Eritrea near Ethiopia erupted throwing ash plumes as high as 13 km into the air. People were asked to move away but for some there was no place where they could move to. This is how tragedy and destruction takes place.

A terrible hurricane named Irene caused extensive damage on the east coast of USA including New York City, in August last year. Justin Gills, in a newspaper article in *New York Times* as reprinted in *The Indian Express* dated August 25, 2011, asked the following important question:

> "Are hurricanes getting worse because of human induced climate change? One group of scientists believe that yes this is happening. The number of such hurricanes and their intensity is increasing. But Thomas Knutson in US government's Geophysical Lab in

Princeton disagrees. He says that on a short-term trend this does seem to happen but over a longer period this trend does not seem to be true ..."

However, there are other scientists who believe that natural disasters result to an extent from excessive exploitation of natural and physical resources.

Man-made Climatic Changes

In addition to these natural disasters, we are all familiar with the environmental degradation that is caused by mankind's exploitation of the earth's natural resources. Examples of these are flooding or landslides that may have natural causes but also occur due to felling of trees and other forms of damage to our environment. As a result of modern-day lifestyles of people, especially in the rich, developed countries, large-scale exploitation of natural and physical resources has become a serious concern today both for the environment as well for all forms of life – human, animal or plant.

The development paradigm that is being followed in most countries, especially the developing ones, is leading to deforestation, denuding the hills and mountains, destroying coastlines due to mining or other projects. Partly as a result of these activities, we see global warming, melting of glaciers, rising of ocean levels, unpredictable weather conditions that cause flooding, excessive or deficient rainfall or landslides.

Recently, a four nation (India, Nepal, Bhutan and Bangladesh) ministerial meeting was held in November 2011 for the protection of the Himalayas which is known for its rich biodiversity. Due to man-made climatic changes, this region is facing forest loss, soil erosion, uneven climate conditions that pose a serious threat to its ecosystem and the people living in these areas. In USA the Grand Canyon, one of America's greatest treasures, is threatened by a huge wave of uranium mining. The famous Taj Mahal in Agra is also adversely affected by the air and water pollution. Similarly, many other areas are in danger. A new study has revealed that as oceans become polluted, there is a threat that coral reefs around the world may become extinct by the end of this century.

John Vidal, in a report published in *The Guardian* and reported in *The Hindu* on 15 June 2011, has pointed out at the extremely abnormal weather conditions in UK, France, Germany, Australia, China and USA last year. He writes about the flooding in Queensland, the once-in-a-100-years drought in southern and central parts of China, and abnormally cold weather in June in UK, etc. Mexico recorded unusually hot temperature of 48.8°C in April leading to drought and wild fires. In October/November of 2011, Thailand including its capital Bangkok witnessed one of the worst flooding in over half a century affecting over 5 million people and causing deaths and destruction on a large scale.

These are all clear signs of natural climatic disasters striking the earth. Are they due to human intervention? No one can say for sure but many people believe that humans are at least partly responsible for these events.

It is well known that the river Ganga (Ganges) that flows eastwards in the northern parts of India is a lifeline for tens of millions of people and is a symbol of India's ancient civilisation, has become extremely polluted. Many people have recently joined the protests by some sections of civil society and different non-governmental organisations (NGOs) near the Prime Minister's official residence demanding that the Prime Minister take some concrete action against pollution of the Ganga. Although efforts by the Indian state and NGOs to clean the river are desirable and necessary, the important question is what needs to be done to arrest the environmental pollution in the first place? What steps are required to avoid the factors causing pollution and averting the environmental crisis?

Several international organisations, including the International Panel for Climate Change (IPCC), are working in the direction of sustaining the environment and suggesting what countries and organisations need to do towards this objective. IPCC had been awarded the Nobel Peace Prize in 2007 jointly with Albert Arnold Gore Jr "for their efforts to build up and disseminate greater knowledge about man-made climate change, and to lay the foundations for the measures that are needed to counteract such change".

Another potential danger that the world is facing is the rising water levels in seas and oceans. Scientific studies suggest that there has been a rise of water levels by about 2 mm per year from 1950 to

2009 due to two main factors: thermal expansion of water as the temperature of water rises and the melting of glaciers and ice sheets due to global warming. The IPCC had projected that the sea levels would rise by about 18 to 50 cm during the twenty-first century. There are of course several uncertainties in this projection.

Happily, there is a contrary view among some scientists. In a conference held in Mumbai recently, *The Hindu* (October 15, 2011) has reported that such alarmist views of rise of water levels are not substantiated on empirical evidence. They report that the observed rise could be due to seasonal variations. There is a view that these alarmist warnings are projected to make money for the insurance companies. In the words of a critic,

> "It is important to realize that climate scare is a massive money maker for the insurance industry. If people believe that climate change and more extreme weather is on the way, then more people will buy property insurance."

Efforts at Restoration of the Environment

There are also some journals that are studying these problems and spreading awareness amongst people and countries to mitigate this problem. In India, there is a well-known journal called *Down to Earth* (DTE) that not only discusses these issues in a simple, readable manner but also highlights efforts by different organisations and individuals to preserve and protect the environment. In its issue of March 1–15, 2010, it reports that villagers of the state of Uttarakhand (in northern India) have peacefully protested against the plans of the National Thermal Power Corporation (NTPC) to build a hydropower electricity generation project in the nearby Gori river. Their protest was directed against the project since it would destroy large areas of forest lands in this region.

Efforts of Sunderlal Bahuguna, an eighty-year-old Gandhian and eco-activist, to protect the forests and trees found in the northern hills of India by his *Chipko* movement (embracing the trees against their being axed), are well known. He and his wife Vimla organised several important *Chipko Andolans* (protests) from 1977 to 1980 in the Kumaon hills of northern India. Lesser known are the efforts of another environmentalist Chandi Prasad Bhatt and his organisation that has played a crucial role in the origins of the *Chipko* movement in 1973. R.C. Guha (2007), the well-known Indian author, writes that:

> "The technique *(Chipko)* itself was suggested by Bhatt for the villagers of Mandal. Since coordinating those early protests against commercial forestry, the Dashauli Gram Swarajya Mandal (DGSM) has focused increasingly on environment restoration. Here it has taken the initiative in organizing women for afforestation work in villages of the Alaknanda valley where its tree planting and protection programmes have been a good deal successful ...".

Guha showers praise in the following words: "These two *Chipko* leaders Bahuguna and Bhatt are among the greatest living Indians. The example of Gandhi animates the lives of both men ..."

Other efforts, especially in the field of education, are also required to highlight and prevent degradation and destruction of the environment. Some efforts have already been made to introduce these topics in our curricula, both at the school and college levels. An American scholar Leslie Sponsel referred in 2009 to the topic called "Quality of Life: Environment, Water, Food, and Health", that has been introduced in Anthropology in some academic institutions. This topic is also of relevance to the issue of environmental degradation. In India, the Supreme Court ruled in 1987 that it was essential for students of Indian schools and colleges to study environmental science as one of the subjects. It is desirable that our education system is able to display the intimate relationship between life on earth and the environment and the importance of sustaining both.

Professor Ranjana Mukhopadhyaya, who teaches Japanese Studies in Delhi University, had recently given a talk on "disaster management in Japan". She pointed out that Japan is particularly prone to earthquakes and the recent earthquake of March of last year was particularly severe resulting in large-scale death and destruction. She informed that among the measures for dealing with these natural disasters, school and college students are given education on what to do when disaster strikes in order to reduce their impact on life and property. The Delhi government carried out in February 2012 a drill to make people aware of different types of disasters that could strike the city and what needed to be done to avoid or limit their damage.

In order to exploit the environment minimally, a deeper appreciation of limiting one's wants and leading simpler lives is also required. This was clearly propagated by Gandhi by his approach to simple and frugal living and avoiding excessive exploitation of the earth's resources. Gandhi felt that this was necessary not only for the protection of the environment but also so that the class differences and mutual suspicion that existed and exist today between the rich who consume more than required and the vast numbers of poor and deprived who are unable to feed themselves and their children adequately, can be minimised. To stress this point, Gandhi had stated in simple language: "There is enough for people's needs but not enough for people's greed". Gandhi himself embodied this principle by wearing only a minimum of clothes to empathise with the India's poor and also by not wasting any food or material items of daily use. Gandhi also inspired many people including Bhatt and Sunderlal Bahuguna as indicated above.

Another person whom he inspired was Madeleine Slade (daughter of an English Admiral), who is better known by the Indian name of Mira Behn after she joined Gandhi's Sabarmati *ashram* in 1925. She wrote in 1949, a year after Gandhi's assassination, about the lifestyles of the affluent that lead to degradation of the environment: "The tragedy today is that educated and moneyed classes are altogether out of touch with the vital fundamentals of existence of our Mother Earth, and the animal and vegetable population which it sustains. The world of Nature's planning is ruthlessly plundered, despoiled and disorganised by man whenever he gets the chance ..."

Gandhi was also critical of modern civilisation with its insatiated craving for material wants. He wrote (*Young India,* 2 June 1927): "The distinguishing characteristic of modern civilisation is an indefinite multiplicity of wants whereas earlier civilisations were forced to have an imperative restriction upon and a strict regulation of these wants ..."

Gandhi was also critical of Nehru's plans for large-scale industrialisation of India for developing the country. He expressed himself in the following words (*Young India*, 20 December 1928):

> "God forbid that India should take to industrialization after the manner of the West. The economic imperialism of a single tiny island kingdom is today keeping the world in chains. If an entire nation of 300 million took to similar economic exploitation, it would strip the world like locusts".

Echoing Gandhi's concerns, R.C. Guha (2007: 115) has stated:

> Without the access to resources and markets enjoyed by those two nations (England and USA), India has had to perforce to rely on exploitation of its own people and the environment. The natural resources of countryside have been channelized to meet the needs of the urban industrial sector while the diversion of forests, water, etc., to the elite having accelerated processes of environmental degradation even as it has deprived rural and tribal communities of their traditional rights of access and use ..."

Mike George, a British scholar and spiritual teacher, has echoed Gandhi's principle by writing in one of his weekly columns that the "true causes of our environmental issues such as resource depletion, climate chaos, biosystem breakdown and atmospheric pollution are missed because there is little spiritual dialogue of any depth or significance at such events". In his words, "All well-meaning citizens must pay heed to these issues of over-exploitation of resources resulting in environmental degradation and climatic changes".

We are faced with a dilemma. We need development and infrastructure – roads, factories, schools and hospitals – for meeting the legitimate requirements and aspirations of people: creating jobs, providing education, homes and healthcare. All these entail increasing energy requirements necessitating building of hydro, thermal and nuclear energy plants with resultant adverse impact on the environment and exploitation of earth's natural resources.

The dilemma is – should we protect the environment at the cost of human needs or should we have rapid development by construction of new infrastructure and dislocation of people? The answer is obvious: we need to do both but we must follow a balanced approach and adopt a suitable developmental paradigm.

It is relevant here to look back in history to the UN initiative to set up the World Commission on Environment and Development (WCED) in December 1983 in order to address the problems of deterioration of the environment and natural resources. This commission is generally referred to as the Brundtland Commission after its Chairperson Gro Harlem Brundtland, who was the former Prime Minister of Norway.

One of the major outcomes of the report of the Brundtland Commission (1987) was how sustainable development was to be viewed. It suggested that there is unity of environment and development and stated that we must work towards a "development that meets the needs of the present without compromising the ability of future generations to meet their own needs".

The complete report was published by Oxford University Press in 1987 under the title *Our Common Future*.

More recently, on 9 August 2010, the UN Secretary-General launched the High-level Panel on Global Sustainability (GSP) to formulate a new blueprint for a sustainable future on a planet under increasing stress resulting from human activities. The panel presented on 30th January 2012 in Addis Ababa (www.un.org/en/gsp (2012)*)* its report called *Resilient People, Resilient Planet: A Future Worth Choosing*. One of the important recommendations is:

> "Continuation of current path of development would put people and planet alike at greatly heightened risk ... we must follow a more sustainable path of development that would enhance human well-being, globalised justice, gender equity and preserve earth's life support systems for future generations".

It is encouraging to see that the problems of sustainable development that do not risk the environment are receiving worldwide attention and possible solutions are being recommended. However, the Gandhian approach of simple living and limiting one's wants is still relevant and important.

Nuclear Disasters

In addition to other natural disasters, we also have the frightful possibility of occurrence of nuclear disasters. Usually it is the leakage of nuclear radiation that affects nearby water bodies and all forms of life – plant, animal and human. Before the last year's Fukushima nuclear accident, we have had two earlier known accidents in nuclear plants.

On March 28, 1979, an accident occurred in the Three Mile Island Nuclear Power Station in Pennsylvania, USA. One of the two reactors experienced a partial meltdown when the uranium fuel rods started to liquefy due to rising temperatures after the coolant flow into the reactor decreased and then stopped. Fortunately, no one was directly injured due to the accident. However, some radioactive radiation and water from the reactor were released into the environment and into a nearby river which was also used for drinking purposes.

The other nuclear disaster occurred on 26 April, 1986 at the Chernobyl Nuclear Power Plant in Ukraine. An explosion and fire released large quantities of radioactive contamination into the atmosphere, which spread over much of Western USSR and Europe. Scientists consider it as the worst nuclear power plant accident in history, along with the Fukushima Daiichi nuclear disaster of March 2011.

The battle to contain the contamination and avert a greater catastrophe ultimately involved thousands of workers and scientists and cost an exorbitant amount which led to affecting even the Soviet economy.

Japanese nuclear scientist Professor Ikuro Anzai delivered a keynote address on 12th October, 2011 in Kyoto in which he talked about the development of nuclear energy in Japan and his personal critical opposition to it for the last 40 odd years. I shall quote from his emotional address in which he also admitted to the academic harassment he faced and how he survived this period through "firstly, by my own personal belief in life with dignity, secondly in solidarity with understanding people in the fields of science and public movements, and thirdly through the support of my partner".

Professor Anzai visited the area of the Fukushima disaster three times (April, May and August 2011) to measure the radiation levels and to sample soils contaminated with radioactive substances (mainly radiation from the element caesium-137) He and his associate found that radiation levels were very high, leading to contaminating the nearby soil and endangering people, especially young people.

It has been reported that experts from IAEA arrived in Fukushima city in October to help in decontamination efforts of the Japanese scientists. They also started a long-term survey of children for thyroid abnormalities which result from exposure to nuclear radiation.

In a report in the *New York Times* as published in *The Hindu* on December 6, 2011, Hiroko Tabuchi and Martin Fackler reported that at least 45 tons of highly radioactive water had leaked from a purification facility at the Fukushima nuclear plant and some of it may have reached the Pacific Ocean, posing a major environmental threat to both wild and marine life.

Reactions after the Fukushima meltdown have been varied and sometimes contradictory. Germany witnessed one of the largest ever anti-nuclear demonstrations demanding that Germany "heed Fukushima" and stop its nuclear energy programmes. As a result, several of its old nuclear energy plants were temporarily shut down in order to assess their safety aspects. Its Chancellor Angela Merkel announced that the country would reduce its dependence on nuclear energy and by 2022 would shut down all its nuclear energy plants.

On the other hand, USA and UK did not seem to be unduly worried about the Fukushima accident. On the contrary they felt that since Fukushima had caused 'so little' harm, they thought they would not follow Germany's example and go ahead with their nuclear energy projects. In the words of an environmentalist writer George Monibiot,

> "I now support (nuclear) technology. Atomic energy has been subjected to one of its harshest of possible tests and the impact on people and the planet has been small ...".

Overall, the feeling in UK is that "given the predicted looming energy and climate crises ahead, we have little choice but to push ahead, as long as we learn the hard lessons of Fukushima".

India has witnessed widespread protests in the southern state of Tamil Nadu against the commissioning of nuclear power plants in Koodankulam. Thousands of people living in close proximity to the plant have been protesting against the plant after the Fukushima accident. Indian scientists say that there is no comparison between the Fukushima plant and this one since the former reactor belonged to the first generation while the present one belongs to the third generation and has the most advanced reactor technology and safety features. Although the Indian government and the Prime Minister himself have tried to reassure the people that the proposed plant is 'safe', the protests are continuing. As a result, the work on the power station has been temporarily halted.

Following the protests in Koodankulam, there has been similar opposition to the construction of other nuclear plants with potential capacity of about 9,000 MWe, near Kovvada in another southern state of India – Andhra Pradesh. Villagers are protesting against dislocation from their traditional homes and for fear of their safety in case of a nuclear accident however remote that possibility is, according to scientists and government spokesmen.

Earlier, when populations of most countries were smaller and more easily manageable, people used to live far off from places which were prone to natural disasters – flooding, volcano eruptions, landslides and the like. Now with pressure on available lands, habitations come up near these areas thus putting themselves and their families and their animals to potential risk. People are compelled to live even near nuclear installations for this very reason.

Mining Disasters

A large number of mining accidents have occurred during the process of mining minerals such as coal. Thousands of miners have died in these accidents. Most of the deaths nowadays occur in developing countries, especially China and some other countries.

Some of the causes for mining accidents are the following:

- leaks of poisonous gases such as hydrogen sulfide or explosive natural gases, especially methane (Terazawa et al., 1985),
- dust explosions due to improper use of explosives underground,
- mining-induced seismicity,
- flooding, and
- general mechanical errors due to malfunctioning mining equipment (such as safety lamps or electrical equipment).

The number of accidents was very large earlier. Deaths of about 1,100 miners were reported in Northern France on 10

March, 1906. Similarly, the Monongah mining accident in West Virginia is considered the worst mining accident of American history where 362 workers were killed in an underground explosion in December 1907.

Fortunately, the number of deaths has decreased substantially due to greater safety measures and use of better technology for mining. But even then in some countries the number of fatalities is still large. In 2006, according to official figures, 4,749 Chinese coal miners were killed in thousands of blasts, floods, and other accidents.

In India, one of the worst coal mining accidents occurred on May 28, 1965 in the Dhanbad coal mine near Dhanbad, then in Bihar. An explosion occurred that led to fire in the mines resulting in deaths of 375 miners.

Disaster Relief

When disasters occur, what type of relief measures are in place? If suitable steps have been taken, the potential consequences of disasters can be mitigated.

There are two types of strategies that can be adopted to avoid or minimise their after-effects: one is preventive and the other post disaster relief measures. Preventive steps can help either to avoid the potential dangers totally or to minimise its adverse effects.

Japan, which is earthquake prone, has specially designed architecture and constructions that will allow buildings to absorb earthquake shocks and movements of the land without falling or crumbling. The other strategy is to have relief measures in place which can be put into operation once a disaster has taken place. Specially designed structures are stocked with adequate supplies of food and drinking water and are also equipped with emergency medical care so that the injured people can be treated or at least receive first aid. There are special signs to help people living nearby to proceed to these structures or camps in emergency after a disaster has struck.

Many Asian countries, including India, Pakistan, Nepal, Thailand, etc., are subject to severe floods that can cause devastation on a huge scale. As already indicated, Thailand witnessed flooding recently that led to a large number of deaths as well as displacing a large number of people.

An unusually massive flooding occurred in July and August 2010 in Pakistan that affected about twenty million people, resulting in loss of human and animal lives and displacement of millions from their homes. It also resulted in vast areas of cropland being submerged in water and destroying grain and other crops. A team of scholars carried out a detailed survey of the affected regions. The results of this survey have been presented by Professor Tatsushi Arai at the APPRA Conference in Kyoto on 12th October, 2011.

Professor Arai pointed out the following grievances that the flood-affected victims felt:

1. Scarcity of food directly resulting from loss of their crops and animals.
2. Absence of relief to rebuild their homes and buy cattle.
3. Structural scarcity arising from disparities in access and distribution of relief material resulting in tensions and conflict because of privileging one group of people over another.

These disasters bring out in stark reality the social dynamics at play in the disaster affected regions where the rich and powerful receive privileged treatment that causes resentment and conflict among the less powerful sections of the society at their unequal treatment. This conflict sometimes leads to violence.

The author of this report suggests that any strategy for dealing with the aftermath of disasters must focus on disaster relief, long-term development and conflict prevention.

It is interesting to note that disaster relief is also implicitly implied in the Universal Declaration of Human Rights that was agreed to by consensus in the United Nations in 1948. Article 28 of this Declaration refers to an international order in which the rights and freedoms set forth can be fully realised. Joseph Wronka (2008) writes that although disaster relief along with rights to cultural diversity, clean environment peace, development, etc., are not explicitly indicated, they emanate from Article 28 of this Declaration.

Conclusion

This article has pointed to several naturally occurring disasters like tornadoes, hurricanes, volcanic eruptions, earthquakes, tsunamis, and those that are largely man-made. Among the latter are flooding, landslides, droughts, pollution, etc., which have natural causes but also result from humankind's unsustainable exploitation of natural resources, mining activities, etc., and resultant global warming.

In addition to disasters referred to above, we also talk of the accidents that sometimes take place when big buildings or bridges collapse or fatalities that result from mining accidents in many parts of the world. Accidents have also taken place in nuclear energy plants leading to fear, death and destruction. Reference is made to the latest nuclear accident in the Fukushima nuclear plant in Japan that has not only polluted the nearby environment by its radiation leakage, but has caused widespread concern about safety aspects of nuclear plants.

We argue that we need to shift to a different development paradigm where excessive exploitation of physical resources is avoided by leading simpler lives and sustaining our environment and different forms of life. For this we need, among other things, a proper education system that inculcates moral values and a shift from our lifestyles that propagate consumerism and destruction of the planet's natural resources. We highlight the Gandhian approach of leading simple, moral lives that will sustain the environment and also bridge the disparities between the affluent and the poor people. We also refer to the efforts of several persons who are helping in sustaining and restoring the environment – persons that Gandhi was able to inspire by his writings and simple, truthful lifestyle. The United Nations is also addressing the problems of environmental damage and has set up several commissions and panels to address the issue of sustainable development.

The question of relief that needs to be provided when disasters of any type take place is also considered. The relief efforts highlight the social dynamics at play that privilege the powerful sections of the society even in terms of relief provided to the victims.

References

Brundtland Commission, *Our Common Future*, Oxford: Oxford University Press, 1987.

Guha, R.C., "Mahatma Gandhi and the Environmental Movement", in Mahesh Rangarajan, (ed.), *Environmental Issues in India,* New Delhi: The Darling Kindersley (India) Pvt. Ltd., 2007, p. 112.

Ikura, Anzai, "Agenda for Peace Research after 3/11", Keynote Speech at the Opening Session of the 2011 International Conference of Asia-Pacific Peace Research Association (APPRA), Kyoto, Japan, 2011.

Sponsel, Leslie E., "Reflections on the Possibilities of Nonkilling Society and Nonkilling Anthropology", in Joam, Evans Pim (ed.), *Towards a Nonkilling Paradigm,* Honolulu: Center for Global Nonkilling, 2009, pp. 35–72.

Terazawa, K. et al., "Methane Asphyxia: Coal Mine Accident Investigation of Distribution of Gas", *Am J Forensic Med Pathol,* September 6(3): 211–14, 1985.

Wronka, Joseph, *Human Rights and Social Justice,* California: Sage Publications, 2008.

www.un.org/en/gsp, *Resilient People, Resilient Planet: A Future Worth Choosing,* 2012.

9

Humour, Witnessing and Cyber Non-violent Action

Current Research on Innovative Tactical Non-violent Actions Against Tyranny, Ethnic Violence and Hatred

CHAIWAT SATHA-ANAND, JANJIRA SOMBATPOONSIRI, JULARAT DAMRONGWITHITHAM AND CHANCHAI CHAISUKKOSOL

From January to the end of March 2012, there have been 32 books published in English that Amazon categorises as works related to non-violence. But, with the word "non-violence" in their titles, there are only eight books including two with the word "non-killing" – a specific type of non-violence, an emerging concept pioneered by Glenn D. Paige, the founder of the Center for Global Nonkilling.[1] These six books deal with Gandhi; Thoreau's essay on civil disobedience; Osho's philosophy of non-violence – though the guru never uses the term; a collection of Wikipedia articles on creative non-violence; methods of achieving peace – which include the 1995 Dayton Peace Accords, the civil rights movement in the United States, and the Nobel Peace Prize; and a study of national movements' choice of violent or non-violent protest with an emphasis on the Palestinian national movement.

This paper is an outcome of Senior Research Scholar's "Nonviolence and Violence in Thai Society" project, supported by the Thailand Research Fund.

Most impressive in terms of its contribution to non-violence research among these six books is the last one – Perlman's extensive research. Using a record that goes back a hundred years to compare the Palestinian with the South African and Northern Ireland movements, she found that a more coherent movement is more conducive to the use of non-violent actions while a more fragmented one tends to generate violence with authority structure that is too weak to prevent escalation.[2]

We believe that such non-violence research that could shed a meaningful light on how to strengthen peaceful change is badly needed in a world plagued with deadly conflicts as well as to strengthen understandings of how non-violent actions work in different contexts. At the latest APPRA conference, held in Kyoto in October 2011, three of us presented our research works on various topics: Janjira Sombatpoonsiri's "Incompatibility?: Examining the relationship between humour, non-violence, and humour as a vehicle for non-violent struggle"; Jularat Damrongviteetham's "Ordinary People and Political Conflict: Peace Witnessing in Thailand"; and Chanchai Chaisukkosol's "Cyber-Nonviolent Response to Hatred". These are parts of a three-year multi-layered projects on "Nonviolence and Violence in Thai Society" headed by Chaiwat Satha-Anand as a Thailand Research Fund's Senior Research Scholar.

Though each research paper is unique in its own way, this paper is an appraisal of the three research papers focussing on the importance of tactical non-violent actions as crucial methods in engaging deadly or potentially deadly conflicts that could prevent them from escalating into violence. These tactical non-violent methods are the use of humour, peace witnessing, and cyber non-violent actions. The paper begins with a brief discussion of the importance of tactical non-violent actions in the contexts of non-violent struggle. Then the use of humour, peace witnessing, and cyber non-violent actions in responding to dictatorship, ethnic violence, and hatred in cyberspace will be elaborated. Their contributions to non-violence research will also be examined. The paper ends with a brief discussion on the need for cutting-edge non-violence research.

Tactical Non-violent Actions

According to Gene Sharp, non-violent action is understood as the waging of conflict by methods of protest, non-cooperation and intervention without physical violence. Non-violent action is identified by what people do, not by what they believe. This type of engaging conflict includes acts of omission and commission as well as a combination of both.[3] Two decades ago, Thomas Weber and Robert J. Burrowes classified four major categories of "non-violence" using two sets of continuum: pragmatic-ideological and the tactical-strategic. The pragmatic-ideological continuum indicates the nature of commitment to non-violence and the approach to conflict that activists utilise, notably the separability/inseparability of means from ends and the attitude towards opponents. But it is the tactical-strategic continuum that is the focus of this paper. The tactical-strategic continuum indicates the depth of analysis – conflict as an issue or a policy problem; the ultimate aim – a change in policy or structure(s) of society; and the operational time frame which non-violent activists use – short or long-term transformation.[4]

Weber and Burrowes suggest that exponents of tactical non-violent actions "use short to medium-term campaigns in order to achieve a particular goal within an existing social framework; their aim is reform."[5] In a University of Peace's glossary of terms used in peace and conflict studies, tactics are defined as "limited and particular actions decided on short-term bases. In conflict situations, tactics refer to such actions during encounters with contending parties. If conducted efficiently, the choice of tactics will be informed by a strategy."[6] For example, it is a strategic choice to use a mass demonstration against a military regime in a struggle for democracy, but the organiser's or leader's decision to conduct demonstrations in a silent and dignified manner as opposed to a boisterous campaign is a tactical choice. As the logic that informs individual encounters or confrontations with the opponents in specific encounters, tactic is normally placed as "subordinate to strategy" or "on the next level down" from policy and strategy.[7]

Four decades ago, Alinsky wrote a book that claimed to be the equal of Machiavelli's *The Prince* as a manual for the have-nots on how to take power away from the haves by creating mass organisations with the purpose of seizing power and giving it to the people.[8] In a central chapter of the book on how to do just that, he defines tactics as "doing what you can with what you have. Tactics are those consciously deliberate acts by which human beings live with each other and deal with the world around them. In the world of give and take, tactics is the art of how to take and how to give."[9] For him, as different from later non-violence theorists' emphasis, tactics are not the product of careful and cold reasons but they arise out of accident, unpredictable reactions to one's actions, necessity and improvisation. Analytical logic comes later – when one needs to appraise his/her position and ponder the risks as well as ways ahead.[10] In this sense, tactics are so human since they are lives themselves. The question is how these human acts which seem to work in ordinary living serve as vehicles to fight injustice and change the world.

The problem of tactics as improvisation or careful analysis, among others, could perhaps be construed from the following research on how people use rather unusual tactics to engage different kinds of conflicts in varied contexts – the use of humour against a dictatorial regime in the Balkan, the use of peace witnessing in the context of ethnic violence in southern Thailand, and the possible use of cyber non-violent actions against hatred in cyber space.

Engaging Dictatorship with Humour[11]

The prime example of using humour as non-violent tactic against a dictatorial regime was the *Otpor* (Resistance) movement in Serbia which deliberately and extensively staged humouristic street performances based on the rhetoric of the Slobodan Miloševiæ regime. This exposed the Serbian public to the absurdity of the regime's propaganda and eventually creating a crisis of legitimacy for the regime and engendered the success of the movement's pro-democracy campaigns in 2000. Here we would use two instances of the use of humour as non-violent tactics to engage the regime through carnivalesque and excorporation:

(1) After the electoral fraud in November 1996, anger and dissatisfaction among the Serbians were on the rise. In an attempt to prevent the escalation of armed uprising against the regime, protest organisers in Belgrade deliberately provided protesters with carnivalesque activities during the four-month demonstrations in 1996–97. Carnivalesque humour demonstrates an aspect where humour transforms antagonism in conflicts through a temporary

inversion of social roles and the transgression of established norms (e.g., water festival in mainland Southeast Asia or the festival of Holi in India),[12] or at times returning to bodily indulgence by subverting authority's control over private life (e.g., people would eat, drink and engage in sexual intercourse without restrictions).[13] Protest organisers encouraged people to throw eggs at state buildings, rather than pelting state authorities with harmful objects. The dull and hateful slogans earlier used by the protesters were replaced with witty ones. Protesters banged pots and pans everyday during the daily broadcast of the state's news programme in an air of emancipated enjoyment. They also replaced politicians' boring speeches with music performances and satirical street theatres. There were also the "citizens' happenings" such as the collective jumping up and down at the green traffic light, which was against the law, and car jamming.

The carnivalesque protests reached its zenith during the eight-day stand-off between the police cordon and demonstrators. The whole scene of anger-loaded, tension-filled stand-off was turned into the liveliest street party ever organised in Belgrade, entitled "Discotheque of Blue Cordon" (*Deskoteka Plavi Kordon*). A provincial sound system was brought in to get the festivity started. For 178 hours, police encountered around 30,000 party goers who ceaselessly danced along to the British punk rocks mixed with traditional Balkan songs. The sound of music was so loud that "all nightclubs in town which normally catered to a student audience suspended their activities, because, even at minus twenty, they could not compete with *Diskoteka Plavi Kordon*".[14] The highlight of the discotheque was the "Miss University Contest", which was organised by students in collaboration with a pro-opposition newspaper, *Demokratija,* to elect the best female protester.[15] The event was followed by the "Mister Police Contest", in which the most popular policeman in the eyes of protesters was selected.[16] Despite signs of clashes and police crackdown, the stand-off ended bloodlessly. Student leaders of the protests attributed this to the carnivalesque activities introduced to joyfully transform the emotion of street demonstrations.[17]

(2) The action "Dinar for a Change" (*Dinar za smenu*) provides an example of how satirical humour works in the mode of 'excorporation' – the process where the subordinates make use of

what is at their disposal in the vast system of domination to emasculate the system itself.[18] The action was launched in the autumn of 1999 as a response to the government's announcement of a new agricultural policy, entitled "A Dinar for Sowing" (*Dinar za setvu*). The policy asked already impoverished Serbians to donate some dinars (Serbian currency) for agricultural improvement. Twisting the policy title, *Otpor* activists announced a parallel policy named "A Dinar for a Change".[19] In front of the National Theatre, at the entrance of the pedestrian street, Knez Mihailova, they placed an empty petrol barrel, pasted with an image of Slobodan Miloševiæ surrounded by the target symbol. Next to the barrel were a stick and instructions: "if you put a dinar inside [the barrel], you can use the provided stick to beat Milosevic's picture".[20] The instruction continues: "if you don't have any coins because of Miloševiæ, hit [the barrel] harder".[21] The action not only aimed to be a channel for Serbians to express their resentment toward the regime, but also brought to the fore the absurdity of the regime's policy. It succeeded because the action's meaning is derived from an already existing propaganda. Instead of blatantly attacking the propaganda, activists used it to their end, twisting its essence to their advantage.

From these examples, we would argue that humour could be seen as an effective non-violent tactic. The concepts of carnivalesque humour and 'excorporation' used here demonstrate that humour subverts domination fundamentally by basing itself on the dominant rhetoric. But it works to twist such rhetoric to absurdity, thereby invalidating the rhetoric's 'truth' claim. This is the 'deconstructive' potency of humour conducive to powerful non-violent resistance. In addition, incorporating carnivalesque activities into protest repertoires can generate peaceful atmosphere of street protests through the production of "another world images" while emitting cheerful emotion. Joyful street protests can then alter anger and resentment that drove people to the streets in the first place. As a result, the positive atmosphere of such tactical non-violent protest would significantly help reduce the likelihood of protest turning into violent riots. In other words, the *Otpor* example demonstrates the use of humour to foster non-violent engagement in conflict against dictatorship without hatred or hateful antagonism that could result in violence.

Engaging Deadly Ethnic Conflict with Peace Witnessing

"Peace Witness Volunteer Group" was formed in Thailand in 2007 during the deadly conflict in southern Thailand which re-exploded in 2004. The three southernmost provinces in Thailand – Pattani, Yala and Narathiwat, with an 80 per cent majority of the Malay Muslims in the area – were forcibly annexed into the new Thai nation state a little more than a hundred years ago. Since then, a combination of factors which include economic deprivations, injustice, bad governance, the proliferation of drugs and crimes have contributed to a deadly protracted conflict between the Thai state/military and groups of nearly invisible insurgents that has killed approximately 5,000 people at the time of this writing.[22]

From November 2006 until June 2007, there were more than 60 protest rallies on different issues such as protest against the arrests of people the locals believed to be innocents, or the killings of local *imams* (religious leaders), pitting local Malay Muslims on one side and the Thai authorities on the other. These protests engendered more tension between state officials and the local Malay Muslims. Initially, Peace Witness Volunteer Group, an NGO (non-governmental organisation) funded by Mahidol university peace institute, chose to be present at these protests aiming to listen to stories from different stakeholders, and then to share these stories from their perspectives with the larger Thai public. Main activities included collecting documents about the situations and taking photos. Peace witness volunteers had been selected on the basis of their faith in non-violence and trained to provide an unarmed presence in-between the government officials and the local people. They believed in the old adage that "in war, truth is the first casualty" and that without "truth", conflict might escalate to become violence. To deter violence, this group believed that they could serve as "the third side" to contain the imminent power struggle by paying attention to possible escalation and thereby help mitigate a potentially deadly conflict.[23] Importantly, they felt that because of their presence as witnesses, government officials would not dare to use violence against the protesters. However after 2007, the number of protests decreased due to the military's decision to suppress all protests, believing that they were instigated by the insurgents. The group then had to adjust their activities by shifting from intervening in confrontations between the two sides with their presence to visiting victims of violence after attacks.

Southern ethnic violence continues amidst the lack of trust between the locals and the government officials. As a result, there are only a few people who would volunteer to serve as witnesses. It is interesting to note that if volunteers were not Malay Muslims, they would need skills and cultural sensitivities in order to properly interact with the locals. On the other hand, if they were Malay Muslims, though they were culturally equipped to serve in just such a context, they often faced a much more complicated problem of staying neutral. Some of the local peace witness volunteers were once victims of state violence or have had their relatives killed or wounded by the authorities. As a result, serving as peace witnesses in real conflict situations where the protesting villagers were on one side and the government security forces on the other, they found it difficult to be neutral. When they saw their relatives, friends, or neighbours facing the officials, they took the protesters' side. As a result, all but two of them eventually decided to leave the peace witness group which continues at the time of this writing.

Peace witnessing is a form of non-violent intervention by a nonpartisan party. According to Gene Sharp, non-violent intervention is a type of methods that actively disrupt the normal operation of policies or the system by deliberate interference, either psychologically, physically, socially, economically, or politically.[24] Sharp also points out that certain methods of non-violent intervention can pose a more direct and immediate challenge to the opponents than non-violent protest and non-cooperation, and may thereby produce more rapid changes. But these methods are usually both harder for the opponents to withstand, and at the same time more difficult for the resisters to sustain because use of these methods may bring more severe repression than other non-violent methods.[25] Robert J. Burrowes, a leading non-violent activist/scholar and a member of the Gulf Peace Team, maintains that one of the reasons why non-violent intervention can cause just such a political disruption is because, apart from any physical intervention, the nature and/or location of the intervention is symbolically meaningful and chosen precisely to delegitimise normal operations. He also advocates the idea that non-violent intervention, especially those that work across borders, should be carried out by grassroots activists to halt or prevent violence or facilitate social change.[26]

Drawing from the Israeli-Palestinian conflict, Rigby[27] suggests that non-violent intervention could be categorised by using its geographical location, style, and goals of actions.

1. Geographical location includes on-site and off-site intervention. On-site intervention refers to actions which involve the physical presence of activists in the zone of conflict. But off-site interventions refer to efforts that do not involve physical presence of the intervening activists in the zone of conflict.
2. Styles of intervention juxtapose non-violent direct action with other conventional political actions. For example, in a near democratic society, non-violent intervention by an NGO in a protest might be acceptable and considered normal. But in a heightened conflict situation such as the occupied territories of Palestine, Tibet, or southern Thailand, the very same act could be discouraged and/or prohibited, and therefore it should be considered unconventional non-violent action.
3. The objectives of the action can be classified as short-term and long-term. Short-term actions aim to curtail the surfacing of violence, while long-term actions seek to bring about solutions for deep-rooted causes of a conflict such as militarism and war. It is also possible that any action can contain within it both short and long-term objectives.

It is important to point out that while non-cooperation relies on the power of number, non-violent intervention, especially peace witnessing, depends primarily on the disciplines and steadfastness of the activists present. Following Rigby's guidelines, peace witnesses in southern Thailand violence operates as on-site intervention with a short-term objective aiming to prevent immediate violence in the context of extreme ethnic violence. Under the circumstances, the degree to which both sides of the conflict accept peace witnesses as "the third side" depends on how their presence is felt and the witnessing is seen. There is indeed a profound relationship between "presence" and "eye witnessing." The presence is significant when an individual is an eyewitness since one never looks at just one thing but always in relations to one's presence. In this sense, peace witnessing is a process of conveying what one has seen – generally endowed with one's own values of finding ways to prevent violence, while trying to retain a neutral position, a difficult but necessary endeavour in working for peace in the context of deadly ethnic conflict.

Engaging Hatred with Cyber Non-violent Action

In the internet age where people with differences are connected in cyber space, prosumers (consumers of information who are simultaneously its producers) express their opinions, share links, and create their own information worlds within and among their communication communities. It is often pointed out that these communities have common goals, participate and share their resources actively. But it is also true that prosumers participate in all kinds of conflict.[28] Though a large part of cyber space discussions are reasonable, prudent and thoughtful, at times they are obscene, rude, narrow-minded and hateful of people who are different in terms of race, gender, religion, and/or political inclination. According to *Hate Directory Report 2010*, internet content related to hate speech is approximately 170 pages long.[29] *Stormfront* (stormfront.org), for example, is the most prominent cyberhate group among the white supremacists.

In Thailand, as a result of a highly polarised political conflict between the yellow and the red shirts movements with strong link to two mass political parties,[30] hate speech has become prevalent in cyber space. From facebooks, hateful comments such as *"Ahh ... don't think you're from heaven, just came up from the true abyss of hell."* Or, *"Red buffalo, better go to Cambodia ... your dad's home country. Don't stay in Thailand anymore"* For the Thais, buffalo is a metaphor for being stupid. Cambodia was mentioned here because Thaksin Shinawatra, the elected prime minister who was ousted in the September 19, 2006 coup d'etat and the icon of the red shirts movement, was a special advisor to the Cambodian prime minister Hun Sen.

Facing the spread of political hatred in today's internet, the use of violence against proponents of hate speech, the tightening of the law and censorship have been encouraged and/or proposed to keep cyber hate speech in check. But these measures are either violent in themselves – if they incite others to do harm to those using hate speech, or backed by violence – such as the use of strict laws to curtail freedom of expression. To deal with hate speech, creative alternatives conducive to open democracy beyond censorship are needed. We would argue that it is necessary for nonviolence research to find ways to deal with this kind of "cyber-violence" non-violently. The use of "electronic civil disobedience", for example, could potentially be used to counter hatred in cyber space.

"Electronic civil disobedience" was developed by the Electronic Disturbance Theatre (EDT), a creative group of people within the Zapatista movement in Chiapas, Mexico. On 29 January, 1998, EDT called global internet users for cyber-action against the Mexican government's decision to bring the country deep into the grips of NAFTA since this globalised ties would systematically further impoverish the Mexican poor. EDT posed five website addresses of ministries which are the symbols of neo-liberalism and asked global users to stage a "virtual sit-in," flooding the request command to all these websites to overload the web-server.[31]

This technique was also employed in other cases, such as the anti-WTO summit in Seattle, November 1999. A group named Electro-Hippies launched this symbolic cyber-action. They got 400,000 unique IP (Internet Protocol) joined in the "virtual sit-in" to overload WTO websites with 600,000 hits.[32]

Though the electronic civil disobedience was not initially developed to deal with hatred and hate speech, we would argue that it can be applied as a non-violent response to hate speech. For example, electronic civil disobedience could be staged against proponents of hate-filled websites and possibly neutralise them. Or a cyberspace response to hatred could sometimes take the form of an online game as well. For example, to counter these hate groups, Microsoft came up with an online game: "Call of Duty 4" where some two million players around the globe join forces through their headsets to blow out hate and racist speeches against the Jews, Asians and the Hispanics, among others.[33]

Comparing cyber and traditional non-violent actions, it could be argued that electronic civil disobedience shares the same philosophy with its traditional predecessor in terms of publicly breaking the laws and the user of this method is prepared to accept consequences. But it goes without saying that while traditional civil disobedience operates on the physical space, the cyber-version works on the internet. Traditional civil disobedience requires the physical body to disobey the power while the electronic version relies very much on a hacker's internet skill and knowledge to create a system or application with global reach for participants to join in from faraway communities. It would be interesting to see how the blending of civil disobedience philosophy with hacker knowledge could work against dominant websites roaming cyber space spreading hatred.

But how effective would cyber non-violent action such as electronic civil disobedience be against hate speech? Admittedly, this kind of cyber non-violent action does not directly deal with the root of hatred,[34] since the aim of this mode of action is neither to eliminate the cause of hatred nor to heal its effects. But then responding to hate speech by shooting or imprisoning the perpetrators does not eliminate the root cause of hatred either. Cyber non-violent action serves instead as an alternative response to hate speech short of violence or censorship.

Using Burrowes' categorisation of non-violence discussed above, it is important to affirm a simple fact that cyber non-violent actions such as electronic civil disobedience are tactics. In fact, most non-violent actions in cyberspace are operating at the tactical level. This is primarily because cyberspace circumstances will never replace other more material or cultural spaces. At best, actions in cyber space act as a new space to supplement or to lead actions in structural or cultural spaces, for example. But its importance lies in the fact that at present it is impossible for other media spaces to act as a field of action against hatred without taking into account cyber space where extreme forms of hate speech could flourish and therefore direct counter electronic form of non-violent actions is extremely necessary. As a result, under such circumstances it might be more urgent and crucial to find ways to creatively respond to hatred in cyber space than to deal with a long-term effort of eliminating hate speech, which would mean finding ways to undermine the deep cultures that continue to legitimise hatred. If hate speech in cyber space is allowed to continue unchecked while negative response such as censorship is encouraged or tolerated, hatred could spiral to the level that it might be even more difficult to prevent such conflict from sliding further into the realm of violence. In this sense, the unchecked prevalence of hate speech would contribute significantly to the intractability of deadly conflicts. That is why it is important to understand how cyber non-violent action as tactics could contribute to a strategic transformation of society where hatred is no longer acceptable.

Conclusion: Innovative Tactical Non-violent Actions and Future Research

Though much has been written about the division between tactical and strategic non-violent actions, and most seem to subsume the importance of non-violent tactics under those of non-violent strategy,[35] Iain Atack has recently argued that such division is artificial in practice since the two objectives of limited and broad structural changes often co-exist within particular cases of non-violent campaigns. This is because such non-violent campaigns often consist of coalitions of different groups with their own objectives, limited among some while extremely broad among others. More importantly, using Gandhi's salt march and his use of salt tax as a reflection of the corruption of British imperialism as an example, Atack points out that tactical non-violent action around a specific issue can indeed be used deliberately in conjunction with much larger objectives.[36]

Based on the three research works discussed above, we would argue that some tactical non-violent actions could be consciously used within a much larger strategic objective while others could be used with a much more limited goal. The use of humour as non-violent action in the case of *Otpor* falls clearly in the realm of connecting a specific tactic within a larger non-violent strategy of fighting dictatorship. But peace witnessing in southern Thailand, on the other hand, often times worked on the premise of preventing confrontations that appeared before the witnesses' very eyes from turning violent. A quarrel in a Malay Muslim village between the gathering crowd and the military about how to transport a corpse of a person shot dead by the authority to the graveyard could easily turn violent but for the non-violent intervention through the presence of peace witnesses. Their goal was not to put an end to the protracted deadly conflict, though this could be the wishes of many, but the immediate prevention of possible violence between the local Malay Muslims and the authority. Their successful prevention, however, could contribute to the ways in which the two sides interact. In addition, from a long-term strategic perspective, a case of successful prevention of violence by peace witnesses could perhaps contribute something to the process of courting the deadly ethnic conflict to its peaceful conclusion in the future. The same could be said about cyber non-violent action. It is true that an online game to counter hate speech or a possible electronic civil disobedience against a cyber hate regime will not put an end to hatred based on racism, homophobia or jingoism. But it will put to rest the understanding that hate speech could go on unchecked in cyber space. Nor will it be allowed to inform and perhaps inspire hate crimes in the real world. In this sense, it could be argued that tactical non-violent action is crucial for countering existing structures that perpetuate violence at present. Therefore, research knowledge on tactical non-violent actions could become increasingly more relevant for those interested in curtailing the tide of violence.

If we look at some of the most remarkable research works on non-violent conflict recently published, they are elaborate case studies that try to convey the messages that non-violent actions did take place to effect political changes around the world and that it is important to understand the ways in which they work through profound analysis of local dynamics.[37] Another important volume demonstrates how non-violent actions work, and through quantitative research shows that they are more effective alternatives in dealing with political conflicts than the use of violence.[38]

Non-violence research works under the three-year research project on "Non-violence and Violence in Thai society" discussed here are somewhat different from these studies, either in terms of theories used, activists' roles and actions' context, or in modern sites that few studies have touched.

In a rather prophetic article on future possibilities for non-violence research published in 2005, Brian Martin expects future non-violence research to "do more". Apart from more case studies and advanced theories, it should also open up new areas of investigation including the role of technology, the absence as well as the presence of action, and new action arenas including cyberspace, among other things.[39]

We would argue that the research works presented here clearly move in Martin's suggested direction. The use of humour as non-violent tactic presents a new challenge in connecting research in the fields of humour studies with non-violent action. Peace witnesses focus on the use of physical bodies to intervene in acute conflict situation that connects the studies of the third side with deadly ethnic conflict. Cyber non-violent action moves into cyber space to find creative ways to confront hatred which include the use of online game. Though it must be noted that humour, peace witnessing and cyber non-violent actions are certainly not stand-alone alternatives but generally work in combination with other actions, both tactical and strategic, they are indeed innovative tactical non-violent actions that people use to fight dictatorship, prevent ethnic conflict from sliding further into violence, and to counter the prevalence of hate speech in cyber space without resorting to censorship.

In a most celebrated account of how to fight modern tyranny, the late Vaclav Havel reflected on the potentials of small acts of defiance, such as refusing to put a party slogan in a greengrocer's window, not voting in a farcical elections, writing letters of protest, listening to or organising a concert of forbidden music. These acts by individuals or groups who refuse to "live a lie" can undermine a system based on ideological lies, and eventually might lead a seemingly monolithic structure of power to disintegration. For Havel, such small acts of "living in truth" are both moral commitment and political.[40] For non-violence researchers, we would argue that these "small acts" Havel proposed are clearly tactical non-violent actions.

These "small acts" are perhaps so powerful because at their hearts, humour as non-violent protest, peace witnessing as non-violent intervention and electronic civil disobedience/online game as tactics are vintage non-violent actions since they empower ordinary people out of desperation and into the course of creative actions that will eventually help foster a less violent world.

Notes

1. See N. Radhakrishnan et al. (eds.) *Towards a Nonkilling World: Festschrift in Honour of Prof. Glenn D. Paige*, Trivandrum: Gandhi Media Centre, 2012.
2. Wendy Pearlman, *Violence, Nonviolence, and the Palestinian National Movement*, Cambridge: Cambridge University Press, 2012.
3. Gene Sharp, *Waging Nonviolent Struggle: 20th Century Practice and 21st Century Potential,* Boston: Extending Horizons Books, 2005, p. 547. For definitions related to non-violent conflict, see also Gene Sharp, *Sharp's Dictionary of Power and Struggle: Language of Civil Resistance in Conflict*, Oxford: Oxford University Press, 2012.
4. See Thomas Weber and Robert J. Burrowes, "Nonviolence: An Introduction," *Peace Dossier* 27 (A Publication of the Victorian Association of Peace Studies) (February 1991), pp. 1–2. It should be noted, however, that in Robert Burrowes' later work, the two axes or continuums are somewhat different. They are: the principled-pragmatic and the reformist-revolutionary continuums. See Robert J. Burrowes, *The Strategy of Nonviolent Defense: A Gandhian Approach*, New York: State University of New York Press, 1996, pp. 98–101.
5. Weber and Burrowes, "Nonviolence: An Introduction," p. 2.
6. Christopher E. Miller, *Glossary of Terms and Concepts in Peace and Conflict Studies* Mary E. King (ed.), Addis Ababa: University for Peace, Africa Programme, 2005, p. 74.
7. Peter Ackerman and Christopher Kruegler, *Strategic Nonviolent Conflict: The Dynamics of People Power in the Twentieth Century,* Westport, Connecticut and London: Praeger, 1997, p. 47.
8. Saul D. Alinsky, *Rules for Radicals: A Pragmatic Primer for Realist Radicals*, New York: Vintage Books, 1972, p. 3.
9. Ibid., p. 126. (Emphasis is mine.)
10. Ibid., p. 165.
11. Janjira Sombatpoonsiri's APPRA paper is based on her extensive research on "The Use of Humor as a Vehicle for Nonviolent Struggle: The Case of the 1996/7 Protests and Otpor, Serbia, 1996–2000," a Ph.D dissertation at La Trobe University and a research project under the Senior Research Scholar project on "Nonviolence and Violence in Thai Society," Thailand Research Fund.
12. See Victoria R. Bricker, *Ritual Humor in Highland Chiapas* (Austin: University of Texas Press, 1973); Mary Douglas, "Jokes," in Douglas (ed.), *Implicit Meanings: Essays in Anthropology* (London & Boston:

Routledge, 1984), pp. 90–114; Mikhail Bakhtin, *Rabelais and His World*, Helen Iswolsky (trans.) (Bloomington: Indiana University Press, 1984), pp. 197–277; James C. Scott, *Domination and the Arts of Resistance* (New Haven & London: Yale University Press, 1990), pp. 172–82; and David Kunzle, "World Upside Down: The Iconography of a European Broadsheet Type," in Barbara A. Babcock (ed.). The *Reversible World: Symbolic Inversion in Art and Society*, Ithaca: Cornell University Press, 1978, pp. 39–90.

13. Bakhtin, *Rabelias and His World*, pp. 296–436.
14. Dejan Sretenoviæ, "Noise," in Darka Radosavljeviæ (ed.) *Graðanski Protest U Srbiji: Šetnja U Mestu/Civil Protest in Serbia: Walking on the Spot*, (Belgrade: B 92, 1997), pp. 86–94; Ivan Pravdiæ, "Student Performances: Guidelines for Possible Analyses or Theatre of the Masses: Walking from Failureville to Never-Never Land," in *Šetnja U Mestu/Walking on the Spot*, pp. 37–42; Mirjana Prosiæ-Dvorniæ, "The Topsy Turvy Days Were There Again: Student and Civil Protest in Belgrade and Serbia, 1996/1997," *Anthropology of East Europe Review* (1998), scholarworks. iu.edu/journals/index.php/aeer/article/viewFile/691/784 (accessed on September 21, 2010); Sreten Voyuviæ, "Protest as an Urban Phenomenon," in ed. Mladen Laziæ, *Protest in Belgrade* (Budapest: Central European University Press, 1999), p. 203; Milena Dragièeviæ-Šešiæ, "The Iconography and Slogans of Civil Society and Civil Protest 96/97," in Nadia Skenderoviæ (ed.) *Civil Society in the Countries in Transition* (Subotica, Serbia: Agency of Local Democracy and Open University Subotica, 1999), pp. 527–40; Stef Jansen, "Victims, Underdogs and Rebels: Discursive Practices of Resistances in Serbian Protest," *Critique of Anthropology* 20 (2000): 49; and Milena Dragiæeviæ-Šešiæ, "The Street as Political Space: Walking as Protest, Graffiti, and the Student Carnivalization of Belgrade," *New Theatre Quarterly* 17 (2001): 74–86.
15. Marina Blagojeviæ, "The Walks in a Gender Perspective," in Mladen Laziæ (ed.) *Protest in Belgrade: Winter of Discontent*, Budapest: Central European University Press, 1999, p. 121.
16. Interview, Milan Milutinoviæ, Belgrade, October 6, 2010; Jansen, "Victims, Underdogs and Rebels: Discursive Practices of Resistances in Serbian Protest", 398. The way police officers were voted on was also quite hilarious. The police identification numbers became the vote number of each officer. In order to vote, students and other protest participants would look at the police's 'belts' and write down the numbers on paper.
17. Interview, Èedomir Antiæ, Belgrade, 8 October, 2010; interview, Ivan Maroviæ, Belgrade, November 1, 2010; interview, Milan Milutinoviæ,

Belgrade, October 6, 2010; interview, Pero Jeliæ, Belgrade, November 15, 2010.

18. John Fiske, *Understanding Popular Culture*, London and New York: Routledge, 1989, pp. 15–19.
19. In Serbian, *setva* means sowing and *smena* means change, dismissal, and purge. Two words are rhymed. So, activists twisted the title of the regime policy for their action that eventually mocked the policy.
20. Interview, Miljia Jovanoviæ, Belgrade, November 13, 2010.
21. Interview, Siniša Šikman, Belgrade, September 19, 2010.
22. See for example, Chaiwat Satha-Anand (ed.) *Imagined Land: Solving Southern Violence in Thailand* (Tokyo: Research Institute for the Languages and Cultures of Asia and Africa, Tokyo University of Foreign Studies, 2009). Most updated data on violence in southern Thailand can be obtained from www.deepsouthwatch.org
23. William L. Ury, *The Third Side: Why We Fight and How We Can Stop*, New York: Penguin Books, 2000, pp. 169–71.
24. Gene Sharp, *Waging Nonviolent Struggle*, p. 42.
25. Ibid., p. 62.
26. Robert J. Burrowes, "Cross-Border Nonviolent Intervention: A Typology," in Yeshua Moser-Puangsuwan and Thomas Weber (eds.), *Nonviolent Intervention Across Borders: A Recurrent Vision*, Hawaii: Spark M. Matsunaga Institute for Peace, 2000, pp. 45–69.
27. Andrew Rigby, "Unofficial Nonviolent Intervention: Examples from the Israeli-Palestinian Conflict," *Journal of Peace Research*, Vol. 32 No. 4 (November 1995), pp. 453–67.
28. Michael Stringlove, "The YouTube Wars: Politics, Religion, and Armed Conflict," *Watching YouTube*, Toronto: University of Toronto Press, 2010.
29. Raymond A. Franklin (compiler), *The Hate Directory.* P.O. Box 121 Woodstock, MD 21163–0121. (2010) retrieved from http://www.hatedirectory.com on July 1, 2010.
30. See an analysis of this complex problem in, for example, John Funston (ed.) *Divided Over Thaksin: Thailand's Coup and Problematic Transition,* Singapore: Institute of Southeast Asian Studies, 2009.
31. Graham Meikle, "Electronic Civil Disobedience and Symbolic Power," in Athina Karatzogianni (ed.) *Cyber Conflict and Global Politics,* (London and New York: Routledge, 2009), pp.177–87; T. Jordan and P.A. Taylor, "Mass Action Hacktivism: Anti-globalisation and the Importance of Bad Technology," in *Hacktivism and Cyberwars: Rebels with a Cause?*, New York: Routledge, 2004, pp. 67–89.

32. http://www.fraw.org.uk/projects/electrohippies/overview.shtml
33. Nicholas K. Geraniols "Hate Speech Corrodes Online Games," Associated Press (AP). April 15, 2010. Retrieved from internet http://www.msnbc.msn.com/id/36572021/on September 7, 2010.
34. For this point, we are indebted to Prof. Tatsushi Arai's comment on Chanchai's paper at the Kyoto APPRA conference, October 2011.
35. For example, Ackerman and Kruegler, *Strategic Nonviolent Conflict*.
36. Iain Atack, "Some Reflections on Transformative Nonviolence," in Luc Reychler, Julianne Funk Deckard and Kevin H.R. Villanueva (eds.), *Building Sustainable Futures: Enacting Peace and Development*, Bilbao: University of Deusto, 2009, p. 239.
37. See especially, Adam Roberts and Timothy Garton Ash (eds.) *Civil Resistance and Power Politics: The Experience of Non-violent Action from Gandhi to the Present*, Oxford: Oxford University Press, 2009. See also a review of this book by Janjira Sombatpoonsiri in *Global Change, Peace and Security*, Vol. 22, Issue 2 (2010).
38. Erica Chenoweth and Maria J. Stephan, *Why Civil Resistance Works: The Strategic Logic of Nonviolent Conflict*, New York: Columbia University Press, 2011.
39. Brian Martin, "Researching Nonviolent Action: Past Themes and Future Possibilities," *Peace and Change*, Vol. 30, No. 2 (April 2005) pp. 247–71.
40. Vaclav Havel et al., *The Power of the Powerless*, London: Hutchinson, 1985.

Part IV

Conflict Transformation in the Asia-Pacific

10

The Transitional Approach between Wars to Peace in Sri Lanka

A Qualitative Conceptual GNH Review

SENTHAN SELVARAJAH

The primary focus of this paper involves the qualitative Gross National Happiness review (GNH review) of the so-called post-war reconstruction, rehabilitation and reçonciliation process in Sri Lanka. This is not an indepth review, but more of a qualitative overview based on the principles of the Gross National Happiness (GNH).

GNH is about defining quality of life in more holistic and psychological terms than Gross National Product (GNP). As Thinley explains, "... while material development measures contribute, undeniably, to enhancing physical well-being, the state of mind, which is perhaps, more important than the body, is not conditioned by material circumstances alone" (Thinley, 2005). In this premise GNH gives equal importance to both "standard of living" and "quality of life" in which "prosperity" is the key realisation of the former and "happiness" is the key realisation of the latter.

Recent researches of the African struggles for political, social and economic power reveal the desires of the people to meaningfully participate in decisions governing their lives, in which happiness is something that can be pursued and acquired (cited in

Melkote and Kandath, 2001: 195). The main consequences of the war is the "absence of happiness", therefore the absence of happiness has a greater chance of triggering violence and crisis in a post-conflict/war environment. The unique feature of the logic of this argument is the relevance of the concept of GNH in the post-conflict/war reconstruction, rehabilitation and reconciliation process. That is, the application of the GNH is much more important for post-conflict/war communities than any other communities.

This paper attempts to explain this relevance and the prospective advantageous of integrating the concept of GNH into the post-conflict reconstruction equation. It is on this explanation and the discussion that this paper reviews the post-war reconstruction, rehabilitation and the reconciliation process in Sri Lanka using the GNH philosophy as the conceptual criterion.

The Vagueness of the Concept of Post-conflict Reconstruction

It is clear that the academic and practical knowledge of transitions between wars to peace is still at its infancy. The post-conflict paradigm developed by the World Bank and the international community does not have the theoretical and practical policy instruments to intervene. Old paradigmatic concepts can do more harm than good.

According to the World Bank definition, post-conflict reconstruction is a process that "supports the transition from conflict to peace in an affected country through the rebuilding of the socio-economic framework of the Society" (World Bank, 1998: 24). As Cheru explains, post-conflict reconstruction provides a good base for a country in order to reach the stage of sustainable development. Post-conflict reconstruction does not solely refer to the reconstruction of actual psychical infrastructure, it also includes all plans to rebuild a society – politically, socially, militarily and economically, and attempts to address the root causes of conflict (Cheru, 2002: 210).

In the definition adopted by the School of Advanced Institutional Studies (SAIS), the post-conflict reconstruction is seen as a process that facilitates the establishment of durable peace and tries to prevent the recurrence of violence by addressing root causes and effects of conflict through reconciliation, institution building and political as well as economic transformation (SAIS, 2006).

The Bond of Prosperity and Happiness

It is very clear from these definitions that the core elements of any post-conflict reconstruction models are "prosperity" and "happiness" on which sustainable peace can grow. However, prosperity and happiness are the two sides of the same coin; they cannot be separated from each other. Therefore, any effort for creating prosperity is bound to be abortive if happiness is lost in the process.

Economic growth is often seen as essential for economic prosperity, and indeed is the main factor that is used as a measure of prosperity. Prosperity is a successful, flour ishing, or thriving condition, especially in financial respects (Kenworthy, 2001). Conversely, the prosperity theory relates to the theory of standard of living.

The definition of standard of living means "a level of material comfort as measured by the goods, services, and luxuries available to an individual, group, or nation" (Merriam Webster online dictionary). Faith M. Williams defines the standard of living as "an ideal or norm of consumption "which may be described "in terms of goods and services of a specific quantity and quality" (cited in Cottam and Mangus, 1942: 177).

It is in this context of the economic conception that the activities of the post-conflict reconstruction are carried out with the view of creating "peace economy", and thereby increasing the (standard of living) prosperity (Collier et al., 2003: 13). Although, post-conflict reconstruction is a holistic approach that includes security, political transition, socio-economic development, human rights and resources mobilisation (NEPAD Secretariat, 2005: IV-V), the post-conflict paradigm developed by the World Bank and other institutions lacks clear strategy of creating "happiness".

Everyone wants happiness and does not want suffering. Suffering is the result of war, but happiness is the result of peace. This denotes that the "feeling of happiness" of the people is the precondition for the lasting peace in any conflict-ridden society. Happiness cannot come purely from material, development and economic aspects of the theory of standard of living, but all these aspects should be very carefully balanced with the psychological satisfaction to have a better quality of life.

Every human being aspires for happiness to have a better quality of life. It is important therefore to balance the economic development with psychological, emotional and sometimes spiritual well-being of the society while realising the economic development for better living standards. What this explanation emphasises is that any society's real development should be measured in terms of prosperity and happiness. Therefore, the long-term and the ultimate goal of any post-conflict/war reconstruction should have parallel strategies for creating (standard of living) prosperity and (quality of life) happiness.

Even though the standard of living and quality of life are two different theories, as we have seen throughout the discussion, some of the aspects of these two theories overlap each other. For example, for Elizabeth Ellis Hoyt, standard of living is "more than material things consumed ... a sum total, not of things, but of satisfactions". According to Thomas D. Elliot, it sometimes refers "to the actual distribution of real income in goods, services and advantages received. In other connections it means rather a set of habitual valuations, of attitudes of insistence towards certain goods and services and advantages" (cited in Cottam and Mangus, 1942: 177).

Observably, the definitions highlighted above consist of the aspects of quality of life. Perhaps, it is the reason why Bennett says that "standard of living is a complex and elusive concept. It is perhaps most vague, and certainly most difficult for the statistician to deal with, when regarded as the per capita quantum of human satisfactions or enjoyments" (cited in Curcio, 2005: 3).

It is based on this vague concept of standard of living that the instruments, concepts and definitions of post-conflict/war reconstruction of World Bank and other organisations have been adapted and defined. This is the reason why the definitions of post-conflict/war reconstruction consist of both the aspects of standard of living and quality of life such as security, socio-economic development, human rights, political transition, etc. However, as already observed above, they lack clear distinctive strategies for creating better standard of living and quality of life, and consequently lack distinctive formulas for measuring these distinctive goals.

It is in this premise that there is a necessity and an opportunity of developing distinctive, but integrated post-conflict/war reconstruction strategies for achieving better standard of living and quality of life with the view to create sustainable peace. Such distinctive strategies will enable researchers to create distinctive measurement formulas to scale the level of standard of living and quality of life in post-conflict societies in order to monitor, evaluate and assess the impact of the post-conflict/war reconstruction programmes and to achieve the best results.

This is where it is proposed that the opportunity of creating such distinct strategies can be derived from the concept of GNH. The next section of this paper attempts to explain the relevance of the GNH in the post-war reconstruction process and the prospective merits of integrating it into the concept of post-war reconstruction.

Relevance of GNH

Gross National Happiness (GNH) is concept introduced by king of Bhutan, Jigme Singye Wang Chuck in 1972. GNH as Thinley explains "is based on the idea that sustainable development should take a holistic approach towards notions of progress and give equal importance to economic and non-economic aspects of well-being, and thereby creating a society in which collective happiness of the people is the ultimate desired outcome" (Thinley, 2005). Manifestly, GNH is a concept constructed on the basis of the already emphasised two important components: standard of living and quality of life.

This is where the relevance of GNH comes into play in the post-conflict/war reconstruction process, which is, as explained earlier, also a concept constructed on the basis of standard of living and quality of life.

Hence, the application of the GNH is much more important for post-conflict communities than any other communities, because as noted earlier one of the main consequences of war is the "absence of happiness", and the absence of happiness has a greater potential of triggering a conflict in a post-conflict environment. It is in this connection there is a great potential of integrating the GNH principles into the post-conflict reconstruction programme and thereby creating the much required distinctive but integrated strategies for achieving better standard of living and quality of life toward sustainable peace and development.

On the other hand, integrating the concept of GNH into the concept of post-conflict reconstruction would create a space and opportunity to develop a measurement mechanism to assess the quality of life (happiness) to guide its practical policies and programmes.

Currently, a country or society's development is measured using the Human Development Index (HDI), developed in 1990 by the United Nations. It considers life expectancy at birth, adult literacy rates and per capita gross domestic product (GDP) (Investopediya, 2001). At present, GDP is the only measure in common use and the best indicator of living standards. Therefore, even in the post-conflict environments, there is no option, other than using the GDP to measure the level of progress of the reconstruction and development.

Nevertheless, GDP is not a specific and suitable criterion to scale the standard of living in post-conflict societies as it generally refers to the level of wealth, material goods and services (education, health, etc.) all of which are quantitative variables, and therefore they fail to measure the level and progress of happiness to assess the state of quality of life.

If any such measurement mechanisms of the post-conflict/war reconstruction programmes have to be effective and result oriented, then they should be able to measure the level of both prosperity and happiness. Also, they should be specific enough in compatible with the post-conflict environment to direct and guide its policies and programmes in the right way.

The Centre for Bhutan Studies has already succeeded in developing GNH indicators in order to translate the GNH philosophy into a metric system (Centre for Bhutan Studies and Alkire et al., 2008: 3–4). This measurement mechanism can be useful to develop an index system for measuring the level of the progress of the "happiness" of the post-conflict/war societies and thereby steer the practical application of the GNH integrated post-conflict reconstruction programmes.

It is outside of the scope of this study to explain in detail about the GNH index developed by the Centre for Bhutan Studies.

However, it is pertinent at this point to briefly and generically highlight the principles and ideals inherent in this methodology, so that the discussion of the next section of the qualitative GNH review of the post-war reconstruction process can be best understood.

The GNH concept was initially divided into four main pillars: promotion of sustainable and equitable socio-economic development, preservation and promotion of culture, conservation of the natural environment, and establishment of good governance. Subsequently, these four pillars were divided by the Centre for Bhutan Studies into nine dimensions that comprise the GNH index. They are: psychological well-being, time use, community vitality, culture, health, education, environmental diversity, living standards and governance (ibid.).

It is in this background of the discussion of the relevance of GNH in the post-conflict/war reconstruction process that the next section of this paper moves on to examine the qualitative aspects of the current post-war reconstruction and reconciliation activities of the Sri Lankan government in the context of the socio-political and economic conditions, and explore if they have the potential of bringing about a just and sustainable reconciliation through a transition.

As stressed at the beginning of this paper, it is not an indepth review nor does it consider the GNH index developed by the Centre for Bhutan Studies (CBS), rather it is a conceptual qualitative review.

Transitional Activities of the Post-war Environment in Sri Lanka

It should be made clear, first of all, that transition and post-war reconstruction is not the same thing. Post-war reconstruction is an utmost aspect in the transition process. The major challenge with the current post-conflict transition process in Sri Lanka is the power sharing between Sinhalese and Tamils to transform the post-colonial Sinhala state to a Confederate/Federal state. The government of Sri Lanka sees this problem as a management exercise whilst the Tamil side sees this issue as a problem of transforming power relations.

The activities that are happening in the post-war period reflect and clearly show this difference between the Sri Lankan government and Tamils in their approach of resolving the conflict. The government undertakes the post-war reconstruction and reconciliation in a way that can complement to its own thinking of power sharing through a management exercise. The government thinks that just improving the standard of living of the people in the North and East through its post-war reconstruction can resolve the conflict between these two races, while it should be noted that the government does not undertake such post-war reconstruction activities wholeheartedly and appropriately for such purposes. The government is reluctant to spend its own money for the post-war reconstruction activities though it spent several billion dollars in the past years for the war. Indeed, the government keeps on asking for financial assistance for the post-conflict reconstruction activities from the international community and the Tamil diaspora.

It should be noted that the government has allocated 1.9 billion dollars for its defence expenditure for this year. This amount is exceeded than the previous years, which are: 1.4 billion, 1.5 billion and 1.6 billion for the years respectively 2007, 2008 and 2009 (Ministry of Finance and Planning of Sri Lanka). This defence expenditure has been increased year by year and even after the end of civil war. There have been no mentionable rehabilitation or reconstruction activities undertaken by the government from its own money even two years after the end of war.

However, there have been a few infrastructure improvements such as highways, roads, recreational facilities, government offices and new buildings constructed by the government, but which cannot be seen as an absolute development. Though, there have been several buildings including houses, schools, temples and shops destroyed during the war time, the government has taken no serious moves to reconstruct them. The president mentioned once that people have to reconstruct their destroyed assets by themselves. Even the non-profit organisations are not independently allowed to carry out their rehabilitation and reconstruction activities by the government (TamilNet, 2010). Indeed, the government is keen in creating Sinhala colonisation and constructing Buddhist temples in the northern and eastern areas.

There has been a significant degree of Sinhala colonisation in different areas of North and East by the government during the last two years. In the name of development, the government has undertaken quite a number of projects under its post-war reconstruction programmes to facilitate and strengthen the Sinhala colonisation with the prime aim of changing the demography in the North and East taken over by the military. The government has also forcibly acquired hundreds of acres of lands owned by Tamil people under its "land grab policy" in order to establish military camps [BBC Sinhala Service, 2010 (a)].

Lack of Good Governance

Even the few post-war reconstruction and development programmes that take place in the Tamils areas do not include the participation of Tamils and their expectations. Contrarily, these activities are carried out with the direct control of the military. The civil administration of North and East is also badly controlled by the military. The example would be that retired army officers are appointed as the governors of North and East provinces. North and East are still heavily militarised, and the due impact on the normal life of the people has been disturbing. This military presence make the people recall the war memories and mirror the traumatic experience, which consequently creates negative impact on the activities that the normal Tamil people try towards their own development.

In a manner, it can be said that keeping a large number of military personnel who were purposely pre-prepared for the war there in the North and East would only make negative impacts on the general people's lives. Such forces who could not re-join with their families seem to be unrest and it can motivate them towards some illegal activities and anti-social activities. A mentionable example would be that a recent desecration of the Greece Devils in the North and East points out the blame on forces (Groundviews, 2011).

Therefore, the presence of the military forces and their control in the civil administration do definitely create a negative impact on the reconciliation process. Hence, it becomes important that much of the troops should be pulled out from North and East. Nevertheless, they cannot be just accommodated in the south of Sri Lanka after taking them from North and East as there is a possibility that they would engage in some illegal activities. In many instances, army deserters have been accused of murder, rape, robbery and other crimes in the south (Kaviratne and Wickremasekera, 2010). Therefore, the only solution left is to dismantle the excessive army battalions and integrate them into normal society, which will in turn help to reduce the defence expenditure and help to create a positive impact in the post-war reconciliation. However, there is no such positive sign so far and the government seems to be keen in sustaining forces in the North and East for a long time and it keeps on convincing the presence of forces by saying that they are used in the development activities of North and East.

Moreover, the government argues that it is paramount for them to keep the military deployment in the North and East in order to face any possible future comeback of the LTTE [BBC Sinhala Service, 2010 (b)]. Nevertheless, the president, ministers and military officials have repeatedly said in the past that "LTTE has been totally destroyed by the security forces and there is no way the LTTE can get revived in the country" (*Indian Express*, 2009). The intention of the government to keep its military in the long term in the Northeast shows the duplicity of the government to create sustainable peace and true reconciliation. The military mood of the government is clearly visible in its announcement in the 2012 budget in which the government proposed a Rs 100,000 grant to every third child born to police personnel (which are 99% Sinhalese) in Sri Lanka. A similar grant was already provided for army soldiers (which are 99% Sinhalese) in the 2011 budget (Haviland, 2011).

Even the rehabilitation activities are not undertaken in a real manner. Thousands of LTTE cadres are still being held in Rehabilitation Centres. Many of them are held under the Prevention of Terrorism Act (PTA) for many years without charges. Under the emergency laws which had been in place on and off since 1971, the government detained thousands of LTTE suspects for a year without bringing them to trial. However, the government in September 2011 removed the emergency law, but invoked the PTA to continue with the Emergency (Weliamuna, 2011 and BBC News, 2011).

Negative Effect on Psychological Well-being

The few freed rehabilitated LTTE cadres continue to be monitored and harassed (Groundviews, 2012). In addition, the government came up with an order soon after the end of war that the national anthem should be sung in Sinhala in the Tamil schools and during official ceremonies. The government was very strict in implementing this order despite the strong resistance from the Tamil politicians and civil society leaders (*Dailymirror*, 2011). All these activities show that the government has no honest intention to create a congenial condition for a sustainable peace through its post-war reconstruction process. These are clearly the activities that negatively affect the psychological well-being of the Tamil people.

Psychological well-being is about peoples' evaluation of their life. As Diener explains, "This evaluation takes two forms: cognitions and affect. The cognitive part is an information based appraisal of one's life that is when a person gives conscious evaluative judgments about one's satisfaction with life as a whole. The affective part is a hedonic evaluation guided by emotions and feelings such as frequency with which people experience pleasant/unpleasant moods in reaction to their lives" (Centre for Bhutan Studies).

Revenging and humiliating activities mentioned above are likely to influence the affective part of the evaluation and create negative mood-swings. These unpleasant moods of several reactions can negatively affect the cognitive based evaluation of one's life as a whole and eventually a community's feeling as a whole. As underlined the psychological well-being is the prime source for happiness, and therefore when the psychological well-being is lost, then happiness is also lost. The absence of happiness in a society is the cause of misery and conflict in that society. This is what started happening among the Tamil people in Sri Lanka in 1950s and 1960s and finally leading to the armed conflict in 1970s.

For example, through the enactment and adaptation of Citizenship Act and the laws of disenfranchisement, the first government of independent Ceylon disenfranchised Tamils of Indian origin Tamils in the hill country, leaving a majority of them stateless (Sivapragasam, 2009: 69). The Sinhala Only Act that was introduced in 1956 resulted in bringing disintegrating tendencies to the Sri Lankan polity and society. In a similar manner in 1957, the government introduced legislation to place the Sinhalese "sri" character on the number plates of all vehicles in the country and forced the Tamils to place the Sinhala letter in their number plates. The government launched massive Sinhala colonisation schemes in the Eastern province soon after the independence in 1948 and Galoya in Batticaloa, Allai and Kathalai in Trincomalee were colonised under pretexts of development (Clarance, 2002).

All these activities aimed at degrading and humiliating the Tamil people which badly affected the psychological well-being of the Tamil community, and consequently led to the armed conflict in 1970s. It is in this same line that many of the current post-war activities of the government should be seen. Like in the past, these activities of the government create a greater risk of negatively impacting the psychological well-being of the Tamil people by creating the feeling of humiliation and insult, and thereby fuelling violence and make the ethnic conflict more complicated.

Conversely, it is clear throughout this discussion that, the so called post-war reconstruction, rehabilitation and development process neither helps to increase the standard of living (prosperity) nor promotes the quality of living (happiness). However, due to some optimistic facts such as the absence of war, assistance from Tamil diaspora and the working of the NGOs have contributed to increase the standard of living among Tamils to a slight extent. But, the living standards of the people, particularly those who live in the rural areas of Vanni and Batticaloa, remain very low, and overall the people in the northeast people are living unhappy life.

The International Crisis Group (ICG), in its recent report, has clearly reflected this ground reality of the Northeast of Sri Lanka. The report states that "deepening militarisation and the lack of accountable governance in Sri Lanka's Northern Province are preventing a return to normal life and threaten future violence. Scene of the most bitter fighting in the civil war, the Tamil-majority North remains under de facto military occupation, with all important policies set by Sinhala officials in Colombo. The slow but undeniable movement of Sinhala settlers into the fringes of the north and other forms of government-supported 'Sinhalisation' are reigniting a sense of grievance and weakening chances for a real settlement with Tamil and other minority parties to devolve power" (ICG, 2012, p. ii).

According to the statistics of the ICG report, 120,000–150,000 houses in the Northern Province are in need of rebuilding or repair, however, only 16,400 new houses have been constructed (ibid.: 7).

An assessment conducted by the UN World Food Programme (WFP) in April 2011, the ICG has found that "livelihoods are still underdeveloped" in the north and that "the substantial non-availability of basic infrastructure and services in many parts of the Northern Province and serious damage to private and public assets provide a challenging environment for households to re-establish their livelihoods" (cited in ibid.).

Referring to the recent assessments by a variety of agencies, the ICG observes the existence of extremely high rates of poverty and food insecurity exists in the cleared areas of North. With high unemployment and poverty at high levels throughout North, people experience a very hard life. Quoting to WFP statistics, ICG notes that in all five districts of the North, more than half the population lives below the poverty line; in Kilinochchi, 26 per cent of households live on less than half the official poverty line (ibid.: 10).

Moreover, ICG finds the situation as worse with lack of jobs or other sources of income. It records that "many people are struggling to buy the food they need to survive. High food prices and poverty have forced many to eat less and/or to borrow money to pay for food". As per the WFP survey, "more than 60 per cent of households in the Northern Province were food insecure, and some 15 per cent severely food insecure" (ibid.).

As explained earlier, 'prosperity' is the central aspect of the standard of living, and the level of prosperity is a precondition and a key essential for happiness to spread and fill in the lives. Therefore, in this connection, standard of living which is one of the main domains of GNH Index, in turn, is one of the important determinants of well-being or happiness. This implies the potential occurrence of dissatisfaction and discontentment among the people who live under adverse living conditions. Particularly various studies on poverty have looked at its causes, effects, and prevalence (Centre for Bhutan Studies).

As Pupavac points out, people's lives have a tenuous coherence, and they feel psychologically vulnerable in the face of any setbacks or obstacles (2006: 16). This is clearly evident in the above references of the ICG report. The vulnerable living conditions of the people tend to create a feeling of 'unsafe' rooted in people's psychological insecurity. This psychological insecurity of psychological construct can greatly influence the political attitudes of people. This shows the connection between the creation of psychological insecurity/discontentment and political attitudes (political psychology), and the possible consequences of psychological insecurity/discontentment on politics.

The post-war parliamentary election results in 2010 can be the evidence of this argument (Sundayleader, 2010). Though the government and its alliances promised excessively regarding the development ideas during the election period, however Tamil people had given their preferred votes to the Tamil National Alliance (TNA) while knowing that their places would be developed if only voted to the government. Nevertheless, they voted for TNA that actually could contribute nothing to the post-war reconstruction and development process, which denotes that these people voted for TNA intending to regain their empowerment and dignity through political rights regardless of their poor living conditions, resulted due to the war. On the other hand, the anger of the people against the government caused due to the psychological insecurity/discontentment of the people over the issues (both material and psychological) discussed earlier in this paper also could have possibly influenced the outcome of this election results. However, the factors of identity politics associated with the quality of life have greater chance of having "superseding effect".

The Message of the People

Overall, this election results clearly indicates how people are unsatisfied and how their psychological well-being has been affected due to the current post-war happenings. Importantly, it is a message of the people that the political rights are the most important ones than their own physical well-being or their material possession. This is, in turn, a clear indication of the necessity of giving importance to the aspect of quality of life which comprises majority of the pillars of the GNH particularly the establishment of good governance associated with the power sharing in the context of the Tamil national question. The message from the people is very clear. That is, they are poor or disadvantaged or sick or do not consume good food or do not go to school not because they lack knowledge or rationality but because they do not have access to opportunities for enhancing their standard of lives and quality of lives. They lack these opportunities because they lack political, social and economic power.

Hence, the election results clearly show that a political solution is an utmost pre-condition in the post-war reconstruction and reconciliation process in Sri Lanka. However, it does not mean that a post-war reconstruction and reconciliation cannot be undertaken without a political solution, but they should be undertaken carefully and honestly with a real intention of creating a sustainable peace in parallel to the peace process.

The 'If' Argument and the Prerequisites

If the post-war reconstruction and reconciliation activities had been undertaken in a spirit of fair play and honesty during the last two years where there was a huge opportunity for such a task, the current situation would have been improved to a greater extent. People would have trusted the government, and subsequently the elections results also would have been at least to some extent positive to the government and there would have been a positive situation where there is great extent of mutual understanding and mutual trust. In turn, such a situation would have created a congenial environment to advance with the peace talks. Neither of them has happened yet, and consequently, proper and genuine post-war reconstruction and reconciliation process remains as the prerequisite to the efforts for political solution at this point of time.

Throughout this discussion, it was observed that both political solution and post-war reconciliation do remain as the interrelated prerequisites to each other. That means, the political solution becomes a meaningful prerequisite for post-war reconstruction and reconciliation. In the same manner, as noted earlier a genuine post-war reconstruction and reconciliation can also be considered as the prerequisite of a genuine political solution. However, in the case of Sri Lanka, as observed neither of these requisites has been successfully fulfilled and this situation has moved the situation further into critical. If there was an honest post-war reconstruction and reconciliation process, it would have led to a situation where there is now a huge extent of happiness and prosperity and would have resulted positively towards a peaceful political solution. In other words, if there was an acceptable political solution suggested to Tamil people, now there would have been a meaningful post-war reconciliation reconstruction taking place. Truly, there was a great opportunity with government to propose a fair and acceptable political solution soon after the end of military conflict. If such a political solution had been proposed soon after the end of war, even the Sinhala hardliners would have had nothing to say against it. But, the government missed the opportunity to propose such a political solution for petty party political reasons.

The current situation seems to be diminishing further between both sides with a shadow of suspicions and disbeliefs. This has further hardened the Tamil side's demand for justice against the war crimes committed during the final stage of the war and their national and transnational politics against the Sri Lankan government. Therefore, as observed above, there is no sufficient fulfilment in both prerequisites to move forward in either direction at this point of time. It is in this deadlock scenario that the contribution of the international community becomes vital and is one of the utmost responsibilities of the international community.

The Duplicity of the International Community

The international community was solemnly silent; when the government of Sri Lanka's discriminated practices agitated the Sinhala-Tamil non-violent conflict in the 1950s, 1960s, 1970s and then it was converted into the form of violent in 1970s. Also, the international community did not do anything when there were more than 40,000 people killed by the Sri Lankan government during the final war in 2009 (UN War Crime Report, 2011: 40–41). In 2005, the tsunami killed the same amount (nearly 40,000) of people in Sri Lanka (Haviland, 2011). The only difference is that the former is a man-made disaster and the latter is the natural disaster. The natural disaster cannot be stopped from happening, but a man-made disaster can be stopped from happening. The international community quickly responded to the tsunami disaster and assistance came from all parts of the world to the Sri Lankan people. They did receive direct assistance from the international community. But, unfortunately, there was not any interference from the international community to stop this man-made disaster during which more than 40,000 people were killed in front of the eyes of the international community. Even after the end of this man-made disaster, the international community failed to step in to directly assist and support the victims of this man-made disaster.

The co-chair countries such as Norway, Japan, US and EU that had been got involved in the Sri Lankan peace process with the aim of bringing a political solution to the Sri Lankan civil conflict simply stepped aside from their involvement after the end of military conflict without accomplishing their responsibility of mooting a political solution. Unfortunately, this shows the duplicity of the involvement of the international community in the Tamil national question.

Still there is a great opportunity for the international community to get involved in the Sri Lankan civil conflict and contribute to bring a just and sustainable solution before the constantly moving conflict cycle turns into second phase of violent. The current allegations of the war crimes against the Sri Lankan government to a great extent can be used well by the international community to moot a fair and sustainable political solution.

Conclusion

The discussion of this paper clearly demonstrates that the current post-war reconstruction, rehabilitation and reconciliation process does not carry any hope or potential of creating a congenial situation in which to achieve a sustainable peace and create a better and more stable future for Tamils in Sri Lanka. Instead, the activities and the programmes that are taking place in the northeast have failed and proved more harmful to the ideal creation of post-war prosperity and happiness and created a deadlock scenario in which progress is conditioned.

The discussion identifies two reasons for this situation. Firstly, the rationality of the discussion of this paper clearly identifies the lack of willingness and genuinity of the Sri Lankan government. Secondly, the scanning of the post-war reconstruction process through the qualitative conceptual GNH review finds the lack of clear integrated post-war reconstruction, rehabilitation and reconciliation strategy built on "standard of living" and "quality of life". This qualitative conceptual GNH review clearly identifies the weaknesses and the shortcomings of the current post-war reconstruction process in the context of "standard of living" and "quality of life".

In turn, the application of this qualitative conceptual GNH review in this discussion shows the relevance and the prospective merits of integrating the GNH principles into the post-conflict/war reconstruction process and developing an index system for measuring the level of the progress of "prosperity" and "happiness" in the post-conflict/war societies. So that, the practical application of the GNH integrated post-conflict reconstruction programmes and policies can be directed and guided in targeted and right manner.

Recommendation

The current situation is that it is only through presenting a reasonable and acceptable political solution that a genuine and meaningful post-war reconstruction can be moved forward towards a sustainable peace in Sri Lanka. But, such a political solution seems a long process at this point of time and uncertainty exists at high level given the described nature of the happenings on the ground.

Nevertheless, relief and assistance to the war-affected people cannot be delayed until that time. There is a pressing need to take immediate steps to embark on a comprehensive programme of resettlement, rehabilitation and reconstruction in the North and East. This can only be done by establishing an interim international assistance mechanism through which Tamil Diaspora organisations and International Development Organisations should be directly able to engage in aiding the resettlement, rehabilitation and reconstruction process. Establishing such a mechanism is a must and an urgent necessity to improve the conditions of the existence of the war-affected people of North and East. This responsibility relies in the hands of the United Nations and the co-chair countries (Norway, Japan, US and EU) that got involved in the Tamil national question. In turn, such an assistance mechanism under the supervision of UN/international community arrangement will greatly assist in advancing and consolidating the negotiation process.

References

Alkire, S., M.E. Santos and E. Ura, "Gross National Happiness and Poverty in Bhutan: Applying the GNH Index Methodology to Explore Poverty", http://www.ophi.org.uk/wp-content/uploads/OPHI-RP-4a.pdf?cda6c1, 2008.

BBC News, "Human Rights Watch Condemns 'draconian' Sri Lankan laws", 8 September 2011. http://www.bbc.co.uk/news/ world-south-asia-14839493, 2011.

BBC Sinhala Service, "Government 'trying to change' Demography", 2 August, 2010. http://www.bbc.co.uk/sinhala/news/story/ 2010/08/ 100802_north_resettlement.shtml, 2010(b).

BBC Sinhala Service, "Government 'trying to change' Demography", 2 August 2011. http://www.bbc.co.uk/sinhala/news/ story/2010/08/ 100802_north_resettlement.shtml, 2011(a).

Centre for Bhutan Studies, "9 Domains", http://www.grossnational-happiness.com/9–domains/

Cheru, F., *African Renaissance: Roadmaps to the Challenge of Globalization,* London: Zed., 2002.

Clarance, W., "Conflict and Community in Sri Lanka", *History Today,* Vol. 52, Issue 7. http://www.historytoday.com/ william-clarance/ conflict-and-community-sri-lanka, 2002.

Collier, P. et al., *Breaking the Conflict Trap: Civil War and Development, Policy*. Washington, DC: World Bank, 2003.

Cottam, H.R. and A.R. Mangus, "Proposed Definition of Standard of Living", *Social Forces*, Vol. 21, No. 2, pp. 177–79, 1942.

Curcio, C., "A New Economic Measure of the Standard of Living: Ranking US Metropolitan Areas", Duquesne University, 2005.

Dailymirror, "National Anthem should be Sung in Tamil in North and East", 9 December 2011. http://www.dailymirror.lk/news/15353–national-anthem-should-be-sung-in-tamil-in-north-and-east-.html.

Fraenkel, J.R. and N.E. Wallen, *How to Design and Evaluate Research*, New York: McGraw-Hill, 1990.

Groundviews, "The Desecration of Graves in Jaffna: Path to Reconciliation?", 8 March 2011. http://groundviews.org/2011/03/08/the-desecration-graves-in-jaffna-path-of-reconciliation/

Groundviews, "Female Ex-combatants of LTTE in Post-war Sri Lanka", 24 February 2012. http://groundviews.org/2012/02/24/female-ex-combatants-of-ltte-in-post-war-sri-lanka/

Haviland, C., "Have More Children, Police Hinted", *BBC News*, Colombo, 21 November 2011. http://www.bbc.co.uk/sinhala/ news/story/2011/11/111121_budget_police.shtml

ICG, "Sri Lanka's North II: Rebuilding under the Military", *Asia Report N°220,* 16 March 2012. http://www.crisisgroup.org/~/media/Files/asia/south-asia/sri-lanka/220–sri-lankas-north-ii-rebuilding-under-the-military.pdf

Indian Express, "LTTE Totally Destroyed: Sri Lanka", 25 May 2009. http://www.indianexpress.com/news/ltte-totally-destroyed-sri-lanka/465483/

Investopediya, "Standard of Living vs. Quality of Life", 20 October 2001. http://www.investopedia.com/articles/financial-theory/08/standard-of-living-quality-of-life.asp#axzz1pZXisxf1

Kenworthy, L., "Middle America's Standard of Living", 2001. http://www.u.arizona.edu/~lkenwor/indv102livingstandards.pdf

Manners, I., "Article name", in *Strategies for Peace: Contributions of International Organisations, States, and Non-State Actors*, Volker Rittberger and Martina Fischer (eds.), Leverkusen Opladen: Barbara Budrich-Esser, 2008.

Melkote, S.R. and K. Kandath, *Critical Issues in Communication*, New Delhi: Sage Publications, 2001.

Ministry of Finance and Planning of Sri Lanka, "Budget Speech" 2007, 2008, 2009, 2010, 2010, 2012, http://www.treasury.gov.lk/index.php?option=com_content&view=article&id=78&Itemid=141

NEPAD Secretariat, "African Post-Conflict Reconstruction Policy Framework, Governance, Peace and Security Programme", June, 2005, available at http://www.nepad.org/2005/aprwforum/PCRPolicy Framework_en.pdf

Pupavac, V., "Humanitarian Politics and the Rise of International Disaster Psychology", in G. Reyes and G.A. Jacobb (eds.), *Handbook of International Disaster Psychology: Fundamentals and Overview*, Praeger Publications, 2006.

Sivapragasam, P., "From Stateless to Citizenship: Upcountry Tamils in Sri Lanka", in B.K. Blitz and M. Lynch (eds.), *Statelessness and the Benefits of Citizenship: A Comparative Study*, Oxford: Oxfor Brookes University, 2009. http://www.udhr60.ch/report/statelessness_paper 0609.pdf

TamilNet, "NGOs Consider Withdrawing from Vanni as Sri Lanka Tightens Restrictions", 23 July 2010. http://www.tamilnet.com/art.html?catid=13&artid=32281

Thinley, J.Y., "What Does Gross National Happiness (GNH) Mean?", The Second International Conference on Gross National Happiness, Rethinking Development, Local Pathways to Global Well-being, St. Francis Xavier University, Antigonish, Nova Scotia, Canada, 2005.

UN War Crime Report, *Report of the Secretary-General's Panel of Experts on Accountability in Sri Lanka*, 2011. http://www.un.org/News/dh/infocus/Sri_Lanka/POE_Report_Full.pdf

Ura, Karma, GNH Methodology. http://www.grossnationalhappiness.com/gnhIndex/intruductionGNH.aspx

Weliamuna, J.C., "Sri Lanka: Lifting of Emergency – Exposing the Sham Exercise?" AHRC-ART-054–201, 2011. http://www.globalpeacesupport.com/globalpeacesupport.com/post/2011/09/19/SRI-LANKA-Lifting-of-Emergency-Exposing-the-sham-exercise.aspx

World Bank, *Post-Conflict Reconstruction: The Role of the World Bank*, Washington: The International Bank for Reconstruction and Development, 1998.

11

Sino-Japanese Reconciliation from a Peace Studies Perspective

LIU CHENG

In terms of practical significance and historical importance, the Sino-Japanese relationship ought to play just as dominant a role in China's foreign relations as Sino-American ties. For a considerable period of time now the Chinese government has attached great importance to improving and reinforcing the Sino-Japanese relationship, not only on account of the importance of the bilateral trade between the two nations, but also because building a good friendship between China and Japan is necessary for a more stable and peaceful Far East. For this reason, Chinese scholars have paid much attention to Sino-Japanese relations, especially at times when the two countries' relations have been tense. For example, in 2003, Professor Shi Yinhong of China's Renmin University in Beijing, concerned about the worsening state of Sino-Japanese relations, published an article entitled "the Sino-Japanese Diplomatic Approach and the 'Diplomatic Revolution.'"[1] His article put forward the idea of a Sino-Japanese diplomatic approach, which emphasised that the Chinese government should take a stance whereby paying a small price in terms of diplomatic concessions would enable both sides to realise a "Diplomatic Revolution." Thus, by looking at the problem by taking international relations and international strategy into consideration, China has no reason to "shut the door" on a closer relationship with Japan. Like the dispute over Taiwan which mars Sino-American ties, Japan's aggressive war against China during the 1930s and '40s has cast a long shadow over the current Sino-Japanese relationship. In the same way that Sino-American relations cannot reach the next level without a proper solution to the Taiwan issue, so the Sino-Japanese relationship, affected by the consequences of the war of aggression against China, is still far from stable. However, China's stance on Japan's former aggression is in a completely different category compared to that of the Taiwan issue. The latter demonstrates a strong attitude by the Chinese government, because the government has time and time again shown the impossibility of giving up sovereignty over Taiwan in exchange for closer Sino-American ties, even as the Chinese side acknowledges certain adjustments could be made to existing policies. Therefore, any Sino-American "Diplomatic Revolution's" success or failure is probably more dependant on changes in the international arena, and especially the attitude of the United States. However, when considering the requisite changes needed for a Sino-Japanese "Diplomatic Revolution", China has played an active part in enunciating the requirements, mainly because the former aggression has touched on national sentiment, which is very important but still less significant than national sovereignty. National sentiment is closely related to the collective memory of the Chinese nation, and in this case the ferocity of the Japanese imperial army has been branded on the Chinese people's memory. This memory has been kept current from generation-to-generation through persistent efforts of the media and other government propaganda. Therefore, as far as China is concerned, two elements should be considered if a Sino-Japanese "Diplomatic Revolution" is to be launched, namely the attitude of the Chinese government and the Chinese people. In other words, can the government stop using the propaganda it has become accustomed to using? Could the Chinese people forgive and forget the atrocities committed by the Japanese army? These two questions focus on core issues in the relationship and thus form preconditions for a Sino-Japanese diplomatic approach which results in a "Diplomatic Revolution."

II

Initially we should discuss the first question: the element of government. Propaganda and education conducted by the Chinese government over many years, commemorating the national humiliation of being invaded, has frequently been linked with nationalism. Whilst economic modernisation is an overwhelming objective for present-day China, at this stage of development the state has to resort to rallying the people in order that all possible resources can be redeployed for that modernisation. The nation-state is the most convenient tool by which these resources can be redeployed and nationalism forms one banner under which the public is mobilised. The term "nation" belongs to a specific historical category, the outcome of which is human development at a certain historical stage. For much of history, the term "nation" was an ambiguous term. Its current connotations did not appear until relatively recently, when the term was combined with that of the word "state," which then gave birth to a self-realisation of the concept of a "nation-state," thus naturally producing and swelling the spirit of nationalism. Nationalism, in fact, triggered the earliest industrial modernisation, and observing the countries that modernised and industrialised first, it can be seen that, without exception, they all raised the banner of nationalism at some time or another. Thus, Britain, the United States and Japan, impelled by nationalism, achieved advanced industrial status ahead of other nations. In these cases, as soon as the target of modernisation was realised, nationalism rapidly lost its meaning, the most remarkable example of which is the foundation of the European Union (EU).

In imperial times China long accepted the notion of a "world" that was centred on the Han civilisation, but in modern times she has slowly developed "nationalism". Traditionally, China possessed a strong sense of cultural superiority, in the form of a "kingdom of heaven" within the Chinese civilisation, and "savage" uncivilised tribes beyond it. When the concept of the kingdom of heaven was prevalent, it was virtually impossible to nurture a strong sense of nationalism, because "China" did not exist as we think of her today in the form of a nation state. On the contrary, China as "all under heaven" could only perpetuate a closed mindset which blindly excluded other ideas and innovations. As a result of the self-centred introspective Chinese world view, the concept of a nation-state formed slowly in modern China. Furthermore, because modernisation did not have a proper framework to start from, the disparities with modernised western pioneers increased. Ultimately, China's closed door was burst open by western guns during the Opium Wars (1840–42, 1856–60). The ancient "China-centred" dream was washed away by the Great Powers with blood and fire. Humiliated in this way, since the 1911 Revolution China realised that it was a political entity with limited power in a diversified world dominated by modernised western powers. Therefore, at this time a national identity as we think of it in the modern sense came into being, and simultaneously Chinese modernisation started, slowly and with great difficulty, almost two hundred years later than in European and North American countries. From then on, nationalism became the most efficient tool for Chinese modernisation. Those who lifted the banner of nationalism won the support and adherence of all the peoples of China. As a latecomer to modernisation, and in its progress towards it, China has been forced to strengthen and hasten modernisation under both internal and external stresses. Consequently, nationalism only came to prominence relatively recently. How is people's nationalism aroused? Practice has shown that the most efficient way to indoctrinate the Chinese masses about nationalism is by extolling the glorious history of China and revealing her humiliating past. As an example of the former, the Chinese people have always been proud of China's "four great inventions;" as an example of the latter the Chinese people have also extolled the virtues of the success of "people's volunteers" in the Korean War (1950–53). Yet it was Japanese aggression towards China, and especially the Nanjing Massacre committed by the Japanese army, that provided the most vivid "material" for the Chinese government to inspire the people to learn by heart.

How does nationalism interact with or affect Sino-Japanese relations? Since Reform and Opening Up started in 1978, China and Japan have made great advances in terms of increasing political contacts, promoting economic and trade cooperation, and building cultural exchange. Yet because nationalism is an inspiring and useful means of enhancing China's modernisation, the Chinese government will not stop criticising Japan's aggression towards China until modernisation is accomplished; nor will China cease propagating and educating the masses that it is patriotic to take precautions from history; it is right for the Chinese not to ignore Japanese prime ministerial visits to the Yasukuni Shrine; and that China cannot disregard distorted commentary in Japanese history textbooks. Because of these complex recurring issues in the bilateral relationship, Sino-Japanese cooperation and amity is always at risk. Under the leadership of the Chinese Communist Party (CCP), new China has modernised rapidly partly as a result of the inspiration from nationalism. After striving for six decades, Chinese modernisation has achieved many accomplishments that it can be rightly proud of, with some cities, such as Shenzhen and Shanghai realising modernisation extremely rapidly. Thus, the present-day China is very close to its objective of complete modernisation. China's modernisation has developed to a relatively higher degree and comprehensive economic power apparently becomes stronger. Within the current wave of globalisation, further development of China's economy will naturally rely upon the development of the world's economy as well, because domestic drivers of an economy as open as China's are not enough to propel economic growth. It is inevitable that China will remain an active member of the World Trade Organisation (WTO) in order to that the economy continues to develop. As the impetus in the initial stage of modernisation has decreased, nationalism has gradually lost its ability to inspire in parallel with the advance of modernisation. Therefore current day China can now consider the possibility of weakening (actually some actions have been taken) the propaganda and education that encourage the nationalistic attitude, and turn instead to other problem-solving mechanisms to enforce international law. Additionally, the Chinese government could gradually lessen the emphasis on the issue of former Japanese aggression, which would then offer an opportunity for a Sino-Japanese diplomatic approach and a "Diplomatic Revolution". However, if the Japanese government is unwilling to thoroughly reflect on its barbarities, the idea of toning down the Chinese government's nationalistic propaganda would almost certainly be slowed down.

III

In fact, nationalist sentiment in China is not only generated by the government, but there is also the new phenomenon of "e-nationalism" (nationalism on the internet). Internet-nationalists are actually fiercer than the government in their condemnation of the Japanese, and it is true that they would like to provoke the government into taking a stronger anti-Japanese stance. Normally the Chinese government prefers to settle political issues by negotiation as it helps the long-term economic development, but this is not the case in the Sino-Japanese relationship because of the poison from Japanese actions during the war. How can I explain it? In my opinion, the reason is that most Chinese cannot separate the bitter historical relationship with militarist Japan from the current day problems with the Republic of Japan. So, apart from the government, the question is whether the Chinese people are willing to forgive the past, which, as mentioned above is another essential element of the Sino-Japanese approach needed for a "Diplomatic Revolution". In a general sense, most people ought to be willing to forget their past sufferings and start afresh. However, in the Chinese people's mind, the barbarities committed by the invading Japanese army on Chinese soil have shaped the Chinese masses' image of Japan as an enemy and this cannot be easily erased. Once a specific representation has been formed in a certain country or society, it usually becomes fixed. Research in social psychology, cultural anthropology, international relations and comparative politics has indicated that even when lacking reliable evidence to convince hostile intention, individuals and groups tend to form and maintain a certain image of the enemy.[2] The enemy image embodies a kind of extremely disgusting emotional element. This is the reason why people tenaciously cling to the established image (of Japan as an invading enemy) while very few Chinese people are likely to seek new information about their former enemy. The image so fixed in people's minds causes hostile reactions, and in return increases the possibility of an antagonistic approach from the opposite side too. This cycle of interactive hostile reactions exacerbates the opponents' image of each other.[3]

In the present climate everyone would like to talk about the agonies that they or their families suffered. What is meaningful to them is the deliberation and debate that has ensued the collective disaster: massacre – a controversial problem in academic circles, too. Should justice have priority or should forgiveness be most important? Of course, there has been no authoritative answer to date, which is why contemporary Sino-Japanese relations are still bedeviled by the history problem.

The noted Japanese scholar on Chinese Studies Professor Mizoguchi Osumi once proposed another way to interpret the memories of misery (sic) between China and Japan, hoping that Chinese people would forgive Japan on the basis of understanding Japan.[4] In general, when talking about this sensitive issue, scholarly thought is generally impartial and even indifferent. However, for common people who endured the Japanese slaughter it is extremely difficult to erase these miserable recollections and hostile feelings. Even scholars themselves are not immune to the influence of public opinion in their own country. If a scholar is from a nation which has indulged in wanton massacre and persecution, then in writing about these events he or she is very likely to be tormented by emotional sentiments. This is the main reason why Chinese and Japanese intellectuals are less likely to agree on ways to resolve the history problem, and this is also an important reason why Professor Shi Yinhong's article received intense scrutiny.

Undoubtedly, to remember the past does not mean that both sides have to bear eternal grudges. Whatever the nature of the calamity, what has been lost in disasters, invasions or massacres will never return, just as the dead can never be brought back. Generally speaking, the key to building friendship between two sides who were formerly enemies is not to focus on the past all the time, but to extinguish the hatred of revenge and extend forgiveness to the enemy. In his book *The Human Condition,* Hannah Arendt points out that "forgiving serves to undo the deeds of the past, whose 'sins' hang like Damocles's sword over every new generation."[5] Marc Gopin considers that forgiveness might introduce a new life to those who have long suffered misery, because in practice this may be more effective than continuing to recall losses and punishing war criminals.[6] South African Bishop Tutu also made it clear that it is possible to "have a future with forgiveness."[7]

The question we now have to consider is whether forgiveness needs one or more presuppositions. The purpose of forgiveness is to become reconciled, therefore the presuppositions of forgiveness are firstly that the people believe that the hostile violator is punished, and secondly that both individual and group pains or hurts are cured. Only when these happen can people look to the future, rather than cling to the pains and hatred of the past. If the wrongdoer tries to avoid or even cover up the past crimes, how can the victims be asked to forgive and forget?

Simon Winsenthal told the following story in his book *The Sunflower*: a Schutzstaffel who had participated in a massacre action on Jews was dying. In his last moments he desired forgiveness from Simon Winsenthal, who was a former prisoner in a concentration camp, but he was refused. For a long time this matter had occupied the author's mind. Should Winsenthal forgive the Schutzstaffel? Twenty years later, *The Sunflower* was reedited and published and included new articles, responses to the book collected by the author from 32 contemporary celebrities. These articles discussed questions about the extent of forgiveness, such as whether repentance alone was sufficient for forgiveness and whether it was possible to forgive but not forget. To the readers' surprise, almost all the celebrities agreed that Winsenthal had the right not to forgive the Schutzstaffel. "Forgiving is a kind of virtue, but butchering the innocent is an unforgivable crime." Someone even held the opinion that "forgiving is ruthless. Forgiveness seems very mild apparently, but it is rather ruthless for those who were slain."[8]

Certainly, forgiveness is an important factor in the progression towards reconciliation. However, it does not necessarily mean that crimes must be pardoned or that one has to close one's eyes to barbarities. One may extend forgiveness while seeking justice, but one also has the right to keep requesting that somebody claim legal responsibility for the crimes or anti-social behaviour.[9] Indeed, forgiveness is a kind of virtue, but is not cheap. Without real repentance, evil cannot be counteracted by righteousness. Any side involved in a conflict has its own history to contend with, and it will never lightly write-off collective memories of a conflict that have formed a part of its identity. However, in order to ensure the

Invading side's memories do not create barriers for future reconciliation, the critical step for their own people is to learn to acknowledge "the truth of past." This is an interactive process as we review history from a different perspective. This is also the foundation of seeking common ground while allowing for differences. If forgiveness truly exists then it needs to include the acknowledgment of past and present memories. More importantly, only when the people believe the past nightmare will not be repeated and when things are progressing in the right direction, can they be relieved from the past painful memories, have their rage pacified, forgive the antagonistic side, and place hope in the future. However, the Republic of Japan has completely abandoned her passive attitude that she strove towards during the Cold War. Her military expenditure is obviously higher than that of other countries apart from America. Worse, legislatively, she has broken her own peaceful constitution, by changing Japan's defensive strategy on the use of armaments to an offensive strategy. For example, Japan's self-defense corps has three times as many tanks as Britain's and a fleet of warships twice as large as the UK.[10] Meanwhile, Japan has been trying to cover its guilt of launching the invasion against China in the 1930s. The Japanese Prime Minister has also turned a deaf ear to the protests of the Chinese, Korean and other Asian peoples, and the clauses in the 1978 *"Sino-Japanese Agreement for Peace and Friendship,"* by insisting on visiting the Yasukuni Shrine (where the souls of Class A Japanese war criminals are enshrined) several times. All these, together with the glorified and distorted records of the aggression in Japanese school history textbooks, are totally unacceptable to the Chinese people. They are not conducive to the removal of the memories of the Japanese invasion still imprinted on the minds of the Chinese people, but they would rather, intensify their anti-Japanese sentiments.

IV

Because long-term China needs to improve its own strategic situation and interests, Professor Shi Yinhong (mentioned at the start of this article) insists firstly on substantially improving Sino-Japanese relations, and secondly on exerting greater effort to attempt a Sino-Japanese centred approach. All known that in the history of international relations, there is no eternal enemy but rather, an eternal interest. Starting from this point, the two Chinese scholars' new reflections upon Japan have emerged completely from the "eternal interest" of China.

However, the main problem is that China's basic interests depend on the degree of Chinese modernisation and development, and therefore both Sino-Japanese ties and Sino-American diplomacy have to comply with and serve this basic interest. As mentioned above, the Chinese government could weaken its nationalistic propaganda (which it has done to some extent already). On May 31, 2003, in St Petersburg, Hu Jintao and Japanese leaders held their dialogue. Although this meeting didn't achieve any agreement in a substantial sense, it showed that the Chinese government held a positive attitude towards Japan. The meeting also displayed the CCP's grace and pragmatism, and even took into consideration Prime Minister Koizumi's visits to the Yasukuni Shrine; these visits being a symbol of reversing the previous judgment of Japanese aggression by Japanese right-wing factions. However, China has not achieved modernisation yet, and is still economically far behind the developed countries, so it has to adopt the developing mode of "sleeping on brushwood and tasting gall" for a period, patriotism should not be abandoned, and nationalism should not be given up. What's more, the diplomatic policy does not exist in a vacuum, rather it is a continuous process, which means that it is impossible to break away from the past. Fundamental adjustments to Sino-Japanese ties will be a long-term interactive process, rather than a decisive breakthrough achieved in a short time. At present, to start and press for Sino-Japanese strategic dialogue and military communication, and create a favourable political and security situation, it is critical to achieve Sino-Japanese strategic reconciliation and cooperation in the twenty-first century. But a continuously pro-active improvement in China's policy toward Japan should be accompanied by a quickening in the pace of Chinese modernisation. China's modernisation needs Chinese people to work together with one heart. As the planner and director of the nation's modernisation, the Chinese government also requires the inspiring and uniting power of nationalism. In other words, the Chinese government may gradually dampen the memory of being trampled by the Japanese but cannot be required to not bring that part of history to our attention. A couple of years ago, during discussions as to whether the name "Memorial Hall of the Victims in Nanjing Massacre by Japanese Invaders" should be changed, some people advised that it be called an "International Peace Centre" instead, yet most people were resolutely opposed to altering the name. The reason is simple. It is because at the present time nationalism is still an essential condition for Chinese modernisation. "Forget not how we have been shamed" is still an important motto used to inspire the Chinese masses. Even when studying twenty-first century globalisation, nationalism might fade away with the declining of a nation-state, but saying this just now, just as Eric Hobsbawm pointed out, is obviously absurd.[11] Nevertheless, the question itself reflects that the Chinese government and people's attitude has been transformed on the issue of the Japanese invasion. Professor Shi and other Chinese scholars' new thoughts on the foreign policy toward Japan provide good examples. The Japanese government should know and understand this and thus make active responses to assist Chinese modernisation.

Uncomfortable memories left by history on any nation are extremely hard to erase. In Japan, on the sixth and ninth of August every year, activities held in order to commemorate the detonation of atomic bombs over Hiroshima and Nagasaki are good examples of this. Of course, America's bombing of atomic bombs on Japan and Japan's invasion of Asian countries during World War Two are obviously issues of a different kind. According to certain recent scholars, the former was a righteous war fought against evil powers, while the latter was an unjust war which should be condemned by all mankind. Hence, it needs a long process of combined effort to erase the disastrous collective memory left by the Japanese invasion. Being the wrongdoer in this historic period, it would be reasonable for the Japanese to have a proactive and constructive attitude. As it has been proved, without the Chinese people's forgiveness of the Japanese invasion, there can be no long-lasting, stable and harmonious Sino-Japanese relations, nor can success take root without the people's fundamental support for the Sino-Japanese approach and "Diplomatic Revolution". Chinese people should look to the future, gradually extinguishing the emotional flames of anger, and reconstruct good Sino-Japanese relations. More importantly, the Japanese government and people should make greater efforts to gain the forgiveness of the Chinese people. There is no reconciliation without forgiveness, but forgiveness cannot lose its appeal to justice and its anticipation of truth. In a word, Sino-Japanese relations should follow the principles of "taking history as a warning" and "facing the future," in that the former is a precondition of the latter.

John Paul Lederach believes that *peace, truth, justice and mercy (or forgiveness)* are core elements of *reconciliation*. In fact, reconciliation is the process whereby these four elements are combined. Truth is the longing for acknowledgment of wrong and the validation of loss, which at the same time is coupled with mercy, which states a need for mutual acceptance, letting go, and hope for a new beginning. Justice is the pursuit of individual and group rights, as well as the pursuit of social reconstruction and restitution. However, justice is also linked with peace, which underscores the need for interdependence, well-being and security. Reconciliation is seen both as a process of encounters and also as a form of social space where people and things come together.[12] In a word, reconciliation is made through the two sides' efforts for a creative realisation of conflict conversion.[13]

On June 12th 2003, the day following the Sino-Japan highest leaders' summit meeting, *Tokyo News* published an editorial claiming that this meeting was "the beginning of new Japan-Chinese relationship".[14] Indeed, Sino-Japanese relations should make a new breakthrough in the twenty-first century. As a neighbouring political power China is actually progressing towards becoming an economic power while Japan as an economic power is also striving for political power. In considering domestic interests or benefits for regional and even global stability, the Sino-Japanese gradual approach is very important. But this depends not only on the Chinese government, but also on the common people; likewise, it is dependant on the Japanese government and people as well.

In conclusion, fundamental improvements in the Sino-Japanese relationship and reconciliation of present conflicts between China and Japan should comply with the following principles. Firstly, both sides should endeavour to reinforce cooperation and solve issues together; secondly, they should strive for a regulated "win-win" target; and thirdly, they need to adopt peaceful methods, respecting and understanding each others interests.

Notes

1. *Journal of Strategy and Management,* Vol. 2, 2003.
2. Janice Gross Stein, "Image, Identity, and Conflict Resolution", in C.A. Crockerp and F.O. Hampson (eds.), *Managing Global Chaos: Sources of and Responses to International Conflict*, Washington, DC: US Institute of Peace, 1996, p. 94.
3. Dean G. Pruitt and Jeffrey Z. Rubin, *Social Conflict*, New York: McGraw-Hill, 1986, pp. 117–18.
4. *Journal of Du Shu*, Vol. 5, 2001, pp. 5–10.
5. Hannah Arendt, *The Human Condition,* New York: Doubleday Anchor, 1959, p. 213. Quoted from Andrew Rigby, *Justice and Reconciliation*, Boulder & London: Lynne Rienner Publishers, 2001, p. 12.
6. Marc Gopin, "Forgiveness as an Element of Conflict Resolution in Religious Culture", in M. Abu-Nimer (ed.), *Reconciliation, Justice and Co-Existence: Theory and Practice*, Lanham, MD: Lexington Books, 2001, p. 98.
7. Desmond Tutu, *No Future without Forgiveness*, Shanghai: Shanghai Wenyi Press, 2002, p. 213.
8. Simon Wiesenthal, *The Sunflower,* New York: Schocken Books Inc. This book was translated into Chinese by Tianjing Renmin Press in 1998.
9. Liu Cheng, *Peace Studies*, Nanjing Press, 2006, p. 42.
10. Yan Xue-Tong and Jin De-Xiang (eds.), *Peace and Security in East Asia*, Beijing: Shishi Press, 2005, pp. 272–44.
11. Eric Hobsbawm, *Nations and Nationalism Since 1780*, Shanghai: Shanghai Renmin Press, 2000, p. 224.
12. John Paul Lederach, *Building Peace: Sustainable Reconciliation in Divided Societies*, Washington, DC: United States Institute of Peace, 1997, pp. 29–30.
13. Peace studies in China started in 2000 when the cooperation was formally established between the World History Study Section at Nanjing University's History Department and the Centre for Peace and Reconciliation Studies in Coventry. Since 2002 several Chinese teachers have been dispatched annually to attend advanced peace

studies at Coventry University in England. Now there are three Peace studies courses for both bachelor and postgraduate students at Nanjing University. Additionally, in 2004 Nanjing University began recruiting peace studies' postgraduates and doctoral candidates. An undergraduate textbook entitled *Peace Studies* was issued in January 2006 (of which I am the author). To mark the formal start of peace studies and peace education in China, an international symposium on peace studies held in March, 2005 received much positive coverage and helped more Chinese comprehend the objectives of peace studies, thereby advancing peace teaching and research work which will hopefully be good news for the Sino-Japanese relationship.

14. http://www.nanfangdaily.com.cn/zm/20030612/xw/tx/200306121121.asp

12

Strait Talk

Activating Peace Potential in Youth-led Civil Society Dialogues Across the Taiwan Strait

TATSUSHI ARAI

This essay explores lessons learned from the ten week-long dialogues that the present author has facilitated since 2005 among young civil society delegates from Mainland China, Taiwan, and the United States.[1] Critical reflections on the repeated patterns of group dynamics demonstrated by fifteen delegates, five from each of the three societies carefully selected each year, reveal useful hypotheses as to how highly-educated young people on both sides of the Taiwan Strait experience: (a) contested worldviews on the history of cross-Strait relations, both experienced firsthand and inherited from past generations, (b) the negotiability of Chinese sovereignty, (c) the enduring relevance of their deep-rooted large-group identities and their emotional attachment to them, and (d) their capacity to empathise with each other, sometimes to the point of crossing boundaries of political correctness.

As demonstrated shortly, the emerging trends in cross-Strait relations – from the advent of direct two-way flights, to the growing number of tourists from both sides – provide an unprecedented opportunity for civil society exchange to deepen and expand. Weeklong conflict resolution dialogues among young delegates from Mainland China, Taiwan, and the United States in impartial American academic settings present a potentially useful model of cross-Strait relationship-building that may be replicated in the region and utilised to activate peace potential inherent in the deepening civil society ties between the two sides. At the same time, these dialogues also offer a unique window of opportunity through which one may observe how the young civil society delegates, who have grown up in the third to fourth generation of the Taiwanese and Mainland Chinese who had experienced the Chinese Civil War in the 1940s firsthand, negotiate the meanings of this historical conflict. Lessons learned from the ten cross-Strait dialogues, therefore, are likely to contain unique insights into the future of the conflict that may not appear frequently in the growing literature on the formal diplomatic relations over the Taiwan Strait.

To define the scope of this inquiry, two points deserve mention at its outset. First, the term 'civil society' is used here in its broadest sense. The concept commonly refers to realms of social interactions that are not led or coerced by the government or the forces of the market. This working definition is more of a vision of an ideal state than an empirical reality, especially in current cross-Strait relations regulated by the two governing authorities and driven by the forces of the market. The position adopted in this paper, however, is that despite all these constraints instituted by the government and the market, there exist emerging realms of people-to-people encounters whose intent and consequences may not be *reduced* to single-minded pursuits of official government agendas or market-driven, profit-seeking activities. Examples of such encounters include, but are not limited to, educational and scholarly exchange, voluntarily organised tourism, and exchanges in sports and arts. This study will focus on the dynamic, ever-changing nature of elastic boundaries of civil society's influence on both sides of the Strait, pushing and pulling the spheres of countervailing influence created by the government and the market. It will contextualise the on-going dialogues among young delegates within this broad conceptualisation of civil society, and attempt to draw potentially generalisable lessons.

The second point worth noting is the geographic scope of the analysis. The fifteen delegates undergoing the week-long dialogue include not only five Taiwanese and five Mainland Chinese representatives, but also five Americans committed to learning about this conflict and taking action to generate positive impact on cross-Strait relations. Although their contributions to the dialogues are significant, especially as informants of American society as a critical stakeholder in cross-Strait relations, this essay will view them in the supplementary background of the inquiry and place the two-party relations between Taiwan and Mainland China in the foreground, as a primary focus. This analytical focus is intended to keep the discussion manageable in scope while it also seeks to provide a basis for a future inquiry into the role of the US government, business communities, and civil society in cross-Strait relations.

With this scope of inquiry in mind, the discussion that follows will be organised in three parts. First, a brief overview of the history of the conflict will be presented, with emphasis on the most recent trends in cross-Strait grassroots exchange since 2008. Second, the rationale and the method of the initiative under study, which will be referred to as Strait Talk, will be outlined in an attempt to articulate a model of civil society exchange aspiring to activate peace potential underlying the emerging trends of people-to-people encounters. Third, a series of four working propositions, enumerated above as (a) to (d), will be discussed as they represent recurring themes in the dialogues that may hold a key to our understanding of the future of cross-Strait relations.

A Synopsis of the Conflict: In Search of Peace Potential in the Evolving Historical Context

The unique contribution that Strait Talk seeks to make in cross-Strait relations is explored in the macro-historical context of the conflict. Despite the unofficial, informal nature of the dialogue process, its participants, together with the present author as their facilitator, are constantly urged to confront the fundamental question that those holding the highest political positions on both sides have been grappling with for decades: *In a nutshell, what is this conflict about at its very core?* Part of the answer, informed by the cumulative experience of Strait Talk, is summarised as follows:

For Mainland China, the stated goal of reunification under One China ultimately finds its roots in the collective commitment to building and restoring a historical coherence of its nationhood and its inviolable territorial integrity. This commitment, in essence, is a search for a rightful place that the People's Republic of China (PRC) seeks to occupy and consolidate in the contemporary world, while at the same, it continuously strives to cope with both unforgettable historical traumas and glories that it is driven to re-enact in times of crisis and hardship. Such collective traumas, some more conspicuous than others, include the "Century of Humiliation" spanning from the mid-nineteenth century, when China lost the Opium War to the British and started falling on the slippery slope of Western and Japanese invasions and colonial exploitation.[2] The most salient national glories, on the other hand, include the establishment of PRC in 1949 under the Chinese Communist Party (CCP), having defeated the Japanese imperial army and driven out the Chinese Nationalist Party, or Kuomintang (KMT), from the mainland. Failure to achieve One China due to the independence movement in Taiwan – the island to which some two million KMT soldiers and followers had fled – would mean a failure to acknowledge CCP's historical victory in the civil war in the late 1940s. Such a failure, by implication, is tantamount to a denial of the rightful status of PRC, a state built on the unspeakable suffering and sacrifice sustained by its founders, who had paid the ultimate price to save their beloved motherland from colonialists, imperialists, and domestic oppressors.

From the Taiwanese perspective, the conflict is not only about the highly-popularised official positions such as reunification under One China, Taiwanese independence, and the status quo of the Taiwan-based Republic of China (ROC) maintaining the unsettled status of diplomatic ambiguity with the mainland. More fundamentally, the conflict is about how twenty-three million inhabitants of diverse ethnic and historical backgrounds – either immigrants from the mainland during the Chinese Civil War in the 1940s or descendants of historical Taiwanese communities that preceded the civil war – can choose their political future on their own, without interference from the mainland. While the search for a contemporary meaning of the Chinese Civil War and the flight of KMT leaders and followers to the island is still alive and will continuously evolve in the Taiwanese national consciousness, the distinct Taiwanese identity – or multiple Taiwanese identities, to be precise – that distinguish themselves from Mainland Chinese are more salient and decisive today than ever before in terms of shaping and reshaping their outlook of the nation's destiny. Because of such a decisive nature of their evolving local identities, many Taiwanese communities of diverse backgrounds – and most certainly the young Taiwanese delegates joining the Strait Talk dialogues – view CCP's reunification policy fundamentally incompatible with the Taiwanese reality on the ground and simply unrealistic. The historical evolution of Taiwanese multi-party democracy, its ever-deepening immersion in the Western-style free market, its dependency on the bilateral security ties with the United States, and the enduring legacy of Japanese colonialism and post-colonial ties have all contributed to crystallising distinct Taiwanese identities striving for freedom of political choice and greater security from perceived threats, imagined or real, from the mainland.

A deeper look into the root causes and dynamics of the conflict over the Taiwan Strait, along this line of thinking, invites us to transcend the oversimplified image of the conflict's essence, which is often reduced to a binary way of pursuing *either* Taiwanese independence *or* reunification under One China. A more fruitful way of exploring future scenarios opens up when we ask: How can we envision the kind of cross-Strait relations in which *both* the Mainland Chinese quest for coherent nationhood and territorial integrity on the one hand, *and* the Taiwanese aspiration for the freedom of political choice and security from perceived Chinese threats on the other, may be fulfilled at the same time? Put another way, what would an acceptable, sustainable mechanism of cross-Strait relations look like that can flexibly accommodate and effectively facilitate these parallel search processes until they come to a mutually respectful way of coexistence?[3] Week-long dialogues between young civil society delegates from both sides of the Strait, joined by their American counterparts, tackle these questions squarely in a way diplomats and government officials might have been unable or unwilling to tackle them. And here lies the significance of Strait Talk's visions and the unique method it employs, as elaborated shortly.

While the long-term, macro-historical trends outlined here contextualise the significance of civil society initiatives of this nature, more recent events in cross-Strait relations enable us to define their immediate focus. According to International Crisis Group (2005), since the late 1980s, when cross-Strait relations started opening up gradually, there have been over 210,000 marriages between the two societies, with 90,000 Mainland Chinese spouses living in Taiwan; Taiwanese tourists make over four million trips to China every year; about one million Taiwanese citizens, out of the entire population of twenty-three million, currently live in the mainland.

In May, 2008, Ma Ying-jeou won the presidential election as a KMT candidate in Taiwan. Ma replaced his predecessor, Chen Shui-bian, who had taken steps during his eight-year presidency to demonstrate Taiwan's readiness toward greater independence from the mainland, based on the backing of the Democratic Progressive Party (DPP), a major opponent of KMT. With KMT rule restored under Ma's leadership, the interactions between the two sides of the Strait have been accelerated at an unprecedented pace. In November 2008, for example, officials on both sides signed agreements that would increase the number of weekly round-trip charter flights to 108, from the previous level of 36, with flights departing daily. These flights link twenty-one cities in the mainland with eight cities in Taiwan. With the introduction of more efficient, improved routing, Taipei-Beijing flights are only two hours long, and Taipei-Shanghai, 80 minutes. Ordinary Chinese citizens are now free to travel to Taiwan as tourists, based on the new arrangement made between the two sides in July, 2008. Consequently, there has been an exponential growth in cross-Strait tourism as illustrated by the following table:

Table 12.1

Number of Mainland Chinese Visitors to Taiwan, 2008–2011[4]

Year	*Number of mainland visitors per year (million)*	*Number of mainland visitors daily*
2008	0.3	900
2009	1.0	2,600
2010	1.6	4,400
2011	1.8	4,900

This dramatic and steady increase in the number of Mainland Chinese visitors to Taiwan is but one visible sign of deepening cross-Strait ties, symptomatic of similar trends in such other realms as mail service, cargo shipments, art exhibits, and educational exchange. As Ma Ying-jeou was reelected as president in January 2012 for his second four-year term, KMT rule under his leadership is expected to sustain these trends for some time to come.

None of these commercial and civil society activities is intended to promote open discussions about how to solve the *political* conflict between the two sides. Yet lessons learned from historical peace processes in other parts of the world – from South Africa to Northern Ireland – suggest that the opening of civil society exchange, if carried out with a robust, sustainable mechanism, humanises each other's image, builds mutual trust, and increases the readiness at the grassroots level to deal non-violently with difficult political choices that will have to be made at the governmental level in the future. With such a long-term, macro-historical perspective – and with a time horizon of decades to generations in mind – what kind of sustained, well-organised civil society exchange across the Taiwan Strait will most effectively prepare the grassroots on both sides to be resilient to war and remain firm on a joint search for peaceful means, especially when the two sides need to face major political choices?

In search of a possible answer to this question, a vision advocated by Strait Talk has been to establish and institutionalise a safe and sustainable social space in which people on both sides can explore various future scenarios of non-violent coexistence that transcend the narrow definitions and static images of One China pitted against Taiwanese independence. Such a social space has to be well-orchestrated and robust enough to provide a sustainable platform of communication where *future scenarios challenging today's political boundaries and taboos can be explored open-mindedly and debated rigorously, and they can even sit for years, perhaps very uncomfortably*. An example of such gradual processes of sensitisation is found in the formerly unacceptable vision of a two-state solution now firmly embedded in Israel-Palestine relations. Such a social space may be replicated and multiplied at different levels of social interaction, including academia, business, tourism, and the media. Its primary function is to familiarise people on both sides with a broadening horizon of seemingly unconventional solutions. Strait Talk, however modest in its scope and influence, seeks to create at least one compelling model of such a social space, as demonstrated in the sections that follow.

Strait Talk: Its Rationale and Methodology

This ongoing dialogue process, Strait Talk, was first conceptualised and implemented in 2005 by student volunteers at Brown University in Rhode Island, USA, with a commitment to generating immediate impact, however preliminary, on stalemated civil society exchange across the Taiwan Strait.[5] It has been held every fall on the Brown campus, and since March, 2009, expanded to include an annual spring workshop at the University of California at Berkeley. Between 2005 and 2011, there have been ten workshops conducted, seven at Brown and three at Berkeley.

For each event, Strait Talk, which subsequently became a US-based non-profit organisation in 2008, recruits highly-qualified English-speaking undergraduate and graduate students, five from each of the three sides, through open advertisement and rigorous selection. Selected participants typically come from top-ranking universities. Special care is taken to assure diversity among them in terms of gender, regional background, and self-reported political orientations in each of the three societies. Selected participants usually include recent university graduates already working as young professionals – for example, as business consultants, lawyers, and journalists – who aspire to contribute to cross-Strait relations through their own professions. In the absence of sustainable official talks across the Taiwan Strait, especially before 2008, the vision of Strait Talk has been to bring together carefully-selected, highly-qualified young civil society delegates with significant academic and professional potential as "pre-influentials" – namely, people with the best chance of becoming influential contributors to such fields as civil society exchange, business, academia, and government service in a near future – for the purpose of week-long joint problem-solving and relationship-building.

The fifteen delegates go through up to forty hours of intensive confidential dialogue that seeks to create a safe and inviting atmosphere for an honest, authentic exchange of ideas and feelings. The dialogue incorporates comparative case studies,[6] in-depth conflict analysis, role reversal between parties, joint brainstorming of future visions, and the use of metaphors, rituals, and storytelling. The week-long dialogue is interwoven with occasional intervals featuring informal activities for socialisation, as well as speakers' series and expert panels on cross-Strait relations. Immediately after these public events, each of the speakers or panelists is invited to an additional small-group session that is usually open only to the fifteen delegates and the dialogue facilitator. The delegates may pose questions to these subject experts about pressing issues and controversies that they may have been debating in their conflict resolution dialogue. Because many of the invited speakers are established scholars with intimate knowledge of the issues under study, or senior practitioners with extensive hands-on experience in this conflict, these intimate small-group sessions provide delegates with an opportunity to do a reality check on their own conflict analyses and future visions that they are discussing in their own dialogue. This intentional effort to integrate the two parallel tracks of learning – confidential problem-solving dialogue *and* consultations with subject experts and senior practitioners – is arguably a unique contribution that Strait Talk aspires to make to the methodology of interactive conflict resolution.[7]

Though the dialogue process itself is confidential to create a safe, inviting atmosphere, its immediate end results include producing a final consensus document with concrete proposals for the future of cross-Strait relations. The final consensus document, which typically consists of political/security, economics, and cultural/civil society components, is presented by the fifteen delegates in a public forum at the end of the event and made available for broader circulation afterwards.[8]

In addition to generating final consensus documents that articulate macro visions of long-term social change, Strait Talk delegates are also invited to form multi-national groups, usually three to four participants each, in order to jointly design small-scale grassroots initiatives that they can start implementing immediately after the workshop, with or without extra funding. These initiatives, referred to as peace projects, vary greatly in scope and content. Recent examples include campus seminars to share the participants' Strait Talk experiences in their respective societies, an interview project that documents and juxtaposes experiences of those who experienced the Chinese civil war on both sides, a high school student exchange across the Strait, and a facilitated dialogue that applies the methodology of Strait Talk to social issues that matter within the participants' own society. Importantly, these peace projects have been used to keep the growing network of Strait Talk alumni engaged, both within each society and across the three sides.

Finally, Strait Talk's contribution to the theory and practice of interactive conflict resolution (ICR) is explored. Following Saunders (2000: 225), ICR is defined as "a well-defined and systematic approach used in small unofficial meetings of persons in tension or violent conflict to stimulate their task together about the problems that divide the groups they identify with and the relationships that underlie those problems."

Among a number of different functions that ICR has been used to practice, Strait Talk focuses on the following three:[9]

1. *Relationship-building*:[10] This task is achieved by bringing potential youth leaders from the two sides of the Taiwan Strait, along with their American counterparts, and forming informal tri-national networks for sustainable relationship-building.
2. *Capacity-building*:[11] This task consists of introducing basic skills in conflict analysis and resolution through exercises of experiential learning and encouraging the participants to practice the acquired skills in their peace projects and other contexts.
3. *Learning and transfer of new insights for long-term macro social change*:[12] This process involves enabling the participants to learn new ways of understanding and tackling the cross-Strait conflict and assisting them in their long-term application of new insights to influence a broader scope of stakeholders through final consensus documents, public presentations, peace projects, and their own vocational commitments.

As a youth-led civil society movement, Strait Talk is primarily concerned with relationship-building (Function 1). As a secondary goal, it provides opportunities for capacity-building (Function 2). Its contribution to policy-oriented learning and its immediate transfer to influential decision makers (Function 3), on the other hand, is limited in scope because its participants, as university students and young professionals, are not engaged in policymaking or large-scale social change. Learning and transfer, therefore, is a long-term aspirational goal of Strait Talk.

Having described the expected impact and scope of Strait Talk with pragmatism, it must also be emphasised that this movement of civil society exchange and relationship-building that started in 2005, against the backdrop of China's anti-secession law, is far from insignificant. A less tangible and conspicuous meaning of this exercise comes to light when one recognises that Strait Talk, as of 2005, was most probably the only application of ICR for an in-depth discussion on the cross-Strait conflict. With the expansion of cross-Strait interactions in business, education, and cultural affairs since 2008, the year in which Ma Ying-jeou assumed presidency in Taiwan, the social climate has shifted noticeably in favour of the kind of civil society exchange that Strait Talk had advocated since 2005. Consistent with the political atmosphere of détente, there has since been a steady presence of Chinese Communist Party members joining each of the Strait Talk dialogues held at Brown University and the University of California at Berkeley. Moreover, Strait Talk held the first dialogue in Hong Kong in 2011 based on the preparation carried out by a mainland participant in the 2009 Berkeley dialogue. This Hong Kong dialogue, in turn, inspired its Taiwanese participants to initiate a Taipei-based Strait Talk symposium, which is due to take place in 2012. Strait Talk has thus grown into a civil society movement comprising four concurrent annual dialogues that take place in the United States, Mainland China, and Taiwan.[13]

Conceptually, Strait Talk represents a social experiment in which a growing number of highly motivated young citizens across the Taiwan Strait engage in relationship-building through ICR, despite the political impasse that continues to divide them. Questions that may be used to evaluate this experiment include:

- In what synergistic ways can Strait Talk work with other civil society initiatives across the Taiwan Strait to generate collective and cumulative impact on peacemaking in the long run?
- To what extent will ICR as a method of relationship-building work in the unique socio-cultural context of East Asia in general and cross-Strait relations in particular? Of interest is whether ICR as a system of applied practice is congruent with the East Asian cultural context, which tends to prioritise collectivist social norms over diverse individual expressions of free will.
- Will this exercise of relationship-building ever evolve into some form of policy-oriented learning and transfer that generates tangible impact on the macro political level? If so, under what circumstances is such impact likely to be generated?

These questions define the unique nature of relationship-building through which Strait Talk contributes to the theory and practice of ICR. While the following analysis falls far short of answering these questions, it will at least illuminate the focus and significance of the social experiment that Strait Talk embodies.

Four Emerging Trends Observed in the Dialogues

Each of the ten workshops was moderated by the same facilitator following more or less the same method. Because the participants were different each time, the present author, as the facilitator, has observed differences and similarities in group dynamics across these ten tri-national groups. This section will highlight four recurring themes that reflect repeated patterns of behaviour and attitude demonstrated by the participants over the years. These themes are:

1. The participants' perceptions, both convergent and divergent between the two sides, about which historical events matter most in shaping their notion of conflict history.
2. Their readiness to question and unpack what may have been considered a non-negotiable basis of sovereignty, especially in terms of unpacking the rationale of One China.
3. The enduring relevance of collective historical attachment to both Chinese nationhood and distinct Taiwanese identities, despite the participants' young age.
4. The participants' ability and willingness to empathise deeply with seemingly incompatible narratives of the other side, often to the point of defying their worldview of political correctness and challenging their own taboos.

It is hypothesised that these patterns summarised in the four themes are not random occurrences and that they are likely to have their social roots and reasons for recurrence. These recurring phenomena, it is further hypothesised, are likely to reflect some larger, deeper trends among the younger generation of well-educated Mainland Chinese and Taiwanese people – who constitute the third or fourth generation of the population that had experienced the Chinese Civil War firsthand in the 1940s – in terms of how they view cross-Strait relations today.

The presentation of each theme that follows builds on concrete episodes of group dynamics observed during the dialogues. Though these episodes are seemingly ideographic at times, they illustrate broader conceptual themes, especially when they are viewed in the context of recurring themes over the years. Having said this, it is duly noted that the empirical validity of these four themes should not be elevated beyond the status of a practitioner's fieldnote, which must be subjected to rigorous empirical examination. These themes are nonetheless promising, one may argue, as areas of social scientific inquiry that merit attention.

Theme 1: Perceptions of Conflict History

A careful observation of the dialogues enables one to hypothesise patterns concerning how young Mainland Chinese and Taiwanese delegates conceptualise the history of their conflict. These patterns have manifested most clearly in terms of which historical events they choose to highlight when they explain why and how their conflict has come to be shaped the way it is today.

One of the exercises introduced at a relatively early stage of the week-long dialogue is a "walk-through history," a method of experiential learning popularised by Joseph Montville[14] and used widely by practitioners of conflict resolution. The way it is applied to Strait Talk is summarised as follows: (a) Mainland Chinese and Taiwanese delegates each form a national team of five individuals, and separately come up with seven to eight significant historical events which in their collective judgment, have shaped the nature of the conflict over the Taiwan Strait; (b) each team will write in large characters the nature of each event and the year of its occurrence (e.g., "1949 the People's Republic of China established") on a notebook-size sheet of paper; (c) seven to eight sheets recording the events selected separately by each team are placed in chronological order on the floor along a single line, with Mainland Chinese delegates' version of events on one side of the line and Taiwanese delegates' version on the other. The purpose of this display is to show two conflict histories side by side, with a physical distance between two consecutive chronological events (e.g., 1949 coming after 1945) created in such a way as to be roughly proportionate to the actual number of intervening years (e.g., four years of interval in this example) between them; and (d) all the delegates are asked to stand and form a single line following the facilitator, who is standing at the beginning of the chronological line. The group follows the facilitator, and slowly and silently walks on the line through the two parallel chronologies, looking to the right and looking to the left. While walking, the delegates are asked to imagine what it might be like to live not only one side of the conflict history but also the other side's; and (e) after experiencing the walk, the group sits on the floor surrounding the two chronologies and shares discoveries and reflections on how their views of conflict history have been shaped in comparison with the alternative view, and why.

A question under study is: Are there any patterns emerging over the years as to how the delegates choose particular historical events to nominate over others? A short answer is *yes*. Comparing the chronologies that different national teams have come up with over the years, one may recognise recurrent events that overlap across the generations of Strait Talk delegates:

The sample chronology presented here is adopted from the 2006 workshop. It reflects the highly unique group dynamics and perceptions of the conflict held by the particular individuals who participated in the dialogue that particular year. When juxtaposed with the chronologies developed by the delegates of the other years, however, one realises that this 2006 version is similar in some important respects to how other Taiwanese and Mainland Chinese teams have demonstrated their interpretations of the conflict history.

At the core of this similarity is the shared perception that their conflict history starts in 1895, when the Treaty of Shimonoseki concluded the Sino-Japanese War and instituted Japanese colonial control over Taiwan. The fact that the delegates on both sides have repeatedly started their chronologies with the same event without much questioning is potentially significant because the young generations on the two sides have acquired their views on this conflict through different history textbooks and different political experiences for identity formation. Though the two sides attach different meanings to 1895 – with the Taiwanese often asserting that their nation was abandoned that year by the mainland[15] – they both share the worldview that the history of the conflict is time-bound thus not open-ended, and that this conflict has its genesis in that same year and in that same trauma-inflicting event. By implication, these young delegates choose *not* to go further back into pre-modern history to seek its origin, at least within the parameters of the exercise that require them to select only seven to eight events of their choosing.

Such a bounded nature of conflict history that started in 1895, however, was sometimes broken when the delegates chose much older events to start their chronologies with. For example, the Mainland Chinese team of 2005 chose as a starting point the establishment of the Qin dynasty (221 BC), which first attained central government control of much of the vast territory that constitutes contemporary China. The rationale presented by the mainland delegates was that the Taiwanese search for independence breaks the historical unity of China that dates back to antiquity, at least up to 221 BC, and therefore it requires serious reconsideration within this larger historical context. Another example of expanding the conflict history beyond 1895 is the 2007 Taiwanese delegates' reference to 1683, when Qing forces from Mainland China captured Taiwan. These Chinese forces, the Taiwanese participants argued, came to Taiwan for establishing nominal control there and preventing the island from falling under foreign rule or otherwise from becoming an anti-Chinese outpost of local rebels. A series of anti-Chinese revolts that had ensued in Taiwan, they argued, sharpened distinct indigenous identities against the mainland conquerors and therefore challenge the assertion that Taiwan has been part of China since antiquity.

Despite these occasional references to events preceding 1895, the general trends of group dynamics among the Taiwanese and Mainland Chinese participants over the years are in favour of defining their conflict as a *contemporary* phenomenon. This implies that they are less inclined to seek its origin in antiquity. It also means that they are less likely to mythologise its genesis and dramatise their ancestors' commitment to the deeply-entrenched official positions being held – One China vs Taiwanese independence. From a practical standpoint of conflict resolution dialogue, this tendency manifests most conspicuously when these young delegates demonstrate their readiness and capacity to treat the conflict as a set of contemporary issues and grievances, which one may argue are more negotiable and malleable than unexplainable myths carried over from time immemorial. This contemporary nature of the conflict, however, is still saturated with seemingly irrational emotions, as will be demonstrated by other propositions that follow.

Theme 2: Negotiability of Sovereignty

Conflict resolution dialogues over the years have also demonstrated the young Mainland Chinese and Taiwanese delegates' willingness and ability to self-reflect on the nationalistic fervour in their respective communities' claims of sovereignty. Through self-reflections – and sometimes through personal confessions of their inner thoughts – each of the national teams has endeavoured to interpret for the other team a deep-seated emotional basis of their notion of inviolable sovereignty. They have also unpacked the multi-faceted nature of sovereignty, especially in the context of discussing both One China and Taiwanese independence. And through such a thorough-going process of unpacking and self-reflective sharing, annual dialogues have arrived at final consensus documents that lay out a wide range of possible political arrangements that transcend the conventional zero-sum mode of thinking characteristic of this conflict.

In the 2009 dialogue at Berkeley, for example, Mainland Chinese delegates responded to their Taiwanese counterparts' questions about the basis of One China and Chinese nationalism underlying that policy. In the present author's experience as a dialogue facilitator in different parts of the world, an emotionally-charged exchange about conflict parties' essential positions, like One China, most often degenerates into antagonistic posturing and position-taking. Yet what had emerged from this particular exchange in 2009, as was often the case in other years, was a self-reflective attempt made by multiple Mainland Chinese delegates trying to help their Taiwanese colleagues see and feel the Chinese inner dilemmas.

The Mainland Chinese narratives shared on this occasion may be summarised as follows: contemporary Chinese nationalism underlying their sovereignty claims is fundamentally irrational but this Chinese version of irrationality has its own internal coherence and rationality. Chinese nationalism becomes most manifest when the nation is faced with great obstacles such as foreign policy crises, natural disasters, and economic recessions. This dramatised sense of national cohesion has little to do with a desire for territorial expansion; it has more to do with the desire for dignity and respect in relation to the world around them. Ordinary Chinese people are not necessarily attached to the anti-secession law of 2005, for they see it as elite politics at the government level. Nor do they necessarily link the proposed reunification of Taiwan and Mainland China to their own economic incentives, despite what many

Taiwanese may suspect. What the Chinese fear most is the loss of their dignity and respect as a result of mishandling these sovereignty issues in general and the secessionist movements in particular. Therefore the Beijing government, and perhaps many of the ordinary Chinese people as well, strongly condemn what they see as the manipulative secessionist movement within Taiwan – especially under the eight-year (2000–8) rule of former President Chen Shui-bian and his DPP party – that challenges the dignified status of Mainland China.

This example of a Mainland Chinese narrative may not represent a consensus view of Mainland Chinese delegates who have joined Strait Talk over the past seven years. But it does illustrate the *tone* of authentic, self-reflective storytelling that they have offered repeatedly. It is significant, one may argue, that these views have been offered repeatedly in the presence of their Taiwanese counterparts, often to the point where the Taiwanese unreservedly verbalised a sense of surprise – or even a complete shift in their image of the Mainland Chinese – at hearing these self-reflections. Though omitted for brevity in this essay, narratives also abound that demonstrate the Taiwanese side of self-reflections, especially on the seemingly non-negotiable nature of Taiwanese identities and their desire for independence, in response to questions posed by the Mainland Chinese.

Another example of growing negotiability over sovereignty was observed in the workshop in 2006, in which mainland delegates endeavoured to unpack the meaning of One China for Taiwanese participants. They distinguished between two levels of sovereignty to explain a multi-faceted meaning of One China – legal and cosmological sovereignty. Their explanation may be summarised as follows:

Legal sovereignty emphasises territorial exclusivity, as well as the rightfulness and capacity of One China to conduct its international relations as its sole representative. It is akin to the Westphalia tradition of exclusive sovereignty in western society. Viewed from this perspective, sovereignty is monolithic, non-negotiable, and non-divisive. China, on the other hand, has also internalised and exercised what may be termed as *cosmological sovereignty* throughout its long history of nation-building. This function of Chinese sovereignty emphasises respect for a China-centred worldview, with a harmonious, integrated image of China as a collectivity of diverse peoples. Cosmological sovereignty represents the Chinese collective consciousness of nationhood that seeks respect from other nations and from its own constituent communities. It highlights inclusivity of different communities under the umbrella of the same Chinese cultural family. Historically, such a "soft" aspect of Chinese sovereignty has been manifest when its central government provided security assurances to nations in its peripheries that regularly paid tributes to the Chinese central authority, thus becoming its suzerains. The central government, while flexible in its exercise of territorial control, has remained firm on one principle: the need to *save face* vis a vis those suzerains and the outside world surrounding China.[16]

Stimulated in part by this exploratory mode of inquiry into Chinese sovereignty, the Taiwanese and Mainland Chinese delegates, together with their American counterparts, then brainstormed a wide range of possible future scenarios that both accommodate and transcend the zero-sum, binary thinking on One China vs Taiwanese independence. Their intent was not to commit themselves to one scenario or another but to broaden their horizon of future scenarios. In their final consensus document, the 2006 delegates conceptualised Chinese nation-building as an ever-evolving, dynamic, and historical process that may comprise one or more of the following phases:[17]

1. One China, as a *unitary state*.
2. China, with *Special Administrative Regions* such as Hong Kong, Macao, and Taiwan under the central government's authority to intervene when necessary.
3. *Chinese federation*, with a single constitution and a central representative government presiding over component states and provinces.
4. *Chinese confederation*, with separate semi-autonomous governing bodies in Taiwan and Mainland China coordinated through a shared central governing mechanism in terms of defense, foreign, and fiscal policy, while each body presiding separately over other matters within its own jurisdiction.
5. *Chinese commonwealth*, comprising of separate independent governments entering an international framework, like the

British Commonwealth, to affirm their common heritage and promote goals of common interest; this option, in effect, accommodates Taiwanese independence.

A similar approach to conceptualise a range of sovereignty arrangements was adopted by a different team at Berkeley in 2009 in its final consensus document, through another dynamic, exploratory process. It is significant, from the dialogue facilitator's point of view, that *all* the Taiwanese and Mainland Chinese delegates, along with their American counterparts, could *unanimously* agree on such a broad spectrum of future political arrangements, while choosing *not* to veto and exclude any of them as a non-starter after hours of often-heated exchanges.

These examples of the young Taiwanese and Mainland Chinese delegates' readiness to self-reflect on the less visible logic of Chinese sovereignty and to explore alternative futures are illustrative of numerous other episodes experienced throughout the seven years of Strait Talk dialogue. The flexibility and openness to unpack their boundaries and taboos, however, were often challenged by their own inner commitment to what they see as unchangeable core identities within them, as the next theme illustrates.

Theme 3: Emotional Attachment to Collective Identities

The conflict resolution workshops have provided a unique window of opportunity through which one may witness how the deep-rooted collective consciousness of Chinese nationhood on the one hand, and ever-evolving, distinct Taiwanese identities on the other, manifest, especially when they come face to face with one another. When these two trends collide through emotional exchange, the collective sense of who they are as Chinese and Taiwanese, respectively, emerges as an assertive and seemingly non-negotiable identity inherited from the past in their body image. At these moments, young dialogue participants, despite their informal status that does not officially represent any constituency back home, are compelled to embody their home communities and their large-group identities, often with tears and emotional outbursts.

A Taiwanese-Mainland Chinese exchange observed during the joint conflict analysis exercise in 2007, among numerous other episodes, illustrates this point cogently. Given the floor first to share their perspective on the roots of the cross-Strait conflict, the

Taiwanese delegates, led by one female spokesperson, started their presentation with a symbolic expression of their inner feelings:

> Once upon a time, there was a new-born baby. Somebody came to take the baby but then left her. The baby was again picked up by somebody else and abandoned again. The baby girl eventually grew up, making an effort to become a truly independent person on her own. But her biological parents suddenly appeared at that point and asserted to reclaim her custody.

One way of interpreting the underlying message of this metaphoric expression is the following: a nebulous, burgeoning sense of Taiwanese collective identity began to sprout, like a new-born baby coming into existence, in response to the Qing Dynasty's conquest of the island starting in the late seventeenth century. At the end of the nineteenth century, Japan emerged as a self-declared "liberator" in East Asia, seized the island from the mainland through the Sino-Japanese War of 1894–5, but abandoned it after pursuing its exploitive, colonial agenda for half a century and being defeated in the Second World War. Mainland China, represented then by the Republic of China under Chiang Kai-shek's Kuomintang (KMT) Party, took the island as a new liberator. But the KMT rule soon revealed its true nature when it led systematic massacres of local opponents in the February 28 incident in 1947, generating a widespread popular sentiment that mainland rulers betrayed the Taiwanese again, reminiscent of what the Taiwanese had experienced in the aftermath of the Sino-Japanese War. As Taiwan had sought to develop as an independent nation for decades and gradually built a prosperous democracy, the mainland government under CCP rule, now distinctly different in character from the Taiwanese offspring growing up, claims its inalienable right to integrate Taiwan back into the Chinese family, often citing its ancient ties to Taiwan, imagined or real.

After these introductory remarks filled with metaphoric expressions, the Taiwanese participants moved to a more formal, systematic account of what they saw as the roots of the current cross-Strait conflict, emphasising that at the core of their grievances was the frustrated need to attain greater respect and self-actualisation in relation to the mainland. The mainland delegates, in turn, offered their conflict analysis, highlighting that historically, lack of unity within the Chinese state has often led to foreign invasions and the disintegration of China. After detailed historical accounts by his team, one mainland delegate concluded the mainland team's remarks: "... but the most important reason for us the Mainland Chinese to want Taiwan to be part of One China is that *we love you*, our Taiwanese people."

This concluding remark by one mainland delegate was followed by another mainland delegate, who was looking intently into the eyes of the Taiwanese counterparts, and added, "... yes, the bottomline of all of this is that *we love you and we want you to come back to us.*" These remarks by the mainland delegates invited the Taiwanese delegates' equally emotional responses, with one Taiwanese participant raising her voice and saying, "We don't want to be part of you. Leave us alone. Let us become who we truly are as an independent community." All the intellectual analyses of the conflict that the two sides had presented up to this point were thrown out of the window through this emotional exchange. The group dynamics had then begun to focus squarely on how passionately individual members of each team could display their large-group identities as if they embodied their national communities.

This episode of 2007 illustrates a manifest pattern of group dynamics that have been recurrent throughout the seven-year history of Strait Talk. This pattern is characterised as a personification of the participants' large-group identities, especially their national identities, that become predominant when these young delegates choose to take up their nations' historical traumas and glories on their own. Interestingly, such a process of personification of their large-group identities was often expressed through, or at least triggered by, the use of family metaphors, as in the reference to parent-child relations in the episode just described.

It is significant that the hardening of the delegates' attitudes through the embodiment of their large-group identities recurred persistently over the years despite the other two concurrent trends of "softening" described earlier, that is, the greater negotiability of perceived conflict history (Theme 1) and sovereignty (Theme 2). It is inferred from these trends that well-educated young "pre-influentials" like the Strait Talk delegates are now growing accustomed to communicating with each other their views on political taboos and boundaries in cross-Strait relations, yet at the same time, they do carry their share of nationalism inherited from the historical past. Raised in the third and fourth generations of the post-Civil War era, these young delegates embody a unique mixture of the present and the past, change and continuity in their respective societies. And there is one more conspicuous trait that they frequently exhibit and that is worth highlighting, for it is likely to complement our understanding of this intricate mixture.

Theme 4: Deep Empathy, Beyond Political Correctness

Empathy is a capacity to put oneself in the shoes of others and look at their relationships from the other side's perspective. While carefully facilitated workshops are generally known to generate empathy between parties, the depth of empathetic exchange between young Taiwanese and Mainland Chinese delegates appears to be somewhat unique from the perspective of comparative peace-making. This unique quality of empathy-building, it seems, has been facilitated in part by the delegates' readiness to take extra steps to examine their own articles of faith and sometimes go as far as demonstrating clear signs of identity shifts.

In the 2009 workshop at Berkeley, for example, a Taiwanese delegate drew on her team's presentation on conflict analysis and added a personal story about how much she regretted treating fellow Taiwanese students of non-Han minority backgrounds in her classrooms at an earlier stage of her education. Her comment was slightly off the track because the discussion was supposed to focus more on the relationship between Taiwan and Mainland China. Yet her storytelling about her own discriminatory treatment of Taiwanese minorities, which was intermittently interrupted by her sobbing and emotional bursts, introduced silence in the circle of dialogue. Other delegates listened intently. A few minutes into this Taiwanese participant's storytelling, a Mainland Chinese delegate seated in front of her offered her reflection on her Taiwanese counterpart's storytelling, summarised as follows:

Growing up in Beijing and educated at mainland schools, she has always believed that despite the tumultuous relationships with Taiwan and her awareness of the Taiwanese long-standing grievances, the small island nation will be integrated as part of One China sooner or later. She came to this dialogue with this worldview, which had been an integral part of her national identity.

She could not foresee any circumstances under which such a deep-rooted belief within her could be changed. But having witnessed her Taiwanese colleagues sobbing with regret and having self-reflected on what they saw as their mistreatment of their own Taiwanese minorities, she now felt compelled to self-reflect on how her country, Mainland China, should treat Taiwanese. "Taiwanese people have their own feelings, and we need to respect them," she remarked. "Maybe the way we have been treating the Taiwanese has not been totally right." While she was sharing her reflections, another mainland delegate, seated next to her, started sobbing quietly.

This episode of 2009 is unique in terms of the highly conspicuous nature of self-reflections transferred from one side to the other. But it is arguably quite common in terms of the way in which Strait Talk dialogues have opened up an unconventional, interactive space over the years for mutual learning in which the participants have voluntarily chosen to re-evaluate and transform their deep-seated assumptions on their own, with radical empathy. It is hypothesised that the method of dialogue facilitation and the informal atmosphere of relationship-building have helped deepen the level of empathy-building. Yet having facilitated dialogues in other parts of the world still undergoing systematic, active violence – from Rwanda to Israel/Palestine – the present author also hypothesises that part of the young Taiwanese and Mainland Chinese delegates' readiness to empathise deeply with one another comes from the fact that they belong to the generation that has no concrete, tangible memory of active warfare with one another. Six decades after the active fighting in the Chinese Civil War, in other words, the origin of their conflict is becoming increasingly more abstract and less tangible, unlike its long-lasting consequences still recognisable in their daily lives. Precisely because of the less tangible nature of the conflict, it is argued that the immediate, tangible experience of in-depth, face-to-face dialogue is likely to have more promise than ever before to transform each other's images that have been considered unchangeable for much of the long history of the cross-Strait conflict.

Conclusion: Envisioning a Way Forward

This essay has explored lessons learned from seven years of experience with Strait Talk, a movement intended to bring together young civil society delegates from both sides of the Taiwan Strait and the United States for joint problem-solving and sustainable relationship-building. At the heart of this historical conflict is the Mainland Chinese search for coherent nationhood and territorial integrity on the one hand, and the Taiwanese desire to determine their own political future and to give full expressions to their diverse and distinct communal identities without Chinese interference on the other. Despite the deeply-entrenched structural nature of this conflict that has essentially remained intact for decades, the most recent trends in cross-Strait relations, catalysed by the Taiwanese election of the KMT president Ma Ying-jeou in May, 2008, have introduced a burgeoning sense of civil society exchange, including an increasing number of ordinary Taiwanese and Mainland Chinese people crisscrossing the Strait through direct flights. Strait Talk builds on these emerging trends and seeks to develop a model of cross-Strait civil society exchange that activates peace potential inherent in these historical trends.

Moreover, Strait Talk, through its emphasis on highly interactive, experiential learning, offers a unique window of opportunity through which young "pre-influentials" who belong to the third to fourth generation of the post-Civil War era come face to face with each other across the Strait, and also with the history of their conflict that they have inherited across generations. Recurrent patterns of their group dynamics suggest at least four potentially generalisable trends about how this generation of highly-educated people have internalised their conflict: (1) both sides view the conflict as a relatively *contemporary* phenomenon thus time-bound in nature, not to be too open-ended or mythologised; (2) the two sides are ready and able to unpack the seemingly nonnegotiable nature of sovereignty – which confronts them either in the form of One China or Taiwanese independence – by way of self-reflecting on the rationality underlying the seemingly irrational attachments to sovereignty; (3) contrary to these two trends, however, the young delegates also carry with them strong emotional attachments to their large-group identities and display them in a highly personalised way when these identities are challenged; (4) representing the third to fourth generation of the post-Civil War era, young delegates on both sides are also ready and able to extend deep empathy with one another when invited to do so through tangible, impactful experience, even to the point of crossing the boundaries of their political correctness.

These emerging trends demonstrated by young delegates in a safe, academic environment may not be readily replicated in the far more complex reality of macro-political dynamics that they will inherit. Nor is there any sign of systematic social change that the two governing authorities may adopt to settle the political status of Taiwan in such a way as to test the robustness of these young delegates' conciliatory capacities. On the other hand, the opportunities presented since mid-2008 at the grassroots level for greater civil society exchange are real and unprecedented beyond doubt, though not necessarily irreversible. If the history of peace processes elsewhere in the world is a guide, these new opportunities arguably carry significant potential for shaping and reshaping the grassroots' readiness either to accept or reject whatever major political choices the two governing authorities may make at some point in the future. From a macro-historical perspective – with decades to generations of a change process in mind – time is ripe today more than ever before to start making concerted strategic efforts across the Strait to create robust, self-adaptive, and sustainable mechanisms of civil society interactions that deepen interdependence and make war unthinkable. Taking concrete steps toward these visions is in the best interest of both sides of the Strait seeing greater regional stability, not only at the civil society and business level but also at the government level. From a long-term historical perspective, therefore, Strait Talk represents the ultimate form of political pragmatism that takes the voices of the future seriously.

Notes

1. In this paper, the terms 'Mainland China' and 'Taiwan' refer to the two sides of the Taiwan Strait, with emphasis on their geographic regions and the populations associated with them.
2. Historians debate whether the discourse of the Century of Humiliation has evolved from China's actual experience in the mid-nineteenth century or in fact, it has been constructed more recently by the rise of contemporary Chinese nationalism (Gries 2004). While this essay does not seek to settle the debate, it acknowledges the active presence of such an emotionally charged discourse as an authentic reality to work on,

regardless of the exact nature of its historical origin and its dynamic evolution.

3. This line of future-oriented thinking that applies the theory of conflict resolution to cross-Strait relations has been explored by some regional experts. See, for example, Bush (2005).
4. The table entries are approximate numbers. The statistics are collected from the official website of the Taiwanese Ministry of Transportation and Communication at: http://admin.taiwan.net.tw/english/statistics/release.asp?relno=6
5. The founder of Strait Talk Johnny Lin was a nineteen-year-old undergraduate student at Brown University at the point of its inception in 2005. He currently co-leads the non-profit organisation as its president. For more information about Strait Talk, visit www.straittalk.org
6. One of the opening exercises invites Taiwanese participants to be in the Indonesian shoes and their Mainland Chinese counterparts to be in the East Timorese shoes as they explore possible solutions to the East Timor-Indonesian conflict in the late 1990s. In this exercise, perceived power relations are reversed between the two sides. American participants split into two subgroups and work with either one side or the other. Arai (2012: 203–208) describes this method of experiential learning, which builds on the conflict parties' own identities to elicit empathy and creativity, as cross-contextual case studies.
7. See below for a more detailed discussion on interactive conflict resolution.
8. On completion of a weeklong workshop each year, fifteen Strait Talk participants travel together to present their consensus document at such US-based organisations as the Council on Foreign Relations, Asia Society, and Asia Foundation, often engaging senior scholars and policy-oriented practitioners in attendance.
9. There is a much broader range of functions that ICR has been used to serve than what this essay has considered. For useful overview of these functions, see Rouhana (2000).
10. ICR has been used to build and transform human relationships across many conflict-affected societies. See, for example, Saunders (1999, 2000) and Diamond and Fisher (1995).
11. ICR's contribution to capacity-building has been well researched and documented. Based on his extensive experience in the facilitation of Israel-Palestine dialogues, for example, Kelman (1995) observes that the ICR workshops that he and his colleagues have carried out helped prepare cadres of Israeli and Palestinian leaders, who subsequently negotiated or otherwise influenced various aspects of the Oslo peace accord in 1993.

12. The research and practice on ICR has focused primarily on how to generate solutions to social conflicts (*learning*) and how to convey the solutions to policymakers and influential stakeholders within each of the societies involved in the conflicts (*transfer*). See Burton (1986), Kelman (1997), and Mitchell and Banks (1996).
13. The author facilitates Brown and Berkeley workshops only. This essay analyses the ten US-based sessions in which the author has directly been involved.
14. Joseph Montville offers a synopsis of walk-through history and its application to conflicts in American society at: www.hopeinthecities.org/node/23241
15. Reflections on the meaning of 1895 offered by a 2009 delegate right after a weeklong dialogue capture this feeling metaphorically: "some see it as a woman being separated from a man while others see it as the birth of a new consciousness."
16. A Mainland Chinese delegate in 2008 even went as far as arguing that the whole notion of sovereignty, especially in line with the Westphalia tradition, is alien to Chinese society. He stated that the Confucian tradition underlying the Chinese ideal of good governance sees a nation in the mirror image of a family. Viewed from this perspective, he continued, the nation-citizen relationship in China is more akin to a father-son relationship bound by lineage and loyalty than to the Western notion of social contract between a state and its citizens who have given consent to its authority. This perspective, though not necessarily shared by all the mainland delegates, is worth noting because it illustrates how far the cosmological basis of sovereignty can possibly expand to override the conventional legal argument, with which Americans, as well as a growing number of young Western-leaning Taiwanese, are more familiar.
17. A list of possible sovereignty arrangements presented here is simplified for brevity and modified for clarity from the original text of the 2006 consensus document. The original text may be obtained by writing to Strait Talk coordinators at: straittalk@gmail.com

References

Arai, Tatsushi, *Creativity and Conflict Resolution: Alternative Pathways to Peace*, London: Routledge, 2012.

Burton, John W., 'The History of International Conflict Resolution'. in *International Conflict Resolution*, edited by E.E. Azar and J.W. Burton, Brighton, UK: Wheatsheaf, 1986.

Bush, Richard, *Untying the Knot: Making Peace in the Taiwan Strait*. Washington, DC: Brookings Institution Press, 2005.

Diamond, Louise and Ronald Fisher, 'Integrating Conflict Resolution Training and Consultation: A Cyprus Example', *Negotiation Journal* 11 (3): 287–301, 1995.

Gries, Peter Hays, *China's New Nationalism: Pride, Politics and Diplomacy*, Berkeley, California: University of California Press, 2004.

International Crisis Group, *China and Taiwan: Uneasy Détente*. <http://www.crisisgroup.org/home/index.cfm?id=3694&l=1> (March 1, 2012), 2009.

Kelman, Herbert, 'Contributions of an Unofficial Conflict Resolution Effort to the Israeli-Palestinian Breakthrough'. *Negotiation Journal* 11: 19–27, 1995.

——, 'Group Processes in the Resolution of International Conflicts', *American Psychologist* 52 (3): 212–220, 1997.

Mitchell, Christopher and Michael Banks, *Handbook of Conflict Resolution: The Analytical Problem-Solving Approach*, New York: Pinter, 1996.

Rouhana, Nadim, 'Interactive Conflict Resolution: Issues in Theory, Methodology, and Evaluation', in *International Conflict Resolution After the Cold War*, edited by P.C. Stern and D. Druckman, Washington, DC: National Academy Press, 2000.

Saunders, Harold, *A Public Peace Process: Sustained Dialogue to Transform Racial and Ethnic Conflicts*, New York: Palgrave, 1999.

——, 'Interactive Conflict Resolution: A View for Policy Makers on Making and Building Peace', in *International Conflict Resolution After the Cold War*, edited by P.C. Stern and D. Druckman, Washington, DC: National Academy Press, 2000.

Appendix

Example of a Walk-Through History: Parallel Chronologies Presented by the 2006 Delegates

Mainland Chinese chronology	*Taiwanese chronology*
1895 Treaty of Shimonoseki, ceding Taiwan to Japan.	1895–1945 Japanese colonial rule of Taiwan.
1943–45 Cairo Declaration and Potsdam Proclamation, both stating the Chinese right to reclaim Taiwan from Japan.	
1947 February 28 incident – Taiwanese uprising met with massacres by the Chinese Nationalist Party, or Kuomintang (KMT).	
1949 People's Republic of China (PRC) established.	1949 KMT, under Chiang Kai-shek's leadership, retreated to Taiwan.
1979 Sino-US communiqué	1979 The US established diplomatic ties with PRC, away from the Republic of China (ROC).
1989 June 4th - Taiwanese President Lee Teng-hui condemned PRC for the Tienanmen incident.	
	1994 The Qiandao Lake incident – Taiwanese tourists killed in China. Taiwan dissatisfied with response, leaning more toward independence.
	1996 First direct vote for Taiwanese national election, triggering a crisis across the Strait, with intensive Chinese military exercises.
	1999 President Lee proposed a special state-to-state relationship with the mainland.
2000 Chen Shui-bian of Democratic Progressive Party (DPP) was elected as Taiwanese president.	2000 DPP came into power with pro-independence slogan, ending half a century of KMT rule.

Note that in the actual exercise of walk-through history, each sheet of paper recording an event was much simpler than the entries into the above matrix. For example, the entry for 1895 was simply "1895 Treaty of Shimonoseki," assuming that all the delegates were intimately familiar with the event.

Index